FILE CLERK ·
GENER.

FILE CLERK · GENERAL CLERK

John C. Czukor

Prentice Hall
New York • London • Toronto • Sydney • Tokyo • Singapore

Ninth Edition

Prentice Hall General Reference
15 Columbus Circle
New York, NY 10023

An Arco Book

Arco is a registered trademark of Prentice-Hall, Inc.
Prentice Hall and colophon are trademarks of Prentice-Hall, Inc.

Library of Congress Cataloging-in-Publication Data

File clerk—general clerk / [edited by] John C. Czukor.—9th ed.
     p. cm.
     At head of title: Arco.
     ISBN 0-671-84714-7
     1. Clerical ability and aptitude tests. 2. Clerks—United States—
Examinations, questions, etc. 3. Filing systems—Examinations,
questions, etc. 4. Civil service—United States—Examinations.
I. Czukor, John C.
JK717.C54F44   1993   92-17676
651.3'743'076—dc20   CIP

Manufactured in the United States of America

2   3   4   5   6   7   8

CONTENTS

HOW TO TAKE A CIVIL SERVICE EXAM

The first step in taking a civil service exam is getting an official announcement from the relevant government agency. You will find the address and telephone number of the nearest Federal Government Personnel Office, the local office of your state civil service commission, and offices of county, municipal, town, and village governments in your telephone book. Call to find out how to get an announcement and application form. Then write or go in person, as instructed. Read the announcement carefully and follow the directions exactly. Fill out the application form carefully and send it along with the required fee.

The government agency to which you have applied will send you an admission blank and instructions for taking the exam. The instructions will include the location, date, time of the exam, and a list of things to bring with you, such as sharpened number-two pencils with erasers, positive identification that includes your picture and/or signature, a watch, and, of course, the admission blank.

Before the exam day find out how to get to the test location. Be sure you know where it is, how to get there, and how long it takes to get there. You might want to make a "dry run" to check out the transportation and time involved. You do not want to be late on test day, and you do not want to be nervous about being late.

The day before the exam, review any subject areas in which you are weak. Then reread this chapter. Sharpen your pencils and put them with your admission blank, identification papers, watch, and whatever other materials you will need to take with you to the test. Get a good night's sleep. Set your alarm for a time that will allow you to eat a good breakfast (if you are scheduled for a morning exam) and to get to the test site on time.

On test day allow ample time for getting to the examination center. Upon entering the exam room, choose a seat with good lighting, good ventilation, and a view of the clock, if possible. If you cannot see the clock, you can always rely on your watch.

A test monitor will hand out papers and will give instructions. Listen closely and follow all of the instructions. If you have any questions, *ask.* There is no penalty for asking questions, even questions that might appear to be foolish. The penalty for misunderstanding instructions might be a low score.

The monitor will give you a test booklet and will tell you the time limits. The booklet may look large, but do not panic. There is plenty of time. Most civil service exams allow thirty minutes for every fifteen questions. You will be able to answer many of the questions in only a few seconds, which will leave you enough time to answer such questions as reading comprehension or arithmetic questions that, by their nature, take longer to read and understand. If you are having trouble answering a particular question, mark that question, go on, and come back to it later.

Once the signal is given to begin the exam, you should:

- READ all the directions carefully. Skipping over the directions or misunderstanding them can lead to your marking a whole series of questions incorrectly.
- READ every word of every question. Be alert for exclusionary words that might affect your answer—words like "not," "most," "all," "every," "least," "except."
- READ all of the choices before you mark your answer. The greatest number of errors are made when the correct answer is the last choice given. Too many people mark the first answer that seems correct without reading through all the choices to find out which answer is *best.*

The following list consists of important suggestions for taking a civil service exam.

Read these suggestions before you go on to the exercises in this book. Read them again before you take the exam. You will find them all useful.

1. Mark your answers by completely blackening the space for the answer you selected.

2. Mark only ONE answer for each question, even if you think that more than one answer is correct. You must choose the best answer. If you mark more than one answer, the scoring machine will give you no credit for that question.

3. If you change your mind, erase completely. Leave no doubt as to which answer you mean.

4. If you do any figuring calculations in your test booklet or on scrap paper, remember to mark your answer on the answer sheet as well. Only the answer sheet is scored.

5. You must mark your answer to every question in the right place. Check often to be sure that the answer number corresponds to the question number. If you find that you have slipped "out of line," you must take the time to find where you went awry and change your answers accordingly.

6. Do not dwell too long on any question. Although you have plenty of time, your time is not unlimited. If you are unsure of your answer, make a mark next to the question in the test booklet so that you may return to the question when you have completed the rest of the exam; but mark your best guess for each question in order.

7. Answer EVERY question. Most civil service exams do not penalize you for wrong answers, and so there is no harm in guessing. If you do not know the answer, eliminate any choices you know are wrong and guess from among the remaining choices. Even a wild guess gives you a chance to get credit for a correct answer. If you have skipped a difficult question to save time during the test, make sure you go back and fill in the answer space, even if you are still not sure of the answer. Do not leave any answers blank on your answer sheet. Even wild guesses are better than no answers at all.

8. Stay alert. Be careful not to mark a wrong answer because you were not concentrating. An example of this type of error might be: The correct answer to a question is choice B, *Dallas,* and you mark choice D instead of B.

9. Check and recheck. There is no bonus for leaving early, and if you finish before the time is up, stay until the end of the exam. Check your answer sheet to be certain that every question has been answered and that every answer has been marked in the right place. Check to be certain that only one answer is marked for each question. Then look back into the question booklet for the questions that you marked as guesses only. This is your opportunity to give any difficult questions more thought and to improve your chances by changing a wild guess into a calculated guess.

GOOD LUCK!

Part One
INTRODUCTION

REPRESENTATIVE CIVIL SERVICE CAREERS

Nearly all states and municipalities use trained business, technical, and professional employees in a variety of fields. College men and women who have prepared for such positions are encouraged to step directly from the classroom into the state and municipal service at the bottom rung of any one of the many career ladders in its numerous departments, institutions, and agencies.

Many state constitutions require that appointments and promotions in the state civil service and all its civil divisions be made according to merit and fitness to be ascertained so far as practicable by examinations. The constitutions further provide that such examinations, so far as practicable, shall be competitive. The entrance positions described in this list are filled competitively by appointment from appropriate civil service eligible lists. Civil service law usually requires that when a vacancy above the entrance level is to be filled, the appointment must be made, if possible, by promotion from among persons holding positions in a lower grade in the department, office or institution where the vacancy exists. This law increases opportunities for advancement of those employees who come into the service at the lowest rung of the state or municipal career ladder, and emphasizes the importance of the recruitment of well-trained, intelligent personnel in these entrance positions.

The following groups of positions outlined should not be considered all-inclusive. While these specifications may present a true picture today, state and municipal services do not remain static. Fluctuations in the labor market, reorganization within departments, and other factors affect revisions.

CLERICAL POSITIONS

Clerical support staff are employed throughout state and municipal government and are at the center of communications throughout these organizations. They perform a wide variety of administrative and clerical duties that are necessary to run and maintain the responsibilities of state and local government.

Sample Exam Announcements

**STATE—MUNICIPAL
ENTRY-LEVEL CLERICAL POSITIONS**

Job Descriptions

Messenger These positions involve sorting and carrying mail, documents, or other materials between offices or buildings. This may involve the operation of a motor vehicle. Lifting and carrying moderately heavy bags or packages is required in the majority of these jobs. A currently valid state driver's license may be required for some jobs.

Clerk I and II Employees in these positions perform clerical duties such as gathering and providing information, sorting, filing, and checking materials. The complexity of these duties varies from limited (Clerk I) to moderate (Clerk II).

Requirements

Applicants must attain passing scores on a written examination to have their names placed on the eligible lists.

Test Information

Written Test The test will consist of a 12-minute Name and Number Checking speed test, and a 70-minute Clerical Abilities test. The type and number of questions for each position are as follows:

Subject Areas	Number of Questions
Messenger	
Perceptual speed and accuracy (name and number checking)	70
Coding (sorting mail)	20
Clerk I	
Perceptual speed and accuracy (name and number checking)	70
Coding (sorting mail)	20
Coding (sorting file material)	10
Filing (alphabetizing)	15
Clerk II and Intermittent Clerk II	
Perceptual speed and accuracy (name and number checking)	70
Coding (sorting mail)	20
Coding (sorting file material)	10
Filing (alphabetizing)	15
Information forwarding (taking telephone messages)	15

Test Results Applicants will receive a Notice of Examination Results in the mail. If they pass the tests, the notice will tell their relative standing on the lists and how long their names will remain on the lists. These lists may be used to fill positions in other comparable job titles.

STATE SECRETARY-TYPIST I

Job Description

Performs secretarial duties which usually involve typing correspondence, reports, and statistical material while acting as a secretary to one or more employees; does related work as required.

Distinguishing Characteristics Works under direct supervision. Performs repetitive and routine work including frequent operation of a typewriter; performs other secretarial duties such as evaluating correspondence, processing mail and typing manifests, advice to vendors and related. Exercises some independent judgment and resourcefulness in laying out work procedures and where work is more repetitive there is added responsibility of finality of action taken, detailed instructions being received when a change in procedure is initiated with advice normally being available relative to unusual or difficult matters. Exercises partial supervision upon assignment over other clerical employees, performing routine tasks including instructions in department procedures and methods.

Examples of Typical Tasks   Performs responsible secretarial duties such as typing forms and correspondence, and completing accounting and financial statements, vouchers, departmental reports, permits or other materials from copy, rough draft, dictating equipment, or general instructions. Maintains routine bookkeeping, financial and cost records where no technical knowledge is required but where frequent procedural problems arise; prepares or checks payrolls, vouchers, requisitions, and purchase orders; maintains personnel, financial and similar records. Gives standard information to other divisions and the public, applying knowledge of departmental rules, regulations, and procedures.

Requirements

Minimum Requirements:

1. Completion of high school or its equivalent, including or supplemented by courses in office procedures and typing or the equivalent.

2. One year's experience in an office or secretarial job or in a position at the level of Secretary Typist Trainee, or any equivalent combination of education and experience.

3. Considerable knowledge of typewriter operations including its functions. Working knowledge of Business English, spelling, and arithmetic. Working knowledge of office practices and procedures. Skill in typing. Ability to maintain fiscal or departmental records and prepare reports from such records. Ability to make arithmetical computations and tabulations accurately and with reasonable speed. Ability to assign, check and review the work of other employees. Ability to establish and maintain effective working relationships with the public and other employees.

4. Must be able to pass a typing test at a speed of 40 words per minute.

Test Information

All applicants must take a typing test.

CITY
BOOKKEEPER I

Test Information

The examination you are scheduled to take is a written, multiple choice test of 104 items. The test contains five sections. Each section consists of items which are similar to job duties performed by Bookkeepers. The following are brief descriptions of the five item types contained on the test.

Section I: *Vocabulary*
This section consists of questions regarding the knowledge of bookkeeping terminology and procedures.

Section II: *Filing*
The test taker is required to answer questions regarding filing terminology. Also in this section, the test taker must perform alphabetical filing.

Section III: *Name/Number Comparison*
This section of the test requires the test taker to determine whether two names or two numbers are alike.

Section IV: *Report Writing*
This section requires the test taker to read a paragraph and then determine the best or most effective method of expressing a selected phrase or sentence.

Section V: *Mathematics*
The test taker is required to calculate simple math functions. This section will include addition, subtraction, multiplication, and division.

STATE
CLERK II

Job Description

Performs varied clerical work involving moderately complex work methods and problems; does related work as required.

Distinguishing Characteristics Works under the immediate supervision of a superior. Performs repetitive, routine work performing a wide variety of clerical functions which require the application of independent judgment and the interpretation of policies and regulations on the basis of training and knowledge gained through experience on the job. Exercises partial supervision over other employees assigning, instructing and supervising a small group of clerical subordinates performing routine operations.

Examples of Typical Tasks Assigns, instructs and supervises a small group of clerical subordinates performing routine operations. Supervises work production and flow in central files, record management, or similar operating unit of moderate size maintaining more complex indexes and files. Makes final checks for proper coding, classification, and mathematical accuracy in compliance with procedures; posts invoices, vouchers, and other fiscal, statistical, and administrative data; prepares routine correspondence; performs the more complex arithmetical and tabulating assignments.

Requirements

Minimum Requirement

1. Completion of a four-year high school course or its equivalent including supplemental courses in business practices.

2. One year experience performing similar clerical work in an office; one year of appropriate formal post-high school training may be substituted for the required experience.

3. Some knowledge of modern office practices, procedures, and equipment. Some knowledge of departmental rules, procedures, and functions. Ability to understand and carry out moderately complex oral and written instructions. Ability to make relatively

complex arithmetical computations and tabulations accurately and with reasonable speed. Ability to make minor decisions on the basis of precedents and regulations and to apply them to work problems. Ability to train, assign, supervise and review work of subordinate employees. Ability to prepare clear and concise oral and written reports. Ability to establish and maintain effective working relationships with other employees and the general public.

STATE—MUNICIPAL CLERICAL/SECRETARIAL POSITIONS

Job Descriptions

Clerk Typist I and II, Intermittent Clerk Typist II   These positions involve typing and clerical duties such as providing information, composing short letters and memos, sorting, filing, and checking materials. These duties vary in complexity from limited (Clerk Typist I) to moderate (Clerk Typist II).

Clerk Stenographer I and II   These positions involve taking dictation and transcribing the notes. Other duties from limited to moderate complexity include typing, providing information, composing letters and memos, and sorting and filing materials.

Library Assistant   Employees in these positions perform moderately complex clerical work in a library, such as maintaining files and records, sorting and shelving books, and checking materials for accuracy.

Requirements

All applicants must achieve a passing score on a written examination.

Test Information

The clerical examination is made up of three major parts: a written test, a typing test, and a stenography test. The parts of the test that you take will depend upon the position(s) for which you have applied. Applicants for Clerk Typist I and II, Clerk Stenographer I and II, and Intermittent Clerk Typist II, must take a typing test. For these job titles, the written test will be weighted 50 percent and the typing test score will be weighted 50 percent. Applicants for Clerk Stenographer I and II must pass a stenography test. The stenography test will not be weighted as part of the final score. You must pass all parts of the test to be considered for employment. Any part of the tests may be cancelled and the weight added to the remaining parts.

Written Test   The written test for these positions contains eight sections. The number of questions an applicant answers will depend upon the position(s) for which he or she has applied. The time alloted for the written test is 1 hour and 42 minutes. The type and number of questions for each position are as follows.

Subject Matter Area	Number of Questions by Job Title	
	Clerk Typist I	Clerk Typist II, Clerk Stenographer I and II, Library Assistant I Intermittent Clerk Typist II
Name and number checking (perceptual speed and accuracy)	65	65
Sorting file material (coding)	10	10
Alphabetizing (filing)	15	15
Taking telephone messages (following directions)	15	15
Capitalization/punctuation/ grammar (language usage)	15	15
Effective expression	10	10
Spelling	25	25
Arithmetic operations	—	15

Typing Test The typing performance test will consist of a 4 minute practice exercise followed by the actual test, which will have an eight-minute time limit. A score of 30 words per minute, after deduction for errors, must be achieved in order to pass the typing performance test. Applicants *may* provide their own typewriters for the typing test.

Stenography Test The stenography test will consist of a three-minute practice exercise followed by the actual test, which will have a three-minute time limit. Dictation will be given at the rate of 80 words per minute. Applicants will have 30 minutes to transcribe their notes into answers on an answer sheet. Applicants for Clerk Stenographer I must not have more than 10% errors on the stenography test. Applicants for Clerk Stenographer II must not have more than 5% errors on the test. Any stenography system including the use of a shorthand machine is acceptable. Applicants who wish to use shorthand machines must provide their own.

CITY
CLERK STENOGRAPHER I

Job Description

The city employs Clerk Stenographers I in all of its operating departments. Under supervision, Clerk Stenographers take dictation, type letters, reports, records and other documents, and perform related clerical duties.

Employees are eligible for a promotional examination upon completion of two years of office experience, which includes a substantial amount of typing or stenography, and at least six months preceding the date of the examination as a regularly appointed employee of the city.

REQUIREMENTS

1. Ability to take dictation at 80 words per minute (wpm) and type at a minimum of 45 wpm.

2. Graduation from high school or successful completion of high school equivalency or G.E.D. test is desirable.

3. Residence in the city within six months of appointment.

Test Information

The examination will include a written test of clerical skills and performance tests of typing and dictation skills. Only electric typewriters will be available. Candidates must receive a minimum qualifying rating on each part of the examination. The minimum speeds needed to qualify are ability to take dictation at the rate of 80 wpm, and typing speed of 45 wpm.

The tests are weighted as follows: Written Test, 5; Typing Test, 1; and Dictation Test, 1.

This is a continuous examination. All qualified candidates will be notified of the date, time and place of the examination. Examination sessions will be scheduled as often as necessary to meet the needs of the City Service.

CITY STENOGRAPHER

Written Test

This is designed to test for knowledge, skills, and/or abilities in such areas as

1. Spelling: These questions are designed to test the candidate's ability to spell words that office employees might encounter in their daily work.

2. Alphabetizing: These questions are designed to test a candidate's ability to file material accurately in alphabetical order.

3. Clerical operations with letters and numbers: These questions are designed to test a candidate's visual perception and basic clerical accuracy in working with alphanumeric characters. The candidate is required to read, compare, check, reorder, and count letters and numbers following specific directions for each question. Knowledge of the alphabet and the ability to count are required.

4. Arithmetic computation: These questions are designed to test a candidate's ability to perform basic computations using addition, subtraction, multiplication, and division. Questions may also involve the use of fractions, decimals, averages, and percents. Word problems are not included in these questions.

A performance test in dictation will be administered on the same day as the written exam. The test involves taking and transcribing dictation of limited difficulty at the rate of 80 words per minute.

A performance test in typing will be administered to candidates who pass the written test and the performance test in dictation. A minimum speed of 35 words per minute is required.

The Commission reserves the right to re-test candidates who fail the typing portion of this examination. This testing would be scheduled at a later date.

Job Description

Performs routine stenographic and clerical work; takes and transcribes dictation; performs related duties as required.

Requirements

Candidates must meet the following requirements on or before the date of the written test: Graduation from high school including or supplemented by courses in stenography and typing. Be sure to indicate when and where you completed the required courses in shorthand and typing.

Satisfactory office experience in clerical work which involved taking and transcribing dictation may be substituted for high school education, including course work, on a year-for-year basis up to a maximum of two years.

Test Information

The examination has three parts: a written test, and performance tests in dictation and typing. Candidates must attain a score of 70 percent in each part of the examination. The eligible list will be established on the basis of the average of the scores received on all parts of the examination.

STATE
ADVANCED CLERICAL/SECRETARIAL POSITIONS

Job Description

All positions involve providing training and guidance to new employees and functioning as a lead worker.

Clerks perform advanced clerical duties which involve gathering and providing information, sorting, filing, and checking materials.

Clerk Typists, in addition to performing the duties above, also type documents of various degrees of complexity and compose letters and memoranda.

Clerk Stenographers, in addition to performing all of the duties above, take dictation of a complex nature and transcribe the notes.

Executive Secretaries perform highly responsible secretarial work as staff assistants to Executive Directors. Supervision may be exercised over a small clerical staff.

Requirements

To speed up test scheduling, your qualifications may not be reviewed until after you have taken the test. Please make sure you meet *all* requirements, because if you *do not*, your test results *will not* be counted. If you are not sure if you qualify, contact one of the Commission's offices.

You must be a state resident, of good moral character, and capable of performing the physical activities of the job.

For promotion examinations, you must have regular or probationary civil service status.

Minimum Requirements

Clerk III (State, Local, and Housing Authority)   Six months as a Clerk II and educational development to the level of high school; OR one year of progressively complex clerical experience and completion of high school; OR six months of complex clerical experience and completion of a post-high school business curriculum; OR any equivalent experience and/or training which provided the required knowledge and abilities.

Clerk Typist III (State, Local, and Housing Authority) Six months as a Clerk Typist II, and educational development to the level of completion of high school; OR one year of progressively complex clerical typing experience and completion of high school; OR six months of moderately complex clerical typing work and completion of a post-high school business curriculum; OR any equivalent experience and/or training which provided the required knowledge, skills, and abilities.

Clerk Stenographer III (State, Local, and Housing Authority) Six months as a Clerk Stenographer II, and educational development to the level of completion of high school; OR one year of progressively complex clerical stenographic experience and completion of a high school business curriculum; OR six months of moderately complex clerical stenographic experience and completion of a post-high school business curriculum; OR any equivalent experience and/or training which provided the required knowledge, skills, and abilities.

Executive Secretary (Housing Authority) Five years of progressively responsible experience in secretarial work. Appropriate formal post-high school secretarial training may be substituted for the required experience on a year-for-year basis up to four years; OR any equivalent combination of experience and training.

Test Information

Applicants must pass all parts of the test to be considered for employment. Any part of the tests may be cancelled by the Commission, and the weight added to the remaining parts.

The clerical examination is made up of three major parts: a written test, a typing performance test, and a stenography performance test. *All applicants must take the written test, which is weighted 100%.* All applicants for Clerk Typist III, Clerk Stenographer III, and Executive Secretary must also pass a typing performance test. All applicants for Clerk Stenographer III and Executive Secretary must also pass a stenography performance test. The performance tests will not be weighted as part of your final score, but will be scored on a pass/fail basis.

Written Test The 2½-hour written test will cover the subject areas noted below.

Subject Areas	Number of Questions
Office procedures and practices	15
Spelling	10
Punctuation and capitalization	10
Grammar	10
Proofreading	35
Arithmetic computations	10
Reports—basis concepts	10
Office management and planning	25
Total	125

Typing Test The typing performance test will have an eight-minute time limit. A score of 30 words per minute, after deduction for errors, must be achieved in order to pass the typing performance test. Applicants *may* provide their own typewriters.

Stenography Test The stenography performance test will have a three-minute time limit. Dictation will be given at the rate of 80 words per minute. Any stenography system is acceptable. Applicants who wish to use shorthand machines must provide their own.

Test Results Employment and promotion lists will be established. Applicants will be notified in writing of their test results.

CLERICAL POSITIONS IN THE FEDERAL SERVICE

Nearly half the jobs in the federal civil service are clerical and the government's demand for clerical workers exceeds the supply. Agencies have not been able to fill all the positions for competent stenographers, typists, office machine operators, and file clerks they need.

In government the title "clerk" describes more positions than it does in private industry. An editor or a writer may be called a clerk (Editorial Clerk), a purchasing agent with fairly important responsibilities may be a clerk (Purchasing Clerk), or an accountant may be called a clerk (Cost Accounting Clerk).

These are the names of some of the government clerical jobs: Clerk-Stenographer, Clerk-Typist, Correspondence Clerk, Dictating Machine Operator, Shorthand Reporter, Mail Clerk, File Clerk, Record Clerk, and Business Machine Operator.

Clerks perform personnel work, auditing and statistical operations, property and supply work, and proofreading. They make blueprints and photostats, prepare payrolls, supply information, work on traffic plans, operate switchboards, decipher codes, and work in engraving and printing plants.

Clerical salaries have risen sharply in recent years, probably exceeding average salaries for similar jobs in private industry. There are usually good opportunities for advancement, and clerk jobs can be the start of a real career in the government.

Here is a typical job announcement for a clerical position.

Clerk, GS-2, GS-3

DESCRIPTION OF WORK

A wide variety of clerical positions will be filled from this examination. Among the basic duties to be performed are, for example: searching for and compiling information and data; indexing, filing, and maintaining records; receiving and routing mail; answering inquiries orally or by correspondence; coding information for mechanical tabulation; maintaining time, leave, payroll, personnel, retirement, or other records; and other similar duties.

BASIS OF RATING

Competitors will be rated on the basis of scores on the verbal abilities and clerical abilities tests. The ratings will be based on a scale of 100. Better performance in the test will be required to establish eligibility at grade GS-3 than at grade GS-2.

HOW MUCH STUDY AND PRACTICE DO YOU REQUIRE?

Start your preparation for the exam by doing the Diagnostic Test. The results of the Test will show how much study and practice you will require in the various subjects that are usually covered by questions on actual examinations. The test consists of 100 questions relating to these areas.

After completing the Diagnostic Test and checking your answers against the Answer Key, enter your score for each subject on the Diagnostic Table. The entries on the Table will pinpoint the subject areas in which you are strong, average, or weak. This will serve as your guide in preparing for the exam. Concentrate your preparation on the areas in which you are weak, but do not neglect the areas in which you are average or strong. Since your score on the actual exam is based on your answers to *all* of the questions, a high score in one area offsets lower scores in other areas.

Following the Answer Key, you will find Explanatory Answers for each question, which explain why the Key Answer is the correct choice. Review all of the Explanatory Answers carefully. The explanations will help you to understand the process of selecting correct answer choices.

Answer Sheet For Diagnostic Test

1 Ⓐ Ⓑ Ⓒ Ⓓ	26 Ⓐ Ⓑ Ⓒ Ⓓ	51 Ⓐ Ⓑ Ⓒ Ⓓ	76 Ⓐ Ⓑ Ⓒ Ⓓ
2 Ⓐ Ⓑ Ⓒ Ⓓ	27 Ⓐ Ⓑ Ⓒ Ⓓ	52 Ⓐ Ⓑ Ⓒ Ⓓ	77 Ⓐ Ⓑ Ⓒ Ⓓ
3 Ⓐ Ⓑ Ⓒ Ⓓ	28 Ⓐ Ⓑ Ⓒ Ⓓ	53 Ⓐ Ⓑ Ⓒ Ⓓ	78 Ⓐ Ⓑ Ⓒ Ⓓ
4 Ⓐ Ⓑ Ⓒ Ⓓ	29 Ⓐ Ⓑ Ⓒ Ⓓ Ⓔ	54 Ⓐ Ⓑ Ⓒ Ⓓ	79 Ⓐ Ⓑ Ⓒ Ⓓ
5 Ⓐ Ⓑ Ⓒ Ⓓ	30 Ⓐ Ⓑ Ⓒ Ⓓ Ⓔ	55 Ⓐ Ⓑ Ⓒ Ⓓ	80 Ⓐ Ⓑ Ⓒ Ⓓ
6 Ⓐ Ⓑ Ⓒ Ⓓ	31 Ⓐ Ⓑ Ⓒ Ⓓ Ⓔ	56 Ⓐ Ⓑ Ⓒ Ⓓ	81 Ⓐ Ⓑ Ⓒ Ⓓ
7 Ⓐ Ⓑ Ⓒ Ⓓ	32 Ⓐ Ⓑ Ⓒ Ⓓ Ⓔ	57 Ⓐ Ⓑ Ⓒ Ⓓ	82 Ⓐ Ⓑ Ⓒ Ⓓ
8 Ⓐ Ⓑ Ⓒ Ⓓ	33 Ⓐ Ⓑ Ⓒ Ⓓ Ⓔ	58 Ⓐ Ⓑ Ⓒ Ⓓ	83 Ⓐ Ⓑ Ⓒ Ⓓ
9 Ⓐ Ⓑ Ⓒ Ⓓ	34 Ⓐ Ⓑ Ⓒ Ⓓ Ⓔ	59 Ⓐ Ⓑ Ⓒ Ⓓ	84 Ⓐ Ⓑ Ⓒ Ⓓ
10 Ⓐ Ⓑ Ⓒ Ⓓ	35 Ⓐ Ⓑ Ⓒ Ⓓ Ⓔ	60 Ⓐ Ⓑ Ⓒ Ⓓ	85 Ⓐ Ⓑ Ⓒ Ⓓ
11 Ⓐ Ⓑ Ⓒ Ⓓ	36 Ⓐ Ⓑ Ⓒ Ⓓ Ⓔ	61 Ⓐ Ⓑ Ⓒ Ⓓ	86 Ⓐ Ⓑ Ⓒ Ⓓ
12 Ⓐ Ⓑ Ⓒ Ⓓ	37 Ⓐ Ⓑ Ⓒ Ⓓ Ⓔ	62 Ⓐ Ⓑ Ⓒ Ⓓ	87 Ⓐ Ⓑ Ⓒ Ⓓ
13 Ⓐ Ⓑ Ⓒ Ⓓ	38 Ⓐ Ⓑ Ⓒ Ⓓ Ⓔ	63 Ⓐ Ⓑ Ⓒ Ⓓ	88 Ⓐ Ⓑ Ⓒ Ⓓ
14 Ⓐ Ⓑ Ⓒ Ⓓ	39 Ⓐ Ⓑ Ⓒ Ⓓ Ⓔ	64 Ⓐ Ⓑ Ⓒ Ⓓ	89 Ⓐ Ⓑ Ⓒ Ⓓ
15 Ⓐ Ⓑ Ⓒ Ⓓ	40 Ⓐ Ⓑ Ⓒ Ⓓ Ⓔ	65 Ⓐ Ⓑ Ⓒ Ⓓ	90 Ⓐ Ⓑ Ⓒ Ⓓ
16 Ⓐ Ⓑ Ⓒ Ⓓ	41 Ⓐ Ⓑ Ⓒ Ⓓ Ⓔ	66 Ⓐ Ⓑ Ⓒ Ⓓ	91 Ⓐ Ⓑ Ⓒ Ⓓ
17 Ⓐ Ⓑ Ⓒ Ⓓ	42 Ⓐ Ⓑ Ⓒ Ⓓ Ⓔ	67 Ⓐ Ⓑ Ⓒ Ⓓ	92 Ⓐ Ⓑ Ⓒ Ⓓ
18 Ⓐ Ⓑ Ⓒ Ⓓ	43 Ⓐ Ⓑ Ⓒ Ⓓ	68 Ⓐ Ⓑ Ⓒ Ⓓ	93 Ⓐ Ⓑ Ⓒ Ⓓ
19 Ⓐ Ⓑ Ⓒ Ⓓ	44 Ⓐ Ⓑ Ⓒ Ⓓ	69 Ⓐ Ⓑ Ⓒ Ⓓ	94 Ⓐ Ⓑ Ⓒ Ⓓ
20 Ⓐ Ⓑ Ⓒ Ⓓ	45 Ⓐ Ⓑ Ⓒ Ⓓ	70 Ⓐ Ⓑ Ⓒ Ⓓ	95 Ⓐ Ⓑ Ⓒ Ⓓ
21 Ⓐ Ⓑ Ⓒ Ⓓ	46 Ⓐ Ⓑ Ⓒ Ⓓ	71 Ⓐ Ⓑ Ⓒ Ⓓ	96 Ⓐ Ⓑ Ⓒ Ⓓ
22 Ⓐ Ⓑ Ⓒ Ⓓ	47 Ⓐ Ⓑ Ⓒ Ⓓ	72 Ⓐ Ⓑ Ⓒ Ⓓ	97 Ⓐ Ⓑ Ⓒ Ⓓ
23 Ⓐ Ⓑ Ⓒ Ⓓ	48 Ⓐ Ⓑ Ⓒ Ⓓ	73 Ⓐ Ⓑ Ⓒ Ⓓ	98 Ⓐ Ⓑ Ⓒ Ⓓ
24 Ⓐ Ⓑ Ⓒ Ⓓ	49 Ⓐ Ⓑ Ⓒ Ⓓ	74 Ⓐ Ⓑ Ⓒ Ⓓ	99 Ⓐ Ⓑ Ⓒ Ⓓ
25 Ⓐ Ⓑ Ⓒ Ⓓ	50 Ⓐ Ⓑ Ⓒ Ⓓ	75 Ⓐ Ⓑ Ⓒ Ⓓ	100 Ⓐ Ⓑ Ⓒ Ⓓ

DIAGNOSTIC TEST

Use this test to pinpoint your strengths & weaknesses.

Time allowed for the entire examination: 4 Hours

1. As a clerk in an office in a city agency, you have just been given a new assignment by your supervisor. The assignment was previously done by another clerk. Before beginning work it is most important that you

   (A) find out who did the assignment previously
   (B) understand your supervisor's instructions for doing the assignment
   (C) notify the other clerks in the office that you have just received a new assignment
   (D) understand how the assignment is related to the work of other clerks in the office

2. Assume that you are a clerk in a city department. Your supervisor has given you an important job that must be completed as quickly as possible. You will be unable to complete the job by the end of the day, and you will be absent from the office for the next few days. Of the following, the most appropriate action for you to take before leaving the office at the end of the day is to

   (A) lock your work in your desk so that the work will not be disturbed in your absence
   (B) ask another clerk in the office to finish the job while you are away
   (C) tell your supervisor how much of the job has been done and how much remains to be done
   (D) leave a note on your supervisor's desk, advising him that you will continue to work on the job as soon as you return to the office

3. Assume that, as a newly appointed clerk in a city department, you are doing an assignment according to a method that your supervisor has told you to use. You believe that you would be less likely to make errors if you were to do the assignment by a different method, although the method your supervisor has told you to use is faster. For you to discuss your method with your supervisor would be

   (A) desirable because he may not know the value of your method
   (B) undesirable because he may know of your method and may prefer the faster one
   (C) desirable because your method may show your supervisor that you are able to do accurate work
   (D) undesirable because your method may not be as helpful to you as you believe it to be

4. Assume that you are responsible for receiving members of the public who visit your department for information. At a time when there are several persons seeking information, a man asks you for information in a rude and arrogant manner. Of the following, the best action for you to take in handling this man is to

   (A) give him the information in the same manner in which he spoke to you

(B) ignore his request until he asks for the information in a more polite manner
(C) give him the information politely, without commenting on his manner
(D) ask him to request the information in a polite manner so as not to annoy other people seeking information

5. As a clerk in a city agency, you are assigned to issue applications to members of the public who request the applications in person. Your supervisor has told you that under no circumstances are you to issue more than one application to each person. A person enters the office and asks for two applications, explaining that he wants the second one in case he makes an error in filling out the application. Of the following, the most appropriate action for you to take in this situation is to

(A) give the person two applications since he may not know how to fill one out
(B) ask your supervisor for permission to give the person two applications
(C) give one application to the person and advise him to come back later for another one
(D) issue one application to the person and inform him that only one application may be issued to an individual

6. Miss Smith is a clerk in the information section of a city department. Of the following, the most desirable way for Miss Smith to answer a telephone call to the section is to say,

(A) "Hello. Miss Smith speaking."
(B) "Miss Smith speaking. May I ask who is calling?"
(C) "Hello. May I be of service to you?"
(D) "Information Section, Miss Smith."

7. It is not good filing practice to

(A) smooth papers that are wrinkled
(B) use paper clips to keep related papers together in the files
(C) arrange the papers in the order in which they will be filed
(D) mend torn papers with cellophane tape

8. Suppose that as a clerk in an office of a city department, you have been assigned by your supervisor to assist Mr. Jones, another clerk in the office, and to do his work in his absence. Part of Mr. Jones's duties is to give routine information to visitors who request it. Several months later, shortly after Mr. Jones has begun a three-week vacation, a visitor enters the office and asks for some routine information that is available to the public. He explains that he had previously received similar information from Mr. Jones. Of the following, the most advisable action for you to take is to

(A) inform the visitor that Mr. Jones is on vacation but that you will attempt to obtain the information
(B) advise the visitor to return to the office after Mr. Jones has returned from vacation
(C) tell the visitor that you will have Mr. Jones mail him the information as soon as he returns from vacation
(D) attempt to contact Mr. Jones to ask him whether the information should be given to the visitor

Answer questions 9 through 18 by referring to the Code Table and directions below.

CODE TABLE

S	N	W	C	T	Q	I	A	J	X
1	2	3	4	5	6	7	8	9	0

DIRECTIONS: The table above provides a corresponding number for each of the ten letters used as codes in the questions. On the first line there are ten selected letters. On the second line there are the ten numerals, including zero. Directly under each letter on the first line there is a corresponding number on the second line. Every question consists of three pairs of letter and number codes. Each pair of codes is on a separate line. Referring to the Code Table above, determine whether each pair of letter and number codes is made up of corresponding letters and numbers. In answering each question, compare all three pairs of letter and number codes. Then mark your answers, as follows:

A. if in none *of the three pairs of codes do* all *letters and numbers correspond*
B. if in only one *pair of codes do* all *letters and numbers correspond*
C. if in only two *pairs of codes do* all *letters and numbers correspond*
D. if in all three *pairs of codes do* all *letters and numbers correspond*

Example:

TQIAJX	567890
TQICCW	567433
JCWQTA	943658

In the Example above, only in two pairs of codes do all of the letters and numbers correspond (on the first and third line). On the second line the number corresponding to the letter C should be 4, not 3. Since in only two of the pairs of codes do all of the letters and numbers correspond, the answer to the Example is C.

9.
JWNAST	932815
CIJNSW	497213
QAXTCJ	680549

10.
WIQWTS	376351
AJIXSN	897012
TAXISQ	580716

11.
SJSWCT	101245
XCTWNI	041327
IJAXCW	728043

12.
XCNIAN	042786
TAJNIX	587290
SCJSCX	149140

13.
WACISJ	284719
IQANXW	768203
WQXJIN	360792

14.
SWTCQA	135468
NJAAWS	298831
XIQTJA	076598

15.
NQTJQI	263067
AXASIC	808174
WCIQTX	347650

16. XQNWCT	062345
IWCXJA	734098
CQNSWT	246135
17. IAIXNA	797028
ATNISN	853712
QIQXNJ	676028
18. SWTJIQ	130967
NQJTSW	268513
CIWAXJ	473809

19. Under a subject filing system, letters are filed in folders labeled according to subject matter. Assume that you have been asked to file a large number of letters under such a filing system. Of the following, the *first* step that you should take in filing these letters is to

    (A) arrange the letters alphabetically under each subject
    (B) determine under which subject each letter is to be filed
    (C) arrange the letters by date under each subject
    (D) prepare cross references for each letter that should be filed under more than one subject

20. Suppose that your supervisor gives you a folder containing a large number of letters arranged in the order of the dates they were received and a list of names of persons in alphabetical order. He asks you to determine, without disturbing the order of the letters, if there is a letter in the folder from each person on the list. Of the following, the best method to use in doing this assignment is

    (A) determine whether the number of letters in the folder is the same as the number of names on the list
    (B) look at each letter to see who wrote it, and then place a light check mark on each letter that has been written by a person on the list
    (C) prepare a list of the names of the writers of the letters that are in the folder, and then place a light check mark next to each of the names on this list if the name appears on the list of persons your supervisor gave you
    (D) look at each letter to see who wrote it, and then place a light check mark next to the name of the person on the list who wrote the letter

Each of the questions 21 through 28 consists of four names. For each question, select the one of the four names that should be third *if the four names were arranged in alphabetical order in accordance with the Rules for Alphabetical Filing given below. Read these rules carefully. Then, for each question, indicate in the correspondingly numbered row on the answer sheet the letter preceding the name that should be* third *in alphabetical order.*

Rules for Alphabetical Filing

Names of Individuals

1. The names of individuals are filed in strict alphabetical order, first according to the last name, then according to first name or initial, and finally according to

middle name or initial. For example: William Jones precedes George Kirk, and Arthur S. Blake precedes Charles M. Blake.

2. When the last names are identical, the one with an initial instead of a first name precedes the one with a first name beginning with the same initial. For example: J. Green precedes Joseph Green.

3. When identical last names also have identical first names, the one without a middle name or initial precedes the one with a middle name or initial. For example: Robert Jackson precedes both Robert C. Jackson and Robert Chester Jackson.

4. When last names are identical and the first names are also identical, the one with a middle initial precedes the one with a middle name beginning with the same initial. For example: Peter A. Brown precedes Peter Alvin Brown.

5. Prefixes such as De, El, La, and Van are considered parts of the names they precede. For example: Wilfred De Wald precedes Alexander Duval.

6. Last names beginning with "Mac" or "Mc" are filed as spelled.

7. Abbreviated names are treated as if they were spelled out. For example: Jos. is filed as Joseph and Robt. is filed as Robert.

8. Titles and designations such as Dr., Mrs., Prof. are disregarded in filing:

Names of Business Organizations

1. The names of business organizations are filed exactly as written, except that an organization bearing the name of an individual is filed alphabetically according to the name of the individual in accordance with the rules for filing names of individuals given above. For example: Thomas Allison Machine Company precedes Northern Baking Company.

2. When numerals occur in a name, they are treated as if they were spelled out. For example: 6 stands for six and 4th stands for fourth.

3. When the following words occur in names, they are disregarded: the, of, and.

Example

  (A) Fred Town   (2) (C) D. Town   (1)
  (B) Jack Towne (3) (D) Jack S. Towne (4)

The numbers in parentheses indicate the proper alphabetical order in which these names should be filed. Since the name that should be filed *third* is Jack Towne, the answer is (*B*).

21. (A) Herbert Restman
    (B) H. Restman
    (C) Harry Restmore
    (D) H. Restmore

22. (A) Martha Eastwood
    (B) Martha E. Eastwood
    (C) Martha Edna Eastwood
    (D) M. Eastwood

23. (A) Timothy Macalan
    (B) Fred McAlden
    (C) Thomas MacAllister
    (D) Mrs. Frank McAllen

24. (A) Elm Trading Co.
    (B) El Dorado Trucking Corp.
    (C) James Eldred Jewelry Store
    (D) Eldridge Printing, Inc.

25. (A) Edward La Gabriel
    (B) Marie Doris Gabriel
    (C) Marjorie N. Gabriel
    (D) Mrs. Marian Gabriel

26. (A) Peter La Vance
    (B) George Van Meer
    (C) Wallace De Vance
    (D) Leonard Vance

27. (A) Fifth Avenue Book Shop
    (B) Mr. Wm. A. Fifner
    (C) 52nd Street Association
    (D) Robert B. Fiffner

28. (A) Dr. Chas. D. Peterson
    (B) Miss Irene F. Petersen
    (C) Lawrence E. Peterson
    (D) Prof. N.A. Petersen

DIRECTIONS for questions 29 through 42:
Each of the questions in this test consists of three names or numbers. For each question, compare the three names or numbers and decide which ones, if any, are exactly the same. Mark your Answer Sheet as follows:

> *Blacken "A" if all three are exactly the same*
> *Blacken "B" if only the first and second are exactly the same*
> *Blacken "C" if only the first and third are exactly the same*
> *Blacken "D" if only the second and third are exactly the same*
> *Blacken "E" if all three are different*

29. 5261383	5261383	5261338
30. 8125690	8126690	8125609
31. W. E. Johnston	W. E. Johnson	W. E. Johnson
32. Vergil L. Muller	Vergil L. Muller	Vergil L Muller
33. Atherton R. Warde	Asheton R. Warde	Atherton P. Warde
34. 2395890	2395890	2395890
35. 1926341	1926347	1926314
36. E. Owens McVey	E. Owen McVey	E. Owen McVay
37. Emily Neal Rouse	Emily Neal Rowse	Emily Neal Rowse
38. H. Merritt Audubon	H. Merriott Audubon	H. Merritt Audubon
39. 6219354	6219354	6219354
40. 2312793	2312793	2312793
41. 1065407	1065407	1065047
42. Francis Ransdell	Frances Ramsdell	Francis Ramsdell

43. The sum of 284.5, 3016.24, 8.9736, and 94.15 is, most nearly,

    (A) 3402.9 (B) 3403.0 (C) 3403.9 (D) 4036.1

44. If 8394.6 is divided by 29.17, the result is most nearly

    (A) 288 (B) 347 (C) 2880 (D) 3470

45. If two numbers are multiplied together, the result is 3752. If one of the two numbers is 56, the other number is

    (A) 41 (B) 15 (C) 109 (D) 67

46. The sum of the fractions 1/4, 2/3, 3/8, 5/6, and 3/4 is

    (A) 20/33 (B) 1 19/24 (C) 2 1/4 (D) 2 7/8

47. The fraction 7/16 expressed as a decimal is

    (A) .1120 (B) .2286 (C) .4375 (D) .4850

48. If .10 is divided by 50, the result is

    (A) .002 (B) .02 (C) .2 (D) 2

49. The number 60 is 40% of

    (A) 24 (B) 84 (C) 96 (D) 150

50. If 3/8 of a number is 96, the number is

    (A) 132 (B) 36 (C) 256 (D) 156

51. An office uses an average of 25 fourteen-cent, 35 seventeen-cent, and 350 twenty-two-cent postage stamps each day. The total cost of stamps used by the office in a five-day period is

    (A) $312.25 (B) $155.55 (C) $430.75 (D) $432.25

52. A city department issued 12,000 applications in 1979. The number of applications that the department issued in 1977 was 25% greater than the number it issued in 1979. If the department issued 10% fewer applications in 1975 than it did in 1977, the number it issued in 1975 was

    (A) 16,500 (B) 13,500 (C) 9,900 (D) 8,100

53. A clerk can add 40 columns of figures an hour by using an adding machine and 20 columns of figures an hour without using an adding machine. The total number of hours it would take him to add 200 columns if he does 3/5 of the work by machine and the rest without the machine is

    (A) 6 (B) 7 (C) 8 (D) 9

54. In 1975, a city department bought 500 dozen pencils at 40 cents per dozen. In 1978, only 75% as many pencils were bought as were bought in 1975, but the price was 20% higher than the 1975 price. The total cost of the pencils bought in 1978 was

    (A) $180 (B) $187.50 (C) $240 (D) $250

55. A clerk is assigned to check the accuracy of the entries on 490 forms. He checks 40 forms an hour. After working one hour on this task, he is joined by another clerk, who checks these forms at the rate of 35 an hour. The total number of hours required to do the entire assignment is

    (A) 5　　　　　　(B) 6　　　　　　(C) 7　　　　　　(D) 8

56. Assume that there is a total of 420 employees in a city agency. Thirty percent of the employees are clerks and 1/7 are typists. The difference between the number of clerks and the number of typists is

    (A) 126　　　　　(B) 66　　　　　(C) 186　　　　　(D) 80

57. Assume that a duplicating machine produces copies of a bulletin at a cost of 2 cents per copy. The machine produces 120 copies of the bulletin per minute. If the cost of producing a certain number of copies was $12, how many minutes of operation did it take the machine to produce this number of copies?

    (A) 5　　　　　　(B) 2　　　　　　(C) 10　　　　　　(D) 6

DIRECTIONS: Questions 58 to 72 each contain a word in capitals followed by four choices of meaning. Choose the definition that most closely corresponds with the word in capitals. On the answer sheet indicate the letter preceding your choice.

58. CAPACITY

    (A) need　　　　(B) willingness　　　　(C) ability　　　　(D) curiosity

59. EXEMPT

    (A) defend　　　(B) excuse　　　　(C) refuse　　　　(D) expect

60. CONFORM

    (A) conceal from view　(B) remember　(C) be in agreement　(D) complain

61. DEVIATE

    (A) turn aside　　(B) deny　　　　(C) come to a halt　　(D) disturb

62. COMPILE

    (A) confuse　　　(B) support　　　(C) compare　　　(D) gather

63. MANIPULATE

    (A) attempt　(B) add incorrectly　(C) handle　(D) investigate closely

64. POTENTIAL

    (A) useful　　　(B) possible　　　(C) welcome　　　(D) rare

65. AUTHORIZE

    (A) write　　　(B) permit　　　(C) request　　　(D) recommend

66. ASSESS

    (A) set a value　(B) belong　　　(C) think highly of　　(D) increase

67. CONVENTIONAL

    (A) democratic   (B) convenient   (C) modern   (D) customary

68. DEPLETE

    (A) replace   (B) exhaust   (C) review   (D) withhold

69. INTERVENE

    (A) sympathize with   (B) differ   (C) ask for an opinion   (D) interfere

70. HAZARDOUS

    (A) dangerous   (B) unusual   (C) slow   (D) difficult

71. SUBSTANTIATE

    (A) replace   (B) suggest   (C) verify   (D) suffer

72. IMMINENT

    (A) anxious   (B) well-known   (C) important   (D) about to happen

Each of the questions 73 through 82 consists of a sentence that may or may not be correct. Examine each sentence carefully and determine whether it is

(A) incorrect because of faulty grammar or sentence structure
(B) incorrect because of faulty punctuation
(C) incorrect because of faulty capitalization
(D) correct

For each question, mark in the correspondingly numbered row on your answer sheet the letter preceding the answer you have selected. The incorrect sentences contain only one error.

73. The office manager asked each employee to work one saturday a month.

74. Neither Mr. Smith nor Mr. Jones was able to finish his assignment on time.

75. The task of filing these cards is to be divided equally between you and he.

76. He is an employee whom we consider to be efficient.

77. I believe that the new employees are not as punctual as us.

78. The employees, working in this office, are to be congratulated for their work.

79. The supervisor entered the room and said, "The work must be completed today."

80. The letter will be sent to the United States senate this week.

81. When the supervisor entered the room, he noticed that the book was laying on the desk.

82. The price of the pens were higher than the price of the pencils.

DIRECTIONS: *Each of the questions 83 through 90 consists of a group of four words. One word in each group is incorrectly spelled. For each question, indicate in the correspondingly numbered row on the answer sheet the letter preceding the word that is incorrectly spelled.*

83. (A) installment   (B) retrieve   (C) concede   (D) dissappear

84. (A) accidentaly   (B) dismissal   (C) conscientious   (D) indelible

85. (A) perceive   (B) carreer   (C) anticipate   (D) acquire

86. (A) plentiful   (B) across   (C) advantagous   (D) similar

87. (A) omission   (B) pamphlet   (C) guarrantee   (D) repel

88. (A) maintenance   (B) always   (C) liable   (D) anouncement

89. (A) exaggerate   (B) sieze   (C) condemn   (D) commit

90. (A) pospone   (B) altogether   (C) grievance   (D) excessive

Answer questions 91 *through* 100 *on the basis of the information in the passage below.*

Microfilm is a method of copying records in miniature. Because of increasing need for information, many organizations are using microfilm as a solution to some of their information problems. Since microfilm cannot be viewed by the naked eye, the micro images are magnified by a reader or reader printer.

Microfilm was first used as a method of saving space or protecting vital records. Today, however, there are additional reasons why an organization would want to preserve records on microfilm rather than in some other way. Microfilm can be used, for example, as an information storage and retrieval tool, as part of an active organizational procedure or system, and to move records from one location to another.

The use of microfilm saves storage space, since one to two cabinets of microfilm hold the equivalent of a hundred cabinets of original records. In fact, microfilmed records will usually occupy only 2 percent of the space taken by records in their original form.

In protecting vital records against loss through disaster, theft, or negligence, microfilm is used by many organizations as a means of ensuring the security of essential information.

As part of an active organizational system or procedure, microfilm is used frequently. Banks use it to microfilm their customers' checks prior to returning them with the bank statement. Most large department stores return original sales slips charged by customers against their accounts with a copy of the customer's monthly statement. Before doing so, however, the stores will microfilm the charge slips to obtain a copy for future reference. Similarly, governmental organizations have found wide application for the use of microfilm.

Finally, microfilm is used to move records from one location to another; the documents are microfilmed and then transmitted by a high-speed electrostatic printer.

91. According to the information in the previous passage, one of the original reasons for using microfilm was to

(A) save time
(B) save money
(C) save space
(D) eliminate telephone work

92. According to the information in the passage above, microfilming can be basically described as a method in which records are

(A) filed
(B) moved
(C) looked at
(D) reduced in size

93. Which of the following is *not* mentioned in the passage above as a use for microfilm?

(A) Destroying outdated records
(B) Protecting vital records
(C) Retrieving information
(D) Moving records

94. According to the information in the passage above, department stores use microfilm to

(A) film shoplifters
(B) keep copies of charge slips
(C) film canceled checks
(D) keep copies of personnel applications

95. According to the information in the passage above, a reader printer is used

(A) as a high-speed duplicator
(B) to view microfilm
(C) to reduce images
(D) as a substitute for the typewriter

96. According to the passage above, an organization will use microfilm to send records from one place to another by

(A) electrostatic printer
(B) mail
(C) messenger
(D) air freight

DIRECTIONS: Answer questions 97 through 100 solely on the basis of the information given in the passage below.

Each year there are more and more time-saving machines designed and manufactured to lighten the work load. Some are simply improved versions of standard equipment such as the typewriter; others are more recent additions to the modern office, such as miniature electronic calculators. Before selecting a new piece of equipment, careful consideration should be given to various important factors: nature of the work, economy, speed, quality of output, operator training time, and service maintenance cost.

For example, assembling and preparing letters, reports, brochures, etc., for mass mailing can be a slow and tiresome process if done by hand. Machines for collating, folding and inserting, addressing, and mailing can save considerable time and cost and reduce fatigue.

Collators gather papers together into sets. Some collators will count, line up, and staple pages, in addition to arranging them in order. Collators come in all sizes and some are high-speed, fully automated models.

If an office staff sends out large amounts of mail to the same people, an addressing machine will eliminate the need to type labels on envelopes. Folding machines fold paper for mailing. They are used for bulk mailings.

Inserting machines carry the mailing operation further by gathering the folded letters or papers and inserting them into envelopes. Some machines will even collect letters, fold and insert them, seal the envelopes, and stamp and address them.

If there is a need to get a lot of correspondence out, it is possible to rent a postage meter. A postage meter automatically seals envelopes and stamps them. It can get the mail out in about a quarter of the time it would otherwise take. The postage meter is taken to the post office periodically and set for the amount of postage purchased.

97. According to the information in the passage above, one recent addition to the office that is used to save time is the

   (A) microprocessor
   (B) word processor
   (C) miniature calculator
   (D) computer terminal

98. According to the information in the passage above, which one of the following is *not* indicated as an advantage of using a postage meter?

   (A) Time can be saved in getting out correspondence
   (B) Letters will be inserted in mailing envelopes
   (C) Mailing envelopes will be sealed
   (D) Mailing envelopes will be stamped

99. According to the information in the passage above, one function of a collator is to

   (A) fold envelopes
   (B) multiply and divide
   (C) insert letters
   (D) staple pages together

100. In the preceding passage, which one of the following is *not* indicated as an important consideration in selecting new office equipment?

   (A) Cost savings
   (B) Time savings
   (C) Training difficulty
   (D) Office morale

Answer Key For Diagnostic Test

Judgment in Office Work

1. B	3. A	5. D	7. B
2. C	4. C	6. D	8. A

Table Coding

9. C	11. A	13. B	15. C	17. A
10. D	12. B	14. D	16. C	18. B

Filing

19. B	21. D	23. B	25. C	27. A
20. D	22. B	24. D	26. D	28. A

Name and Number Comparison

29. B	33. E	37. D	40. A
30. E	34. A	38. C	41. B
31. D	35. E	39. A	42. E
32. A	36. E		

Arithmetic

43. C	48. A	53. B
44. A	49. D	54. A
45. D	50. C	55. C
46. D	51. D	56. B
47. C	52. B	57. A

Vocabulary

58. C	63. C	68. B
59. B	64. B	69. D
60. C	65. B	70. A
61. A	66. A	71. C
62. D	67. D	72. D

Correct Usage—Grammar, Punctuation, Capitalization

73. C	75. A	77. C	79. D	81. A
74. D	76. D	78. B	80. C	82. A

Spelling

83. D	85. B	87. C	89. B
84. A	86. C	88. D	90. A

Reading Comprehension

91. C	93. A	95. B	97. C	99. D
92. D	94. B	96. A	98. B	100. D

Explanatory Answers

Elucidation, clarification, explication, and a little help with the fundamental facts covered in the previous test. These are the points and principles likely to crop up in the form of questions on future tests.

1. **(B)** This question requires the selection of the most important of the choices given. It is of primary importance that the recipient of work instructions clearly understand them. Finding out who performed the work previously may be of some importance on occasion because the present performer of the work may refer to the person who performed the work previously for clarification if needed. However this reason is subordinate to understanding work instructions given by the supervisor.

2. **(C)** There is only one course of action to be taken in this situation. Your supervisor is expecting you to complete the job by a certain time. If you find that you cannot fulfill his expectations, he should be notified so that he may take appropriate action.

3. **(A)** Suggestions that are offered for work improvement are usually appreciated by a supervisor. There is no harm in presenting your point of view to your supervisor. If you present a better method of work performance, it will be appreciated.

4. **(C)** A receptionist must continue to act in a courteous manner no mater how rude visitors may get. The use of courtesy is infectious; it is likely to influence rude visitors to alter their manner.

5. **(D)** Your orders have been specific. There has been no room left for you to alter them. The visitor's reason for requesting an additional application is that he may make a mistake while filling out the original. This is not reason enough for you to disobey your instructions; he should be careful while completing his application.

6. **(D)** When answering a telephone it is proper to identify the section of an agency and the person answering the telephone to the caller at once.

7. **(B)** The use of paper clips to keep related papers together in a file is unsatisfactory. They are likely to become dislodged. Other types of more permanent paper fasteners should be used. The other three choices are satisfactory procedures for preparing papers for filing.

8. **(A)** The key phrases in this question are "to do his work" and "which is available to the public." Your assignment is to act in the absence of Mr. Jones and do his work, and since the information is available to the public, it should be dispensed to the visitor.

9. **(C)** In the pairs of codes on the first and third lines all letters and numbers correspond. On the second line the number corresponding to the letter I should be 7, not 9.

10. **(D)** In the pairs of codes on all three lines all of the letters and numbers correspond.

11. **(A)** In none of the pairs of codes on any of the three lines do all of the letters and numbers correspond. On the first line the number corresponding to J should be 9, not 0. On the second line the number corresponding to T should be 5, not 1. On the third line the number corresponding to J should be 9, not 2.

12. **(B)** In the pairs of codes the letters and numbers correspond only on the third line. On the first line the number corresponding to the letter N should be 2, not 6. On the second line the number corresponding to the letter J should be 9, not 7, and on the same line the number corresponding to I should be 7, not 9.

13. **(B)** In the pairs of codes the letters and numbers correspond only on the second line. On the first line the number corresponding to W should be 3, not 2. On the third line the number corresponding to J should be 9, not 7, and on the same line the number corresponding to I should be 7, not 9.

14. **(D)** In the pairs of codes on all three lines all of the letters and numbers correspond.

15. **(C)** In the pairs of codes on the second and third lines all of the letters and numbers correspond. On the first line the number corresponding to T should be 5, not 3.

16. **(C)** In the pairs of codes on the first and second lines all of the letters and numbers correspond. On the third line the number corresponding to C should be 4, not 2, and on the same line the number corresponding to Q should be 6, not 4. Also on the same line the number corresponding to N should be 2, not 6.

17. **(A)** In none of the pairs of codes on any of the three lines do all of the letters and numbers correspond. On the first line the number corresponding to A should be 8, not 9. On the second line the number corresponding to N should be 2, not 3. On the third line the number corresponding to J should be 9, not 8.

18. **(B)** In the pairs of codes all of the letters and numbers correspond only on the third line. On the first line the number corresponding to T should be 5, not 0. On the second line the number corresponding to J should be 9, not 8.

19. **(B)** This process is frequently referred to as coding. The first step in this process would be the determination of the subject each piece of material is to be filed under.

20. **(D)** The simplest way to find out if there is a letter from each person on the list is to look at each letter in the sequence they are arranged and check off the writers' names on the list. If, after having looked at all the letters, there is a check mark next to each name on the list, there must be a letter in the folder from each person listed.

21. **(D)**
    (A) Herbert Restman (2)
    (B) H. Restman (1)
    (C) Harry Restmore (4)
    (D) H. Restmore (3)

22. **(B)**
    (A) Martha Eastwood (2)
    (B) Martha E. Eastwood (3)

    (C) Martha Edna Eastwood (4)
    (D) M. Eastwood (1)

23. **(B)**
    (A) Timothy Macalan (1)
    (B) Fred McAlden (3)
    (C) Thomas MacAllister (2)
    (D) Mrs. Frank McAllen (4)

24. **(D)**
    (A) Elm Trading Co. (4)
    (B) El Dorado Trucking Corp. (2)
    (C) James Eldred Jewelery Store (1)
    (D) Eldridge Printing, Inc. (3)

25. **(C)**
    (A) Edward La Gabriel (4)
    (B) Marie Doris Gabriel (2)
    (C) Marjorie N. Gabriel (3)
    (D) Mrs. Marian Gabriel (1)

26. **(D)**
    (A) Peter La Vance (2)
    (B) George Van Meer (4)
    (C) Wallace De Vance (1)
    (D) Leonard Vance (3)

27. **(A)**
    (A) Fifth Avenue Book Shop (3)
    (B) Mr. Wm. A. Fifner (2)
    (C) 52nd Street Association (4)
    (D) Robert B. Fifner (1)

28. **(A)**
    (A) Dr. Chas D. Peterson (3)
    (B) Miss Irene F. Peterson (1)
    (C) Lawrence E. Peterson (4)
    (D) Prof. N. A. Petersen (2)

Questions 29 through 42:

    After a careful review of these questions, the correct answers are self-explanatory. These questions test your powers of observation and your ability to pay attention to details. Although accuracy is the obvious key to answering these questions, it is also important that they should be completed at a reasonable speed. With practice, speed in answering these types of questions can be improved significantly.

    43. **(C)**
       284.5
     3016.24
         8.9736
        94.15
       ──────
    3403.8636 or 3403.9 (answer)

44. **(A)**

$$
29.17 \overline{)8394.60} \quad \begin{array}{r} 287 + \quad \text{(answer)} \end{array}
$$

$$
\begin{array}{r}
5834 \\ \hline
2560\ 6 \\ \hline
2333\ 6 \\ \hline
227\ 00 \\ \hline
204\ 19 \\ \hline
2\ 81
\end{array}
$$

45. **(D)**

To find the missing number in this multiplication problem, simply divide the given multiplied number into the product.

$$
56 \overline{)3752} \quad 67 \text{ (answer)}
$$

$$
\begin{array}{r}
336 \\ \hline
392 \\
392
\end{array}
$$

46. **(D)**

$$\frac{1}{4} = \frac{6}{24}$$

$$\frac{2}{3} = \frac{16}{24}$$

$$\frac{3}{8} = \frac{9}{24}$$

$$\frac{5}{6} = \frac{20}{24}$$

$$\frac{3}{4} = \frac{18}{24}$$

$$\frac{69}{24} = 2\frac{7}{8}$$
(answer)

$$2\frac{21}{24} \text{ reduced to } 2\frac{7}{8}$$

$$
24 \overline{)69}
$$

$$
\begin{array}{r}
48 \\ \hline
21
\end{array}
$$

47. **(C)**

$$\frac{7}{\cancel{16}4} \times \frac{\cancel{100}^{25}}{1} = \frac{175}{4} = .4375 \text{ (answer)}$$

48. **(A)**

$$50\overline{)\,.100}$$
$$\underline{100}$$

.002 (answer)

49. **(D)**
40% is equal to ⅖, therefore ⅕ of 60 here is equal to 30, and ⅘, or the whole number, is 5 × 30 or 150.

50. **(C)**

$$\frac{3}{8} = 96$$

$$\frac{1}{8} = 32$$

$$\frac{8}{8} = 8 \times 32 = 256 \text{ (answer)}$$

51. **(D)**
DAILY STAMP USE

$$
\begin{aligned}
25 \times 14¢ &= \$ \ 3.50 \\
35 \times 17¢ &= \ 5.95 \\
350 \times 22¢ &= \underline{77.00} \\
&\ \$86.45 \text{ Daily}
\end{aligned}
$$

$86.45 × 5 days = $432.25 (answer)

52. **(B)**

1979 —	12,000	(given information)
1977 —	15,000	increase of 25%, or 3,000
		(¼ × 1200) from 1979 figure
1975 —	− 1,500	10% (1,500) fewer than 1977
	13,500	(answer)

53. **(B)**

$$\frac{3}{\cancel{8}} \times \overset{40}{\cancel{200}} = 120 \text{ by machine}$$

120 ÷ 40 = 3 hours

$$\frac{2}{\cancel{8}} \times \overset{40}{\cancel{200}} = 80 \text{ by hand}$$

80 ÷ 20 = 4 hours

4 + 3 = 7 hours (answer)

54. **(A)**

(1975)   500
            .40
         ─────
         $200.00

(1978) 25% of 500 = 125

500 − 125 = 375

$.40 × 120% = $ .48
                   375
               ─────
                 $ .48
                 ─────
                 30 00
                 15 00
               ─────
               $180.00 (answer)

55. **(C)**

   490 total
  − 40 first hour
  ─────
   450 balance to be done

40 first clerk
35 second clerk
─────
75 together one hour

       6 hours   6 hours
75)450   + 1 hour
  450   ─────
  ───   7 (answer)

56. **(B)**

30% is equal to $\frac{3}{10}$

$\frac{3}{10} \times \overset{42}{420} \times 126$ clerks

$\frac{1}{7} \times \overset{60}{420} = 60$ typists

   126
 − 60
 ─────
   66 (answer)

57. **(A)**

$12 ÷ 2¢ = 600 copies $\overset{6\ 00}{.02\overline{)12.00}}$

600 ÷ 120 = 5 minutes (answer)

Questions 58 through 72:

The use of the dictionary is recommended in reviewing these questions. It is advisable that you look up the meaning of all words of which you are unfamiliar —both correct and incorrect. When you encounter new or not quite familiar words, the use of the dictionary is the only sure way to increase your vocabulary.

73. **(C)** *Saturday* should be capitalized, as are all of the days of the week.

74. **(D)** Correct. *Neither* or *nor* calls for a singular verb.

75. **(A)** you and *him.* Following a preposition (*between*) both pronouns in the sentence must be in the objective case.

76. **(D)** Correct. The object of the verb *consider* is *whom;* therefore, the personal pronoun is correctly in the objective case.

77. **(A)** ". . . punctual as *we."* The personal pronoun should be in the nominative case, since it is the subject of the verb *are.*

78. **(B)** The commas are unnecessary. If we eliminated the phrase the commas set up, it would change the meaning of the sentence.

79. **(D)** Correct. Since the sentence gives the exact words of the supervisor, his statement is correctly enclosed between quotation marks.

80. **(C)** *Senate* is part of a proper noun and should be capitalized.

81. **(A)** *Lying* is correct. When an object is resting on a surface or a person is in the act of reclining, use *lie, lay* (past tense), *lying.*

82. **(A)** *Price,* the subject of the sentence is singular. Therefore, it takes a singular verb, *was.* It is a common error to make the verb agree with the noun next to it in the sentence, in this case with *pens* instead of the subject.

83. **(D)** di*s*appear

84. **(A)** accidental*l*y

85. **(B)** ca*r*eer

86. **(C)** advantag*e*ous

87. **(C)** gua*r*antee

88. **(D)** an*n*ouncement

89. **(B)** s*ei*ze (one of the exceptions to the *i*-before-*e* rule)

90. **(A)** pos*t*pone

91. **(C)** First sentence of the second paragraph.

92. **(D)** First sentence of the first paragraph.

93. **(A)** The destruction of original records is not mentioned, although it is often done.

94. **(B)** Fifth paragraph, third sentence.

95. **(B)** Last sentence of the first paragraph.

96. **(A)** Final paragraph.

97. **(C)** First paragraph, second sentence.

98. **(B)** Read the last paragraph. The postage meter does not insert letters into envelopes.

99. **(D)** Third paragraph, second sentence.

100. **(D)** Office morale is not mentioned at all in this passage.

Use of the Diagnostic Table

In the Diagnostic Table below, there are three lines for every subject area listed in the Answer Key. Each line shows the number of correct answers, indicating whether your knowledge in that area is strong, average, or weak.

Count the number of your correct answers in each subject area and enter your scores on the appropriate lines of the Diagnostic Table. Your scores of correct answers on the table will pinpoint the areas in which you need more study and practice to improve your test performance.

Diagnostic Table

Subject Area	Correct Answers		Your correct answer score
Judgment in Office Work	8 7 0–6	←Strong→ ←Average→ ←Weak→	
Table Coding	9–10 7–8 0–6	←Strong→ ←Average→ ←Weak→	
Filing	9–10 7–8 0–6	←Strong→ ←Average→ ←Weak→	
Name and Number Comparisons	13–14 10–12 0–9	←Strong→ ←Average→ ←Weak→	
Arithmetic	13–15 11–12 0–10	←Strong→ ←Average→ ←Weak→	
Vocabulary	13–15 11–12 0–10	←Strong→ ←Average→ ←Weak→	
Correct Usage	9–10 7–8 0–6	←Strong→ ←Average→ ←Weak→	
Spelling	8 7 0–6	←Strong→ ←Average→ ←Weak→	
Reading Comprehension	9–10 7–8 0–6	←Strong→ ←Average→ ←Weak→	

Part Two

REVIEW OF SUBJECTS AND PRACTICE TESTS

Study Materials and Practice Tests

Study materials and practice tests are provided for the various subjects covered by questions on actual exams. Before starting on the practice tests for a subject area, review the study material for that subject. This will give you the necessary background knowledge to answer those questions. The study material will refresh your knowledge of what you have learned in school and will also cover additional information directly related to office work.

For test questions that measure the ability to perform clerical office work, no study materials are provided because answering these questions requires no prior special knowledge. They test powers of observation and attention to detail. Accuracy and speed are crucial to achieve a high score on these tests. Although you cannot study for questions relating to clerical abilities, you can improve your score significantly by extensive practice. This book provides numerous clerical-ability tests of various kinds, which will enable you to increase your score through practice.

Answer Sheet For Judgment In Office Work Practice Test

1 Ⓐ Ⓑ Ⓒ Ⓓ	18 Ⓐ Ⓑ Ⓒ Ⓓ	35 Ⓐ Ⓑ Ⓒ Ⓓ Ⓔ
2 Ⓐ Ⓑ Ⓒ Ⓓ	19 Ⓐ Ⓑ Ⓒ Ⓓ	36 Ⓐ Ⓑ Ⓒ Ⓓ Ⓔ
3 Ⓐ Ⓑ Ⓒ Ⓓ	20 Ⓐ Ⓑ Ⓒ Ⓓ	37 Ⓐ Ⓑ Ⓒ Ⓓ Ⓔ
4 Ⓐ Ⓑ Ⓒ Ⓓ	21 Ⓐ Ⓑ Ⓒ Ⓓ	38 Ⓐ Ⓑ Ⓒ Ⓓ Ⓔ
5 Ⓐ Ⓑ Ⓒ Ⓓ	22 Ⓐ Ⓑ Ⓒ Ⓓ	39 Ⓐ Ⓑ Ⓒ Ⓓ Ⓔ
6 Ⓐ Ⓑ Ⓒ Ⓓ	23 Ⓐ Ⓑ Ⓒ Ⓓ	40 Ⓐ Ⓑ Ⓒ Ⓓ Ⓔ
7 Ⓐ Ⓑ Ⓒ Ⓓ	24 Ⓐ Ⓑ Ⓒ Ⓓ	41 Ⓐ Ⓑ Ⓒ Ⓓ Ⓔ
8 Ⓐ Ⓑ Ⓒ Ⓓ	25 Ⓐ Ⓑ Ⓒ Ⓓ	42 Ⓐ Ⓑ Ⓒ Ⓓ Ⓔ
9 Ⓐ Ⓑ Ⓒ Ⓓ	26 Ⓐ Ⓑ Ⓒ Ⓓ	43 Ⓐ Ⓑ Ⓒ Ⓓ Ⓔ
10 Ⓐ Ⓑ Ⓒ Ⓓ	27 Ⓐ Ⓑ Ⓒ Ⓓ	44 Ⓐ Ⓑ Ⓒ Ⓓ Ⓔ
11 Ⓐ Ⓑ Ⓒ Ⓓ	28 Ⓐ Ⓑ Ⓒ Ⓓ	45 Ⓐ Ⓑ Ⓒ Ⓓ Ⓔ
12 Ⓐ Ⓑ Ⓒ Ⓓ	29 Ⓐ Ⓑ Ⓒ Ⓓ	46 Ⓐ Ⓑ Ⓒ Ⓓ Ⓔ
13 Ⓐ Ⓑ Ⓒ Ⓓ	30 Ⓐ Ⓑ Ⓒ Ⓓ	47 Ⓐ Ⓑ Ⓒ Ⓓ
14 Ⓐ Ⓑ Ⓒ Ⓓ	31 Ⓐ Ⓑ Ⓒ Ⓓ	48 Ⓐ Ⓑ Ⓒ Ⓓ Ⓔ
15 Ⓐ Ⓑ Ⓒ Ⓓ	32 Ⓐ Ⓑ Ⓒ Ⓓ	49 Ⓐ Ⓑ Ⓒ Ⓓ Ⓔ
16 Ⓐ Ⓑ Ⓒ Ⓓ	33 Ⓐ Ⓑ Ⓒ Ⓓ	50 Ⓐ Ⓑ Ⓒ Ⓓ Ⓔ
17 Ⓐ Ⓑ Ⓒ Ⓓ	34 Ⓐ Ⓑ Ⓒ Ⓓ Ⓔ	

JUDGMENT IN OFFICE WORK PRACTICE TEST

Time: 60 minutes. 50 questions.

DIRECTIONS: Select from the choices offered in each of the following the one that is correct or most nearly correct.

1. An invoice is usually a

   (A) check   (B) bond   (C) bill   (D) inventory

2. A letter that contains payment of a bill is called

   (A) a collection letter
   (B) a letter of remittance
   (C) an adjustment letter
   (D) an order letter

3. An enforceable business agreement is called

   (A) a contract   (B) a bill of lading   (C) an invoice   (D) a statement

4. An assignee is

   (A) a series of payments made periodically
   (B) a legal seizure of valuables
   (C) a state of insolvency
   (D) one to whom property is turned over

5. "A clerk in a city agency should realize that each letter he sends out in response to a letter of inquiry from the public represents an expenditure of time and money by his agency." Of the following, the most valid implication of this quotation is that such a clerk should

   (A) use the telephone to answer letters of inquiry directly and promptly
   (B) answer mail inquiries with lengthy letters to eliminate the need for further correspondence
   (C) prevent the accumulation of a large number of similar inquiries by answering each of these letters promptly
   (D) use simple, concise language in answer to letters of inquiry

6. Assume you are the receptionist for Mr. Brown, an official in your department. It is your duty to permit only persons having important business to see this official; otherwise, you are to refer them to other members of the staff. A man tells you that he must see Mr. Brown on a very urgent and confidential matter. He gives you his name and says that Mr. Brown knows him, but he does not wish to tell you the nature of the matter. Of the following, the best action for you to take under these circumstances is to

   (A) permit this man to see Mr. Brown without further question, since the matter seems to be urgent

(B) refer this man to another member of the staff, since Mr. Brown may not wish to see him
(C) call Mr. Brown and explain the situation to him, and ask him whether he wishes to see this man
(D) tell this man that you will permit him to see Mr. Brown only if he informs you of the nature of his business

7. Suppose that you are assigned to the information window of a city department where you come into daily contact with many people. On one occasion a man asks you for some information in a very arrogant and rude manner. Of the following, the best reason for you to give this man the requested information politely is

(A) he may not mean to be rude; it may just be his manner of speech
(B) it is the duty of city employees to teach members of the public to be polite
(C) he will probably apologize for his manner when he sees that you are polite
(D) city employees are expected to be courteous to the public

8. A city agency whose employees come into frequent contact with the public can gain public approval of its work most effectively by

(A) distributing pamphlets describing its objectives and work to the people who come into contact with the agency
(B) encouraging its employees to behave properly when off duty so as to impress the public favorably
(C) making certain that its employees perform their daily services efficiently and courteously
(D) having its officials give lectures to civic groups, describing the agency's efficiency and accomplishments

9. A visitor to an office in a city agency tells one of the clerks that he has an appointment with the supervisor of the office, who is expected shortly. The visitor asks for permission to wait in the supervisor's private office, which is unoccupied at the moment. For the clerk to allow the visitor to do so would be

(A) desirable; the visitor would be less likely to disturb the other employees or to be disturbed by them
(B) undesirable; it is not courteous to permit a visitor to be left alone in an office
(C) desirable; the supervisor may wish to speak to the visitor in private
(D) undesirable; the supervisor may have left confidential papers on his desk

10. Assume that you are a newly appointed clerk in a city agency. While your superior is at a conference that may last for several hours, a visitor enters the office and asks you for information on certain of your agency's procedures with which you are not familiar. Of the following, the best action for you to take is to

(A) ask the visitor to return to the office later in the day when your superior will have returned
(B) ask the visitor to wait in the office until your superior returns
(C) ask a more experienced clerk in your office to answer the visitor's questions.
(D) advise the visitor that the information that he is seeking will be given to him if he writes to your superior

11. Assume that you are one of several clerks employed in the office of a city department. Members of the public occasionally visit the office to obtain

information. Because your desk is nearest the entrance to the office, most of these visitors direct their inquiries to you. One morning when everyone, including yourself, is busy, a visitor enters the office and asks you for some readily available information. Of the following, the best action for you to take is to

(A) disregard his question in the hope that he will direct his inquiry to another clerk
(B) inform him politely that you are busy now and ask him to return in the afternoon
(C) give him the requested information concisely but courteously and then continue with your work
(D) advise him to write a letter to your department so that the information can be sent to him

12. A clerk notices that a visitor has just entered the office. The other clerks are not aware of the visitor's presence. The most appropriate of the following actions for the clerk to take is to

(A) attend to the visitor immediately
(B) continue with his/her own work and leave the visitor to one of the other clerks
(C) cough loudly to direct the attention of the other clerks to the presence of the visitor
(D) continue with his/her work unless the visitor addresses him directly

13. Of the following, the most appropriate greeting for a receptionist to use in addressing visitors is

(A) "Please state your business."
(B) "May I help you?"
(C) "Hello. What is your problem?"
(D) "Do you wish to see someone?"

14. A clerk in a city agency informs Mr. Brown, an applicant for a license issued by the city agency, that the application filed by him was denied because he lacks eighteen months of the required experience. Shortly after the applicant leaves the agency's office, the clerk realizes that Mr. Brown lacks only six months of the required experience. Of the following, the most desirable procedure to be followed in connection with this matter is that

(A) a printed copy of the requirements should be sent to Mr. Brown
(B) a letter explaining and correcting the error should be sent to Mr. Brown
(C) no action should be taken because Mr. Brown is not qualified at the present time for the license
(D) a report of this matter should be prepared and attached to Mr. Brown's application for reference if Mr. Brown should file another application

15. Suppose that you are the secretary to Mr. Smith, the administrative official who is responsible for securing special equipment, supplies, and services for your department. In carrying out his duties, Mr. Smith interviews agents of companies interested in having your department utilize their products and services. You have been informed by Mr. Smith that he does not wish to see certain agents. The best one of the following methods that you may use in denying an interview to one of these unwelcome representatives is to

(A) inform him frankly and bluntly that Mr. Smith has left specific instructions that certain agents are not to be granted interviews
(B) tell him that Mr. Smith has left the office and will not return that day

(C) take his calling card, note the reason for his call, and then tell him that he will be notified by mail or telephone when Mr. Smith wishes to see him
(D) make a note of the nature of his business; then inform him that Mr. Smith will be busy for the remainder of that day and request him to return to the office at a later date

16. As a secretary to a division chief, you may receive requests for information that you know should not be divulged. Of the following replies you may give to such a request received over the telephone, the best one is

(A) "I regret to advise you that it is the policy of the department not to give out this information over the telephone."
(B) "If you hold on a moment, I'll have you connected with the chief of the division."
(C) "I am sorry that I cannot help you, as we are not permitted to give out any information regarding such matters."
(D) "I am sorry, but I know nothing regarding this matter."

17. You overhear two of your fellow workers, a typist and a file clerk, quarreling during working hours. The best of the following procedures for you to follow immediately is

(A) reprimand both workers for creating a disturbance
(B) pay no attention to the quarrel
(C) report the matter to your superior
(D) defend the abused person

18. Accuracy is of greater importance than speed in filing chiefly because

(A) city offices have a tremendous amount of filing to do
(B) fast workers are usually inferior workers
(C) there is considerable difficulty in locating materials that have been filed incorrectly
(D) there are many varieties of filing systems that may be used

19. "Many persons dictate so rapidly that they pay little attention to matters of punctuation and English, but they expect their stenographers to correct errors." This statement implies most clearly that stenographers should be

(A) able to write acceptable original reports when required
(B) good citizens as well as good stenographers
(C) efficient clerks as well as good stenographers
(D) knowledgeable in correct English usage

20. "A typed letter should resemble a picture properly framed." This emphasizes

(A) accuracy   (B) speed   (C) convenience   (D) neatness

21. Of the following, the chief advantage of the use of a mechanical check writer is that it

(A) guards against tearing in handling the check
(B) decreases the possibility of alteration in the amount of the check
(C) tends to prevent the mislaying and loss of checks
(D) facilitates keeping checks in proper order for mailing

22. Of the following, the chief advantage of the use of a dictating machine is that

(A) the stenographer need not take rapid dictation
(B) the person dictating tends to make few errors
(C) the dictator may be dictating letters while the stenographer is busy at some other task
(D) the usual noise in an office is lessened

23. In the absence of specific instructions, the best of the following things for a clerk to do when his/her superior does not wish to interview a visitor is to tell the visitor that

(A) the superior is too busy to see him, and let the visitor go
(B) the superior is out, and ask the visitor to come back another day
(C) the superior will be busy for some time and cannot see him, but that you as his/her secretary will be glad to help in any way you can
(D) the superior is not in, and let him go

24. One of your assignments is the filing of correspondence. You are about to file a letter, addressed to the superintendent and stamped with a receipt date of a week ago, when you realize that the major part of the signature has been torn away. In order to determine under what name the letter is to be filed, the best of the following actions for you to take *first* is to

(A) read the letter for possible clues as to the identity of the writer
(B) show the letter to another clerk in your office and ask what he/she would do
(C) ask the superintendent if he/she remembers the name of the writer of the letter
(D) ask the mail clerk if he/she remembers the name of the writer of the letter

25. Suppose that you have been assigned to proofread a typed copy of a mimeographed report with another clerk. The mimeographed report was prepared in another department, and the copy prepared in your own office. Your supervisor has asked you to make corrections neatly in ink. You are reading aloud from the mimeographed report while the other clerk follows the copy. You notice an obvious spelling error in the mimeographed report that has been repeated in the copy. Of the following, the best action to take is to

(A) correct the spelling error on the mimeographed report only
(B) return the mimeographed report for correction to the department that prepared it
(C) correct the spelling error on both the mimeographed report and copy
(D) leave the spelling error in both the mimeographed report and the copy

26. Assume that you are delivering incoming mail to the office in which you are working. After you have opened a letter addressed to the chief, you discover that the envelope is marked "personal." Of the following, the best action for you to take is to

(A) reseal the letter and say nothing about it in order to avoid any unpleasantness
(B) deliver the letter in the opened envelope and wait to see if anything happens
(C) read the letter and if it does not really seem to be of a personal nature, deliver it without the envelope
(D) deliver the letter in the opened envelope and explain what happened

27. A salesman has a card index file of his customers arranged alphabetically according to their last names. He/she wants to identify for easy reference those of his/her customers residing in each of the five boroughs of New York City. Of the following, the most helpful for the purpose of easy reference would be to

(A) insert in a folder the card of each customer that resides in the same borough
(B) use different-size cards for customers residing in each of the five boroughs
(C) use different-color cards for customers residing in each of the five boroughs
(D) underline the borough in the addresses of customers on each card

28. Assume that you are a storeroom clerk in charge of keeping a card inventory that contains a separate card for each type of article, such as sheets, towels, pillowcases. These articles are obtained from a central purchasing agency under specified code numbers. A single code number usually applies to a rather large group of articles; for example, the above-mentioned items would have a single code number indicating linens. Of the following, the best procedure is to file the cards

(A) first alphabetically, then by code number
(B) first by code number, then alphabetically within each code number
(C) alphabetically, disregarding code number
(D) by code number only

29. One of your duties as a clerk may be to answer routine credit inquiries concerning the employees of your department. These inquiries generally ask for confirmation of employment and salary. However, you have received a letter which, in addition to the usual request, asks for an opinion as to whether or not the credit of the person involved is good. Of the following, the best action for you to take *first* is to

(A) refer the letter of inquiry to your supervisor before making any reply
(B) give a favorable reply, since the employee probably needs the article he wishes to buy
(C) consult the person involved and ask him whether or not he can afford this purchase
(D) ask other employees in the department what they know of this person's financial condition

30. Suppose that a typist in your office has just finished typing a report prepared by you. You are about to proofread the copy with her. She suggests that she read aloud from the original while you check the copy. Compared with the alternative of your reading from the original while the typist checks her own work, this procedure is

(A) more desirable; the typist will have an opportunity to detect errors in the original report
(B) less desirable; the typist should have the opportunity to discover her own errors
(C) less desirable; you are given the opportunity to review your own report once more
(D) more desirable; whenever possible, a person's work should be checked by someone else, rather than by himself/herself

31. Suppose that you are a clerk assigned to the employment office of a hospital. One of your duties is to conduct preliminary interviews with people seeking low-salaried jobs, such as laundry workers and kitchen helpers. You know that at the present time such help is hard to get. An applicant tells you that he has worked at the hospital before. You look up his record and find that he was frequently absent from work. Of the following, the best action for you to take is to

(A) tell him that his past record prevents further employment
(B) refer him to the head of the division in which he seeks employment, after explaining the circumstances to the division head

(C) tell him to report for work immediately

(D) tell him to seek employment at some other institution

32. Suppose that you have been adding a typed list of amounts of money, extending over several pages. You have computed a subtotal at the end of each page. The grand total you have found should check with an amount given to you by your supervisor, but is too large by seven dollars. Of the following, the step you should take *first* in order to detect your error in the computation is to

(A) check the addition of the subtotals

(B) verify the accuracy of each subtotal

(C) add all the figures, disregarding the subtotals

(D) add the column immediately left of the decimal point, since that is where the error occurs

33. Your supervisor has given you instructions concerning the method to be used in doing a certain job. You do not understand the reasons for these instructions. For you to ask your supervisor to explain his reasons would be

(A) wise; you will probably do a better job if you understand the whole picture

(B) unwise; a supervisor is not required to explain the reasons for his/her instructions

(C) wise; you will probably gain the confidence of your supervisor

(D) unwise; you will be wasting your supervisor's time

34. Suppose that you are a clerk assigned to the information desk in your department. Your function is to give information to members of the public who telephone or call in person. It is a busy period of the year. There is a line of seventeen people waiting to speak to you. Because you are constantly being interrupted by telephone calls for information, however, you are unable to give any attention to the people waiting in line. The line is increasing in length. Of the following, the best action for you to take is to

(A) explain courteously to the people in line that you will probably be unable to help them

(B) advise the people at the end of the line that you will probably not reach them for some time and suggest that they come back when you are less busy

(C) ask the switchboard operator to answer telephone requests for information herself/himself instead of putting the calls on your extension

(D) ask your supervisor to assign another clerk to answer telephone calls so that you can give your full attention to the people in line

(E) take care of all of the people in the line before answering any more telephone calls

35. One of your duties as a clerk may be to deliver mimeographed copies of administrative orders to administrators in your department. It is not necessary for an administrator to sign a receipt for his/her copy of an order. One of the administrators to whom you are requested to deliver a copy of an order is not at his desk when you make your usual tour of the offices. Of the following, the best action for you to take is to

(A) keep this order until a later order is issued and then deliver both orders at the same time

(B) wait until you meet the administrator in the corridor and give him his copy in person

(C) leave a note on the administrator's desk requesting him to call at the mail room for his copy

(D) wait at the administrator's desk until he returns

(E) leave the administrator's copy of the order on his desk

36. One of your duties as a clerk may be to deliver interoffice mail to all of the offices in the department in which you work. Of the following, the best procedure for you to follow before you deliver the letters is, in general, to arrange them on the basis of the

(A) offices to which the letters are to be delivered

(B) dates on which the letters were written

(C) specific persons by whom the letters were signed

(D) offices from which the letters come

(E) dates on which the letters were received in the mail room

37. Suppose that your supervisor has asked you to type a copy of a statistical table. In general, the best method for checking the copy to make certain that it is absolutely accurate is to

(A) type a second copy of the table and compare the two copies

(B) have another clerk read the original table aloud to you while you read the copy

(C) compare all totals in the two tables, for if the totals check the copy is probably accurate

(D) check the one or two points in the table at which an error is most likely to be made

(E) examine the copy to determine whether all entries look reasonable

38. Of the following, the most important caution to observe before beginning work on a new task assigned to you by your supervisor is that

(A) you understand fully the relationship of that task to the general function of your department

(B) you know precisely how long the task will take to complete

(C) you will be able to finish the task within a week or two

(D) you understand fully your supervisor's instructions for doing the task

(E) the other clerk in the office knows what your assignment is

39. As a clerk, you may be assigned the duty of opening and sorting the mail coming to your department. The one of the following that is the best reason for not discarding the envelopes in which letters come from members of the public until you have glanced at the letters is that

(A) it is sometimes necessary to return a letter to the writer in the original envelope

(B) the subject of a letter can, of course, be determined only from the letter itself

(C) the envelopes should usually be filed together with the letters

(D) members of the public frequently neglect to include a return address in their letters

(E) the precise bureau in the department to which a letter should be forwarded sometimes cannot be determined from the envelope

40. Suppose that your supervisor has asked you and another clerk to proofread a stencil. The other clerk is reading rapidly to you from the original copy while you are checking the stencil. For you to interrupt his reading and make an immediate notation of each error you find is

(A) wise; you might otherwise forget to note the error
(B) foolish; such action slows down the reading
(C) foolish; such action demonstrates that the copy is not accurate
(D) wise; such action demonstrates that the rate of reading may be increased
(E) foolish; interruptions waste time

41. One of the administrators in your department cannot find an important letter left on his desk. He believes that the letter may accidentally have been placed among a group of letters sent to you for filing. You look in the file and find the letter filed in its correct place. Of the following, the best suggestion for you to make to your supervisor in order to avoid repetition of such incidents is that

    (A) file clerks should be permitted to read material they are requested to file
    (B) correspondence files should be cross-indexed
    (C) a periodic check should be made of the files to locate material inaccurately filed
    (D) material sent to the file clerk for filing should be marked "O.K. for filing"
    (E) only authorized persons should be permitted to take materials from the files

42. One of your duties as a clerk is to keep a file of administrative orders by date. Your supervisor often asks you to find the order concerning a particular subject. Since you are rarely able to remember the date of the order, it is necessary for you to search through the entire file. Of the following the best suggestion for you to make to your supervisor for remedying this situation is that

    (A) each order bear conspicuously in its upper lefthand corner the precise date on which it is issued
    (B) old orders be taken from the file and destroyed as soon as they are superseded by new orders, so that the file will not be overcrowded
    (C) an alphabetic subject index of orders be prepared so that orders can be located easily by content as well as date
    (D) dates be eliminated entirely from orders
    (E) the content of each order be summarized briefly at the end of the order

43. As a clerk, you are regularly assigned to the information desk of your department. When you report for work at 9 A.M. one morning, you find four people waiting to speak to you. When the first person, Mr. Williams, explains his problem, you realize that his case is unusual and that it will be necessary to make an exhaustive search of record files in other parts of the building. There is no other clerk available to help you. For you to explain the situation to Mr. Williams and to ask him to be seated until you have had an opportunity to speak to the other persons who are waiting would be wise chiefly because

    (A) to answer the questions of the other persons may requre a very brief time
    (B) Mr. Williams was probably not the first to arrive, although he was the first to speak to you
    (C) every person seeking information from the department should be asked to wait a short time
    (D) one of the other persons waiting may be able to supply the information in which Mr. Williams is interested
    (E) unusual problems should not be given preference over routine matters

44. Assume that, as a clerk, you are assigned to the information desk of your department. A man makes a request on which, according to your instructions, action cannot be taken unless a detailed application form has been filled out and

filed. You therefore hand a blank form to this person and request that he fill it out. He looks briefly at the form and then tells you that he does not have the necessary information immediately available. His records, he tells you, are at home. For you to advise him to fill out the form at home and to mail it to the department, instead of asking him to attempt to guess at the necessary information, would be wise chiefly because

(A) he may not be able to determine accurately, by only a brief inspection, whether the necessary information is immediately available
(B) inaccurate information on an application form may lead to a considerable waste of time
(C) mail is generally acceptable as a way of delivering official documents
(D) needless work would be created if the application must be returned to the man for additional information
(E) the department would gain an additional day or two to act on his request

45. Suppose that you are assigned to the mail room in your department. It is your duty to open incoming letters and to route them to the appropriate offices. Of the following, the best reason for you to become thoroughly acquainted with the functions and procedures of the various offices in your department is that

(A) many letters are addressed to the department rather than to a specific office or individual
(B) routine letters should be answered without referring them to another office
(C) an accurate directory of departmental employees is an invaluable aid to the mail clerk
(D) letters concerning important matters of policy should be acknowledged before they are referred to another office
(E) it would require too much time for the clerk to open every letter before forwarding it to the proper office

46. You are assigned the duty of receiving applications filed in person at your department. Applications filed by mail are handled by another clerk. The one of the following that is the best reason for glancing through an application being filed in person, before accepting that application, is that

(A) the person filing the application may not be the applicant
(B) false information on the application may be detected
(C) obvious mistakes in filling out the form should be brought to the attention of the person filing the application before he/she leaves
(D) there may be sections of the application uncompleted
(E) each applicant should be held strictly accountable for the number of forms wasted because of careless or avoidable errors

47. Usually, the use of a money order is preferable to sending currency in ordinary mail because

(A) money orders bear interest at the rate of 2 percent
(B) money orders may be deposited or cashed in banks
(C) there is less chance of theft
(D) proof of identity is not required in cashing a money order at a post office

48. While you are working at the information desk of your department, a man requests certain application forms which, he claims, are being distributed by your department. As far as you know, no such forms are being distributed by your department. For you to question the man as to the reason for his request would be

(A) wise; such information may indicate that he should contact another department

(B) unwise; he is obviously well-informed concerning the availability of the forms

(C) unwise; valuable time will be wasted if he is mistaken

(D) unwise; his reason for requesting the forms is immaterial in view of the fact that the forms are not available

(E) unwise; he may wish to obtain the forms for a friend or relative

49. One of the duties to which you as a clerk may be assigned is the distribution of mail from the central mail room to the various departmental offices. Of the following, the best reason for waiting until all of the mail has been sorted before you begin to distribute the mail is that

(A) more mail can be carried at any one time

(B) you can devote time to other duties

(C) mail can be distributed immediately on being received in the mail room

(D) fewer trips to the departmental offices will be required

(E) no office will receive more mail than it can handle at any one time

50. Suppose that your supervisor has asked you to work on five long-range assignments simultaneously. In general, for you to change regularly every two or three hours from one assignment to another would be

(A) wise; greater variety would be introduced into your work

(B) unwise; getting ready and putting away the material necessary for each assignment would consume excessive time

(C) wise; approaching a new task with a fresh mind would enable you to work more efficiently

(D) unwise; you would be unable to devote equal time to each assignment

(E) wise; no one assignment could be completed before the others

Answer Key for Judgment in Office Work Practice Test

1. C	18. C	35. E
2. B	19. D	36. A
3. A	20. D	37. B
4. D	21. B	38. D
5. D	22. C	39. D
6. C	23. C	40. A
7. D	24. A	41. D
8. C	25. C	42. C
9. D	26. D	43. A
10. C	27. C	44. B
11. C	28. B	45. A
12. A	29. A	46. C
13. B	30. D	47. C
14. B	31. B	48. A
15. C	32. A	49. D
16. C	33. A	50. B
17. B	34. D	

TESTS OF ALPHABETIZING AND FILING

Even though the computer has taken over the job of storing and retrieving much information, paper handling is still a vital aspect of office work. Correspondence and records kept on paper must be systematically stored and easy to find.

To this end, files are established according to some system. Whatever the system in your office may be, you will quickly learn it. No matter how the system is cross-referenced and how papers are actually filed, the base of the system must be the alphabet. If you know the rules of alphabetical filing, you will easily adapt to the specifics of your office's methods.

In testing your clerical aptitude, the prospective employer will be testing your mastery of alphabetic filing and your ability to learn and to adapt to the specific filing system used in that office. Since your ability to learn and to follow a filing system depends largely on your ability to follow instructions, the directions for answering filing questions may be quite complicated. Be sure that you fully understand the directions before you attempt to answer any filing questions.

On some clerical examinations, a short list of rules for filing precedes the test questions. If your exam has such a list of rules, read it very carefully. If any information contradicts your own understanding of the rules of filing, disregard your own method and follow the printed rules precisely. If no rules precede your filing questions, then you must draw on your own knowledge of the rules of alphabetizing and filing.

Even though you know the alphabet as well as you know your own name, when faced with an alphabetizing or filing test, you may find yourself getting flustered. Rather than having to run through the alphabet repeatedly in your head, take a few seconds to write out the alphabet across the top of the page in your test booklet. Having the alphabet before you for ready reference can save time in answering these questions and prevent careless errors.

Rules for Alphabetic Filing

Names of Individuals

RULE 1: The names of individuals are filed in strict alphabetical order, first according to last name, then according to first name or initial, and finally according to middle name or initial. For example, *George Allen* comes before *Edward Bell,* and *Leonard P. Reston* comes before *Lucille B. Reston.*

RULE 2: When last names and first initials are the same, the one with the initial comes before the one with the name written out. For example, *A. Green* comes before *Agnes Green.*

RULE 3: When first and last names are the same, the name without a middle initial comes before the one with a middle name or initial. For example, *John Doe* comes before both *John A. Doe* and *John Alan Doe.*

RULE 4: When first and last names are the same, the name with a middle initial comes before the one with a middle name beginning with the same initial. For example, *Jack R. Hertz* comes before *Jack Richard Hertz.*

RULE 5: A quick summary of rules 2, 3, and 4 reads: "Nothing comes before something and less comes before more."

Example:

King	King, Dorothy
King, D.	King, Dorothy A.
King, D. A.	King, Dorothy Anne
King, D. Anne	

The same rule applies to the filing of businesses and organizations. Thus, *A.A.A. Exterminating* is filed before *Atlas Exterminating*.

RULE 6: Prefixes such as *De, O', Mac, Mc,* and *Van* are filed exactly as written and are treated as part of the names they come before. Ignore apostrophes for purposes of filing. For example, *Robert O'Dea* is filed before *David Olsen*, and *Gladys McTeague* is filed before *Frances Meadows*.

RULE 7: Foreign names are filed as spelled. Prefixes are not considered separately. Likewise, foreign language articles (*le, La, Les, El,* etc.), whether they begin with a lower case or capital letter, are considered part of the name with which they appear.

Example:

Da Costa, Carl	De Takacs, Maria
D'Agnota, Ugo	L'Aiglon
Des Verney, Elizabeth	Les Miserables

RULE 8: Hyphenated surnames are indexed as though the hyphen joined the two parts, making one. Thus, *Lyttonet, Amadeus* is filed before *Lytton-Strachey, John*.

RULE 9: Abbreviated names are treated as if they were spelled out. For example, *Chas.* is filed as *Charles*, and *Thos.* is filed as *Thomas*.

RULE 10: Titles and designations, such as *Dr., Mr., Prof., Jr.,* or *II*, are given last consideration in filing.

Names of Business Organizations

RULE 11: The names of business organizations, institutions, and buildings are filed according to the order in which each word in the name appears, *except* where these names include the full names of individuals.

Example:

General Electric Company	General Mills
General Foods	General Telephone and Telegraph

RULE 12: Where the names of firms, corporations, institutions, and buildings include the full names of individuals, the firm names are filed under the rules for filing individual names.

Example:

Rice, Bernard, and Co.	Rice Electronics
Rice Delivery Service	Rice, Francis P.
Rice, Edward, and Sons Ltd.	

RULE 13: When *the, of, and,* or an apostrophe are parts of a business name, they are disregarded for purposes of filing.

RULE 14: Names that include numerals should be filed as if the numerals were spelled out. Thus, *10th Street Bootery* is filed as *Tenth Street Bootery*.

Example:

> 8th Avenue Bookshop = Eighth Avenue Bookshop
> 5th Street Church = Fifth Street Church
> 4th National Bank = Fourth National Bank
> 7th Avenue Restaurant = Seventh Avenue Restaurant

RULE 15: When the same names appear with different addresses, arrange them alphabetically according to town or city, considering state only where there is a duplication of town or city names.

Example:

> American Tobacco Co.   Norfolk, VA
> American Tobacco Co.   Osceola, FL
> American Tobacco Co.   Quincy, IL
> American Tobacco Co.   Quincy, MA

RULE 16: Abbreviations are alphabetized as though the words were spelled out in full.

Example:

> Indus. Bros. of America = Industrial Brothers . . .
> Indus. Bldrs. of America = Industrial Builders . .

RULE 17: Hyphenated firm names are treated as *separate* words.

Example:

> Oil-O-Matic Heating Co.
> Oilimatic Heating Co.

RULE 18: Compound geographic names written as separate words are always treated as separate words.

Example:

> West Chester
> West Milton
> Westchester
> Western Chicago Railway
> Westinghouse

RULE 19: Bureaus, boards, offices, and departments of government are filed under the name of the chief governing body. For example, *Bureau of the Budget* would be filed as if written *Budget, Bureau of the*.

Answer Sheet For Filing Practice Tests

Test 1

1 Ⓐ Ⓑ Ⓒ Ⓓ Ⓔ   11 Ⓐ Ⓑ Ⓒ Ⓓ Ⓔ   21 Ⓐ Ⓑ Ⓒ Ⓓ Ⓔ
2 Ⓐ Ⓑ Ⓒ Ⓓ Ⓔ   12 Ⓐ Ⓑ Ⓒ Ⓓ Ⓔ   22 Ⓐ Ⓑ Ⓒ Ⓓ Ⓔ
3 Ⓐ Ⓑ Ⓒ Ⓓ Ⓔ   13 Ⓐ Ⓑ Ⓒ Ⓓ Ⓔ   23 Ⓐ Ⓑ Ⓒ Ⓓ Ⓔ
4 Ⓐ Ⓑ Ⓒ Ⓓ Ⓔ   14 Ⓐ Ⓑ Ⓒ Ⓓ Ⓔ   24 Ⓐ Ⓑ Ⓒ Ⓓ Ⓔ
5 Ⓐ Ⓑ Ⓒ Ⓓ Ⓔ   15 Ⓐ Ⓑ Ⓒ Ⓓ Ⓔ   25 Ⓐ Ⓑ Ⓒ Ⓓ Ⓔ
6 Ⓐ Ⓑ Ⓒ Ⓓ Ⓔ   16 Ⓐ Ⓑ Ⓒ Ⓓ Ⓔ   26 Ⓐ Ⓑ Ⓒ Ⓓ Ⓔ
7 Ⓐ Ⓑ Ⓒ Ⓓ Ⓔ   17 Ⓐ Ⓑ Ⓒ Ⓓ Ⓔ   27 Ⓐ Ⓑ Ⓒ Ⓓ Ⓔ
8 Ⓐ Ⓑ Ⓒ Ⓓ Ⓔ   18 Ⓐ Ⓑ Ⓒ Ⓓ Ⓔ   28 Ⓐ Ⓑ Ⓒ Ⓓ Ⓔ
9 Ⓐ Ⓑ Ⓒ Ⓓ Ⓔ   19 Ⓐ Ⓑ Ⓒ Ⓓ Ⓔ   29 Ⓐ Ⓑ Ⓒ Ⓓ Ⓔ
10 Ⓐ Ⓑ Ⓒ Ⓓ Ⓔ   20 Ⓐ Ⓑ Ⓒ Ⓓ Ⓔ   30 Ⓐ Ⓑ Ⓒ Ⓓ Ⓔ

Test 2

1 Ⓐ Ⓑ Ⓒ Ⓓ   11 Ⓐ Ⓑ Ⓒ Ⓓ   21 Ⓐ Ⓑ Ⓒ Ⓓ
2 Ⓐ Ⓑ Ⓒ Ⓓ   12 Ⓐ Ⓑ Ⓒ Ⓓ   22 Ⓐ Ⓑ Ⓒ Ⓓ
3 Ⓐ Ⓑ Ⓒ Ⓓ   13 Ⓐ Ⓑ Ⓒ Ⓓ   23 Ⓐ Ⓑ Ⓒ Ⓓ
4 Ⓐ Ⓑ Ⓒ Ⓓ   14 Ⓐ Ⓑ Ⓒ Ⓓ   24 Ⓐ Ⓑ Ⓒ Ⓓ
5 Ⓐ Ⓑ Ⓒ Ⓓ   15 Ⓐ Ⓑ Ⓒ Ⓓ   25 Ⓐ Ⓑ Ⓒ Ⓓ
6 Ⓐ Ⓑ Ⓒ Ⓓ   16 Ⓐ Ⓑ Ⓒ Ⓓ   26 Ⓐ Ⓑ Ⓒ Ⓓ
7 Ⓐ Ⓑ Ⓒ Ⓓ   17 Ⓐ Ⓑ Ⓒ Ⓓ   27 Ⓐ Ⓑ Ⓒ Ⓓ
8 Ⓐ Ⓑ Ⓒ Ⓓ   18 Ⓐ Ⓑ Ⓒ Ⓓ   28 Ⓐ Ⓑ Ⓒ Ⓓ
9 Ⓐ Ⓑ Ⓒ Ⓓ   19 Ⓐ Ⓑ Ⓒ Ⓓ   29 Ⓐ Ⓑ Ⓒ Ⓓ
10 Ⓐ Ⓑ Ⓒ Ⓓ   20 Ⓐ Ⓑ Ⓒ Ⓓ   30 Ⓐ Ⓑ Ⓒ Ⓓ

Test 3

1 Ⓐ Ⓑ Ⓒ Ⓓ   15 Ⓐ Ⓑ Ⓒ Ⓓ
2 Ⓐ Ⓑ Ⓒ Ⓓ   16 Ⓐ Ⓑ Ⓒ Ⓓ
3 Ⓐ Ⓑ Ⓒ Ⓓ   17 Ⓐ Ⓑ Ⓒ Ⓓ
4 Ⓐ Ⓑ Ⓒ Ⓓ   18 Ⓐ Ⓑ Ⓒ Ⓓ
5 Ⓐ Ⓑ Ⓒ Ⓓ   19 Ⓐ Ⓑ Ⓒ Ⓓ
6 Ⓐ Ⓑ Ⓒ Ⓓ   20 Ⓐ Ⓑ Ⓒ Ⓓ
7 Ⓐ Ⓑ Ⓒ Ⓓ   21 Ⓐ Ⓑ Ⓒ Ⓓ
8 Ⓐ Ⓑ Ⓒ Ⓓ   22 Ⓐ Ⓑ Ⓒ Ⓓ
9 Ⓐ Ⓑ Ⓒ Ⓓ   23 Ⓐ Ⓑ Ⓒ Ⓓ
10 Ⓐ Ⓑ Ⓒ Ⓓ   24 Ⓐ Ⓑ Ⓒ Ⓓ
11 Ⓐ Ⓑ Ⓒ Ⓓ
12 Ⓐ Ⓑ Ⓒ Ⓓ
13 Ⓐ Ⓑ Ⓒ Ⓓ
14 Ⓐ Ⓑ Ⓒ Ⓓ

Test 4

1 Ⓐ Ⓑ Ⓒ Ⓓ Ⓔ	11 Ⓐ Ⓑ Ⓒ Ⓓ Ⓔ	21 Ⓐ Ⓑ Ⓒ Ⓓ Ⓔ	31 Ⓐ Ⓑ Ⓒ Ⓓ Ⓔ
2 Ⓐ Ⓑ Ⓒ Ⓓ Ⓔ	12 Ⓐ Ⓑ Ⓒ Ⓓ Ⓔ	22 Ⓐ Ⓑ Ⓒ Ⓓ Ⓔ	32 Ⓐ Ⓑ Ⓒ Ⓓ Ⓔ
3 Ⓐ Ⓑ Ⓒ Ⓓ Ⓔ	13 Ⓐ Ⓑ Ⓒ Ⓓ Ⓔ	23 Ⓐ Ⓑ Ⓒ Ⓓ Ⓔ	33 Ⓐ Ⓑ Ⓒ Ⓓ Ⓔ
4 Ⓐ Ⓑ Ⓒ Ⓓ Ⓔ	14 Ⓐ Ⓑ Ⓒ Ⓓ Ⓔ	24 Ⓐ Ⓑ Ⓒ Ⓓ Ⓔ	34 Ⓐ Ⓑ Ⓒ Ⓓ Ⓔ
5 Ⓐ Ⓑ Ⓒ Ⓓ Ⓔ	15 Ⓐ Ⓑ Ⓒ Ⓓ Ⓔ	25 Ⓐ Ⓑ Ⓒ Ⓓ Ⓔ	35 Ⓐ Ⓑ Ⓒ Ⓓ Ⓔ
6 Ⓐ Ⓑ Ⓒ Ⓓ Ⓔ	16 Ⓐ Ⓑ Ⓒ Ⓓ Ⓔ	26 Ⓐ Ⓑ Ⓒ Ⓓ Ⓔ	36 Ⓐ Ⓑ Ⓒ Ⓓ Ⓔ
7 Ⓐ Ⓑ Ⓒ Ⓓ Ⓔ	17 Ⓐ Ⓑ Ⓒ Ⓓ Ⓔ	27 Ⓐ Ⓑ Ⓒ Ⓓ Ⓔ	37 Ⓐ Ⓑ Ⓒ Ⓓ Ⓔ
8 Ⓐ Ⓑ Ⓒ Ⓓ Ⓔ	18 Ⓐ Ⓑ Ⓒ Ⓓ Ⓔ	28 Ⓐ Ⓑ Ⓒ Ⓓ Ⓔ	38 Ⓐ Ⓑ Ⓒ Ⓓ Ⓔ
9 Ⓐ Ⓑ Ⓒ Ⓓ Ⓔ	19 Ⓐ Ⓑ Ⓒ Ⓓ Ⓔ	29 Ⓐ Ⓑ Ⓒ Ⓓ Ⓔ	39 Ⓐ Ⓑ Ⓒ Ⓓ Ⓔ
10 Ⓐ Ⓑ Ⓒ Ⓓ Ⓔ	20 Ⓐ Ⓑ Ⓒ Ⓓ Ⓔ	30 Ⓐ Ⓑ Ⓒ Ⓓ Ⓔ	40 Ⓐ Ⓑ Ⓒ Ⓓ Ⓔ

Test 5

1 ___	26 ___	51 ___
2 ___	27 ___	52 ___
3 ___	28 ___	53 ___
4 ___	29 ___	54 ___
5 ___	30 ___	55 ___
6 ___	31 ___	56 ___
7 ___	32 ___	57 ___
8 ___	33 ___	58 ___
9 ___	34 ___	59 ___
10 ___	35 ___	60 ___
11 ___	36 ___	61 ___
12 ___	37 ___	62 ___
13 ___	38 ___	63 ___
14 ___	39 ___	64 ___
15 ___	40 ___	65 ___
16 ___	41 ___	66 ___
17 ___	42 ___	67 ___
18 ___	43 ___	68 ___
19 ___	44 ___	69 ___
20 ___	45 ___	70 ___
21 ___	46 ___	71 ___
22 ___	47 ___	72 ___
23 ___	48 ___	73 ___
24 ___	49 ___	74 ___
25 ___	50 ___	75 ___

Test 6

1 Ⓐ Ⓑ Ⓒ Ⓓ Ⓔ	4 Ⓐ Ⓑ Ⓒ Ⓓ Ⓔ	7 Ⓐ Ⓑ Ⓒ Ⓓ Ⓔ
2 Ⓐ Ⓑ Ⓒ Ⓓ Ⓔ	5 Ⓐ Ⓑ Ⓒ Ⓓ Ⓔ	8 Ⓐ Ⓑ Ⓒ Ⓓ Ⓔ
3 Ⓐ Ⓑ Ⓒ Ⓓ Ⓔ	6 Ⓐ Ⓑ Ⓒ Ⓓ Ⓔ	9 Ⓐ Ⓑ Ⓒ Ⓓ Ⓔ

Test 7

1 Ⓐ Ⓑ Ⓒ Ⓓ   5 Ⓐ Ⓑ Ⓒ Ⓓ   8 Ⓐ Ⓑ Ⓒ Ⓓ
2 Ⓐ Ⓑ Ⓒ Ⓓ   6 Ⓐ Ⓑ Ⓒ Ⓓ   9 Ⓐ Ⓑ Ⓒ Ⓓ
3 Ⓐ Ⓑ Ⓒ Ⓓ   7 Ⓐ Ⓑ Ⓒ Ⓓ   10 Ⓐ Ⓑ Ⓒ Ⓓ
4 Ⓐ Ⓑ Ⓒ Ⓓ

Test 8

1 Ⓐ Ⓑ Ⓒ Ⓓ   5 Ⓐ Ⓑ Ⓒ Ⓓ   9 Ⓐ Ⓑ Ⓒ Ⓓ
2 Ⓐ Ⓑ Ⓒ Ⓓ   6 Ⓐ Ⓑ Ⓒ Ⓓ   10 Ⓐ Ⓑ Ⓒ Ⓓ
3 Ⓐ Ⓑ Ⓒ Ⓓ   7 Ⓐ Ⓑ Ⓒ Ⓓ   11 Ⓐ Ⓑ Ⓒ Ⓓ
4 Ⓐ Ⓑ Ⓒ Ⓓ   8 Ⓐ Ⓑ Ⓒ Ⓓ   12 Ⓐ Ⓑ Ⓒ Ⓓ

Test 9

1 Ⓐ Ⓑ Ⓒ   3 Ⓐ Ⓑ Ⓒ   5 Ⓐ Ⓑ Ⓒ   7 Ⓐ Ⓑ Ⓒ
2 Ⓐ Ⓑ Ⓒ   4 Ⓐ Ⓑ Ⓒ   6 Ⓐ Ⓑ Ⓒ   8 Ⓐ Ⓑ Ⓒ

Test 10

1 Ⓐ Ⓑ Ⓒ Ⓓ   5 Ⓐ Ⓑ Ⓒ Ⓓ   8 Ⓐ Ⓑ Ⓒ Ⓓ
2 Ⓐ Ⓑ Ⓒ Ⓓ   6 Ⓐ Ⓑ Ⓒ Ⓓ   9 Ⓐ Ⓑ Ⓒ Ⓓ
3 Ⓐ Ⓑ Ⓒ Ⓓ   7 Ⓐ Ⓑ Ⓒ Ⓓ   10 Ⓐ Ⓑ Ⓒ Ⓓ
4 Ⓐ Ⓑ Ⓒ Ⓓ

Test 1

TIME: 30 minutes. 30 questions.

DIRECTIONS: In each of the following questions there is a name enclosed in a box, and a series of four other names in proper alphabetic order. The spaces between the names are lettered (A), (B), (C), (D), and (E). Decide where the boxed name belongs in proper alphabetic order in that series, then blacken the capital letter of your choice on your answer sheet.

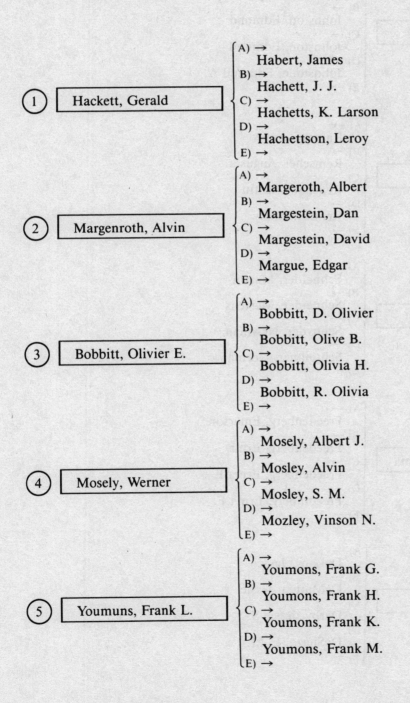

1. Hackett, Gerald

A) →
Habert, James
B) →
Hachett, J. J.
C) →
Hachetts, K. Larson
D) →
Hachettson, Leroy
E) →

2. Margenroth, Alvin

A) →
Margeroth, Albert
B) →
Margestein, Dan
C) →
Margestein, David
D) →
Margue, Edgar
E) →

3. Bobbitt, Olivier E.

A) →
Bobbitt, D. Olivier
B) →
Bobbitt, Olive B.
C) →
Bobbitt, Olivia H.
D) →
Bobbitt, R. Olivia
E) →

4. Mosely, Werner

A) →
Mosely, Albert J.
B) →
Mosley, Alvin
C) →
Mosley, S. M.
D) →
Mozley, Vinson N.
E) →

5. Youmuns, Frank L.

A) →
Youmons, Frank G.
B) →
Youmons, Frank H.
C) →
Youmons, Frank K.
D) →
Youmons, Frank M.
E) →

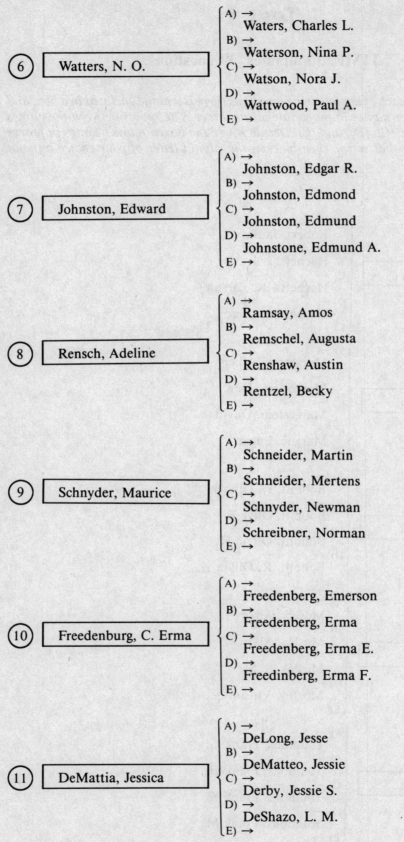

⑥ Watters, N. O.
- A) →
  Waters, Charles L.
- B) →
  Waterson, Nina P.
- C) →
  Watson, Nora J.
- D) →
  Wattwood, Paul A.
- E) →

⑦ Johnston, Edward
- A) →
  Johnston, Edgar R.
- B) →
  Johnston, Edmond
- C) →
  Johnston, Edmund
- D) →
  Johnstone, Edmund A.
- E) →

⑧ Rensch, Adeline
- A) →
  Ramsay, Amos
- B) →
  Remschel, Augusta
- C) →
  Renshaw, Austin
- D) →
  Rentzel, Becky
- E) →

⑨ Schnyder, Maurice
- A) →
  Schneider, Martin
- B) →
  Schneider, Mertens
- C) →
  Schnyder, Newman
- D) →
  Schreibner, Norman
- E) →

⑩ Freedenburg, C. Erma
- A) →
  Freedenberg, Emerson
- B) →
  Freedenberg, Erma
- C) →
  Freedenberg, Erma E.
- D) →
  Freedinberg, Erma F.
- E) →

⑪ DeMattia, Jessica
- A) →
  DeLong, Jesse
- B) →
  DeMatteo, Jessie
- C) →
  Derby, Jessie S.
- D) →
  DeShazo, L. M.
- E) →

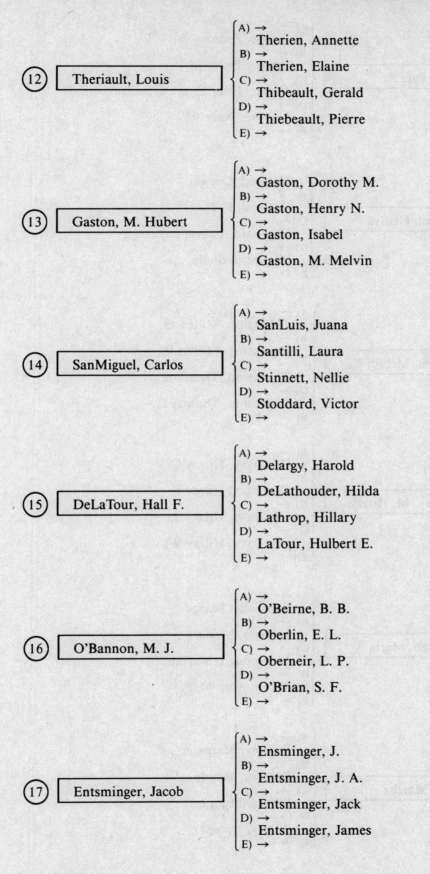

(12) Theriault, Louis
A) →
Therien, Annette
B) →
Therien, Elaine
C) →
Thibeault, Gerald
D) →
Thiebeault, Pierre
E) →

(13) Gaston, M. Hubert
A) →
Gaston, Dorothy M.
B) →
Gaston, Henry N.
C) →
Gaston, Isabel
D) →
Gaston, M. Melvin
E) →

(14) SanMiguel, Carlos
A) →
SanLuis, Juana
B) →
Santilli, Laura
C) →
Stinnett, Nellie
D) →
Stoddard, Victor
E) →

(15) DeLaTour, Hall F.
A) →
Delargy, Harold
B) →
DeLathouder, Hilda
C) →
Lathrop, Hillary
D) →
LaTour, Hulbert E.
E) →

(16) O'Bannon, M. J.
A) →
O'Beirne, B. B.
B) →
Oberlin, E. L.
C) →
Oberneir, L. P.
D) →
O'Brian, S. F.
E) →

(17) Entsminger, Jacob
A) →
Ensminger, J.
B) →
Entsminger, J. A.
C) →
Entsminger, Jack
D) →
Entsminger, James
E) →

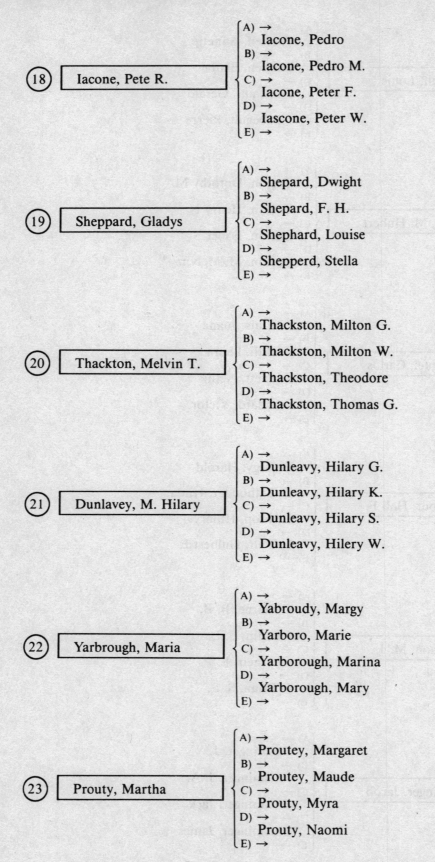

(18) Iacone, Pete R.
- A) →
  Iacone, Pedro
- B) →
  Iacone, Pedro M.
- C) →
  Iacone, Peter F.
- D) →
  Iascone, Peter W.
- E) →

(19) Sheppard, Gladys
- A) →
  Shepard, Dwight
- B) →
  Shepard, F. H.
- C) →
  Shephard, Louise
- D) →
  Shepperd, Stella
- E) →

(20) Thackton, Melvin T.
- A) →
  Thackston, Milton G.
- B) →
  Thackston, Milton W.
- C) →
  Thackston, Theodore
- D) →
  Thackston, Thomas G.
- E) →

(21) Dunlavey, M. Hilary
- A) →
  Dunleavy, Hilary G.
- B) →
  Dunleavy, Hilary K.
- C) →
  Dunleavy, Hilary S.
- D) →
  Dunleavy, Hilery W.
- E) →

(22) Yarbrough, Maria
- A) →
  Yabroudy, Margy
- B) →
  Yarboro, Marie
- C) →
  Yarborough, Marina
- D) →
  Yarborough, Mary
- E) →

(23) Prouty, Martha
- A) →
  Proutey, Margaret
- B) →
  Proutey, Maude
- C) →
  Prouty, Myra
- D) →
  Prouty, Naomi
- E) →

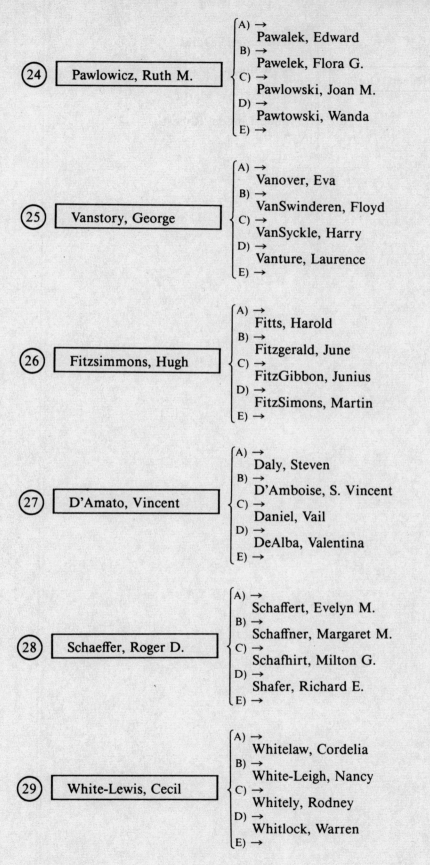

(24) Pawlowicz, Ruth M.
- A) →
- Pawalek, Edward
- B) →
- Pawelek, Flora G.
- C) →
- Pawlowski, Joan M.
- D) →
- Pawtowski, Wanda
- E) →

(25) Vanstory, George
- A) →
- Vanover, Eva
- B) →
- VanSwinderen, Floyd
- C) →
- VanSyckle, Harry
- D) →
- Vanture, Laurence
- E) →

(26) Fitzsimmons, Hugh
- A) →
- Fitts, Harold
- B) →
- Fitzgerald, June
- C) →
- FitzGibbon, Junius
- D) →
- FitzSimons, Martin
- E) →

(27) D'Amato, Vincent
- A) →
- Daly, Steven
- B) →
- D'Amboise, S. Vincent
- C) →
- Daniel, Vail
- D) →
- DeAlba, Valentina
- E) →

(28) Schaeffer, Roger D.
- A) →
- Schaffert, Evelyn M.
- B) →
- Schaffner, Margaret M.
- C) →
- Schafhirt, Milton G.
- D) →
- Shafer, Richard E.
- E) →

(29) White-Lewis, Cecil
- A) →
- Whitelaw, Cordelia
- B) →
- White-Leigh, Nancy
- C) →
- Whitely, Rodney
- D) →
- Whitlock, Warren
- E) →

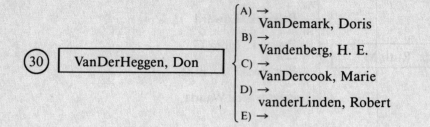

(30) | VanDerHeggen, Don

A) →
VanDemark, Doris
B) →
Vandenberg, H. E.
C) →
VanDercook, Marie
D) →
vanderLinden, Robert
E) →

Test 2

TIME: 30 minutes. 30 questions.

DIRECTIONS: Each of the following exercises consists of a capitalized word that is to be filed correctly. Indicate the word before *which the capitalized word should be filed by blackening the letter preceding that word on your sheet.*
In the following example the correct answer is (B).

Example
HARMONY
(A) Growth   (B) Hegemony   (C) Holdout   (D) Indicator

1. BIOGRAPHY:
   (A) Bible   (B) Bibliography   (C) Bilge   (D) Biology

2. DRAMA:
   (A) Drawing   (B) Drayton   (C) Dreyfus   (D) Drugs

3. INQUISITION:
   (A) Industry   (B) Insurance   (C) International   (D) Interne

4. LUGUBRIOUS:
   (A) Lucretius   (B) Lumber   (C) Luther   (D) Lutheran

5. OCEANIC:
   (A) Occult   (B) Ohio   (C) Oklahoma   (D) Optics

6. ENGLAND:
   (A) Engineering   (B) English   (C) Engraving   (D) Entomology

7. IRRIGATION:
   (A) Ireland   (B) Irish   (C) Iron   (D) Irving

8. MARINE:
   (A) Margolin   (B) Marketing   (C) Mary   (D) Maryland

9. PALEONTOLOGY:
   (A) Pacific   (B) Painting   (C) Palestine   (D) Paltry

10. ASIATIC:
    (A) Ascetic   (B) Assyriology   (C) Astronomy   (D) Astrophysics

11. ENTOMOLOGY:
    (A) Endocrine   (B) Erasmus   (C) Eskimo   (D) Etching

12. GREAT BRITAIN:

(A) Grant   (B) Greece   (C) Greek   (D) Greeley

13. JAPAN:

(A) Jackson   (B) James   (C) Japanese   (D) Java

14. MENUS:

(A) Melville   (B) Mennonites   (C) Merchandising   (D) Meredith

15. PEDAGOGY:

(A) Peace   (B) Pediatrics   (C) Penman   (D) Penology

16. ARCHIVES:

(A) Archaeology   (B) Architecture   (C) Arctic   (D) Arkansas

17. HAGIOGRAPHY:

(A) Hamilton   (B) Hardy   (C) Hawaiiana   (D) Hays

18. LEGEND:

(A) Legacy   (B) Legal   (C) Legislation   (D) Legislative

19. METALLURGY:

(A) Metal   (B) Mete   (C) Meteorology   (D) Methodist

20. PHILIPPINE:

(A) Philately   (B) Philology   (C) Philosopher   (D) Philosophy

21. MONTAIGNE:

(A) Monastic   (B) Money   (C) Montana   (D) Mountain

22. LANGUAGES:

(A) Land   (B) Landscape   (C) Lanier   (D) Lantern

23. ANATOMY:

(A) Anabaptistica   (B) Anarchism   (C) Annuals   (D) Anthropology

24. CONFEDERATE:

(A) Congregational   (B) Connecticut   (C) Conrad   (D) Contamination

25. FOOD:

(A) Florida   (B) Folklore   (C) Foreign   (D) Forestry

26. LITERATURE:

(A) Lincoln   (B) Lithograph   (C) Lithuanian   (D) Liturgy

27. MICROSCOPY:

    (A) Michigan   (B) Middle   (C) Military   (D) Milton

28. PHYSICS:

    (A) Physiocrat   (B) Physical   (C) Physician   (D) Psychical

29. CATHOLIC:

    (A) Catacombs   (B) Catalogs   (C) Catechisms   (D) Cattle

30. FRANCE:

    (A) Franciscan   (B) Franklin   (C) Fraternity   (D) Free

Test 3

DIRECTIONS: In Column I you will find four names to be filed. The names are lettered *w*, *x*, *y*, and *z*. In Column II are four possible orders for alphabetizing those names. You are to choose the arrangement that constitutes the correct filing order according to the rules for alphabetic filing and mark the letter that precedes the correct order.

Examples:

Column I		**Column II**	
1. (w)	Jane Doe	(A)	x, y, z, w
(x)	Janet Doe	(B)	w, z, y, x
(y)	J. A. Doe	(C)	y, z, w, x
(z)	J. Ann Doe	(D)	z, w, x, y

Ⓐ Ⓑ Ⓒ Ⓓ

The correct way to file these names is

(y)	Doe, J.A.
(z)	Doe, J. Ann
(w)	Doe, Jane
(x)	Doe, Janet

So the correct answer is (C).

Column I		**Column II**	
2. (w)	Thomas McLain	(A)	y, w, z, x
(x)	McLain Trucking Co.	(B)	z, y, w, x
(y)	T. J. McLain	(C)	x, w, y, z
(z)	McLain & Sons	(D)	y, x, w, z

Ⓐ Ⓑ Ⓒ Ⓓ

The correct answer is (B) because the names should be filed in the following order:

(z)	McLain and Sons
(y)	McLain, T. J.
(w)	McLain, Thomas
(x)	McLain Trucking Co.

TIME: 24 minutes. 24 questions.

		Column I		**Column II**

1.
   (w) Devine, Sarah   (A) x, y, z, w
   (x) Devine, S.   (B) z, x, y, w
   (y) Devine, Sara H.   (C) y, x, z, w
   (z) Devin, Sarah   (D) z, y, x, w

2.
   (w) Bennet, C.   (A) y, x, z, w
   (x) Benett, Chuck   (B) x, w, y, z
   (y) Bennet, Chas.   (C) z, x, y, w
   (z) Bennett, Charles   (D) z, y, x, w

3.
   (w) Rivera, Ilena   (A) w, x, z, y
   (x) Riviera, Ilene   (B) z, w, y, x
   (y) Rivere, I.   (C) w, y, z, x
   (z) Riviera Ice-Cream Co.   (D) x, z, w, y

4.
   (w) Corral, Dr. Robert   (A) x, w, y, z
   (x) Carrale, Prof. Robert   (B) z, y, w, x
   (y) Corren, R.   (C) w, y, z, x
   (z) Corret, Ron   (D) x, z, w, y

5.
   (w) Chas. A. Levine   (A) w, y, x, z
   (x) Kurt Levene   (B) z, y, x, w
   (y) Charles Levine   (C) x, z, y, w
   (z) Kurt E. Levene   (D) x, w, y, z

6.
   (w) Majorca Leather Goods   (A) w, y, x, z
   (x) Robert Maiorca and Sons   (B) x, y, z, w
   (y) Maintenance Management Corp.   (C) y, z, x, w
   (z) Majestic Carpet Mills   (D) y, x, z, w

7.
   (w) Prof. Geo. Kinkaid   (A) z, y, x, w
   (x) Mr. Alan Kinkaid   (B) z, x, y, w
   (y) Dr. Albert A. Kinkade   (C) z, y, w, x
   (z) Kincade Liquors Inc.   (D) z, w, y, x

	Column I		**Column II**
8.	(w) Charles Green	(A)	z, y, x, w
	(x) Chas. T. Greene	(B)	x, z, w, y
	(y) Charles Thomas Greene	(C)	w, x, z, y
	(z) Wm. A. Greene	(D)	w, x, y, z
9.	(w) Doris MacAllister	(A)	y, w, z, x
	(x) D. McAllen	(B)	w, x, z, y
	(y) Lewis T. MacBride	(C)	w, y, x, z
	(z) Lewis McBride	(D)	w, z, x, y
10.	(w) John Foss Insurance Co.	(A)	w, y, x, z
	(x) New World Stove Co.	(B)	z, x, w, y
	(y) 14th Street Dress Shop	(C)	w, x, z, y
	(z) Arthur Stein Paper Co.	(D)	y, z, w, x
11.	(w) 6th Ave. Swim Shop	(A)	x, w, y, z
	(x) Sport Shoe Store	(B)	x, y, z, w
	(y) The Sky Ski School	(C)	y, z, w, x
	(z) 23rd Street Salon	(D)	w, y, x, z
12.	(w) Charlotte Stair	(A)	z, y, x, w
	(x) C. B. Stare	(B)	z, x, y, w
	(y) Charles B. Stare	(C)	z, w, x, y
	(z) Elaine La Stella	(D)	z, x, w, y
13.	(w) Gold Trucking Co.	(A)	w, y, z, x
	(x) 8th Ave. Garage	(B)	x, y, z, w
	(y) The First National Bank	(C)	z, x, y, w
	(z) The Century Novelty Co.	(D)	x, z, w, y
14.	(w) Robert B. Pierce	(A)	x, w, z, y
	(x) R. Bruce Pierce	(B)	y, x, w, z
	(y) Ronald Pierce	(C)	w, z, x, y
	(z) Robert Bruce Pierce	(D)	x, y, z, w
15.	(w) Four Seasons Sports Club	(A)	w, z, y, x
	(x) 14 Street Shopping Center	(B)	y, w, z, x
	(y) Forty Thieves Restaurant	(C)	z, w, y, x
	(z) 42nd St. Theaters	(D)	z, y, w, x
16.	(w) James Rothschild	(A)	x, z, w, y
	(x) Julius B. Rothchild	(B)	x, w, z, y
	(y) B. Rothstein	(C)	z, y, w, x
	(z) Brian Joel Rothenstein	(D)	z, w, x, y

Column I	**Column II**

17.
(w) George S. Wise
(x) S. G. Wise
(y) Geo. Stuart Wise
(z) Prof. Diana Wise

(A) w, y, z, x
(B) x, w, y, z
(C) y, x, w, z
(D) z, w, y, x

18.
(w) 10th Street Bus Terminal
(x) Buckingham Travel Agency
(y) The Buckingham Theater
(z) Burt Tompkins Studio

(A) x, z, w, y
(B) y, x, w, z
(C) w, z, y, x
(D) x, w, y, z

19.
(w) National Council of American Importers
(x) National Chain Co. of Providence
(y) National Council on Alcoholism
(z) National Chain Co.

(A) w, y, x, z
(B) x, z, w, y
(C) z, x, w, y
(D) z, x, y, w

20.
(w) Dr. Herbert Alvary
(x) Mr. Victor Alvarado
(y) Alvar Industries
(z) V. Alvarado

(A) w, y, x, z
(B) z, w, x, y
(C) y, z, x, w
(D) w, z, x, y

21.
(w) Joan MacBride
(x) Wm. Mackey
(y) Roslyn McKenzie
(z) Winifred Mackey

(A) w, x, z, y
(B) w, y, z, x
(C) w, z, x, y
(D) w, y, x, z

22.
(w) 3 Way Trucking Co.
(x) 3rd Street Bakery
(y) 380 Realty Corp.
(z) Three Lions Pub

(A) y, x, z, w
(B) y, z, w, x
(C) x, y, z, w
(D) x, y, w, z

23.
(w) Miss Rose Leonard
(x) Rev. Leonard Lucas
(y) Sylvia Leonard Linen Shop
(z) Rose S. Leonard

(A) z, w, x, y
(B) w, z, y, x
(C) w, x, z, y
(D) z, w, y, x

24.
(w) Jane Earl
(x) James A. Earle
(y) James Earl
(z) J. Earle

(A) w, y, z, x
(B) y, w, z, x
(C) x, y, w, z
(D) x, w, y, z

Test 4

TIME: 13 minutes. 40 questions.

DIRECTIONS: One of the five classes of employment, lettered (A) to (E), may be applied to each of the individuals listed below. Place on the answer sheet the capital letter of the class in which that name may best be placed.

Class of Work

(A) Clerical   (B) Educational   (C) Professional   (D) Mechanical   (E) Art

Name and Occupation

1. John M. Devine — Stenographer
2. G. D. Wahl — Lawyer
3. Harry B. Allen — Typewriter repairman
4. M. C. Walton — Elevator maintainer
5. Lewis E. Reigner — Typist
6. John G. Cook — Electrician
7. H. B. Allen — Civil engineer
8. Walter E. Jenkins — Physician
9. Clifford H. Wrenn — Telephone operator
10. H. A. Schwartz — Plumber
11. Harry Gruber — Locksmith
12. Ely Fairbanks — Sculptor
13. Abraham Hohing — Radio repairman
14. Samuel Tapft — Laundry driver
15. William M. Murray — Advertising layout person
16. Hyman E. Oral — Motion picture operator
17. L. A. Kurtz — Director of a nursery school
18. Richard H. Hunter — Painter of miniatures
19. Lewis F. Kosch — Saxophone player
20. Marion L. Young — Assistant director of a university extension program
21. Karl W. Hisgen — Printer
22. E. T. Williams — Administrative Assistant
23. H. B. Enderton — Mechanical Engineer
24. Robert F. Hallock — Proofreader
25. Joseph L. Hardin — Dentist
26. E. B. Gjelsteen — Chemist
27. Carter B. Magruder — Coppersmith
28. Wilber R. Pierce — Flutist
29. Russell G. Smith — Carpenter
30. Wilber S. Nye — Singer
31. David Larr — Instructor in barbering
32. Oliver M. Barton — Band Leader
33. E. Oliver Parmly — Word processor
34. C. Parul Summerall — Blacksmith
35. Louis Friedersdorff — Research scientist
36. Daniel E. Healy — Director of worker's education in an industrial union
37. Howard Kessinger — Player of tympani
38. John B. Horton — Secretary
39. Frank S. Kirkpatrick — Supervisor of a filing system
40. William H. Bertsch — Oil burner Installer

Test 5

Time: 20 minutes. 75 questions.

DIRECTIONS: As an aid in filing, the alphabet is often broken up into divisions, the number depending upon the amount of material comprehended by the filing system. In this exercise we are using 30 divisions. File each of the following names in its proper division by writing to the right of each name the number of the alphabetic division in which it should be placed. For example, Yerington, the first name in the test, should be filed under Y since Yerington begins with Y. Now, since in the code XYZ is 30, 30 is the answer which is written to the right of Yerington.

Alphabetic Code

A – 1	D – 7	IJ – 13	N – 19	St – 25
B – 2	E – 8	K – 14	O – 20	T – 26
Bi – 3	F – 9	L – 15	PQ – 21	UV – 27
Br – 4	G – 10	M – 16	R – 22	W – 28
C – 5	H – 11	Me – 17	S – 23	Wi – 29
Co – 6	Ho – 12	Mo – 18	Si – 24	XYZ – 30

1. Yerington
2. Hawthorne
3. Tonopah
4. Loveloch
5. Reno
6. Ely
7. Picohe
8. Winnemucca
9. Goldfield
10. Elko
11. Austin
12. Eureka
13. Fallon
14. Gardnerville
15. Genoa
16. Millers
17. Iono
18. Jarbridge
19. Minden
20. Luning
21. Jiggs
22. Uvada
23. Roderick
24. Montello
25. Nyala
26. Sutcliffe
27. Oreana
28. Vya
29. Shoshone
30. Rawhide
31. Forman
32. Washburn
33. Wahpeton
34. Crosby
35. Finley
36. Bowbells
37. Jamestown
38. Minnewaukau
39. Cavalier
40. Cando
41. Grafton
42. Cooperstown
43. Willistown
44. Fargo
45. Stanley
46. Devils Lake
47. Ellendale
48. Steele
49. Hillsboro
50. Mandan
51. Lakota
52. Rolla
53. Amida
54. Minot
55. Dickinson
56. Towner
57. Manning
58. Eckman
59. Fessender
60. Lisbon
61. Cadillac
62. Ithaca
63. Alpehn
64. Leland
65. Mason
66. Petoskey
67. Stanton
68. Munising
69. Adrian
70. Caro
71. Mio
72. Pontiac
73. Monroe
74. Allegan
75. Fling

Test 6

Time: 5 minutes. 9 questions.

DIRECTIONS: Consider each group of names as a unit. Determine in what position the name printed in **bold letters** *would be if the names in the group were correctly arranged in alphabetical order. If the name in bold letters should be first, print the letter A; if second, print the letter B; if third, print the letter C; if fourth, print the letter D; and if fifth, print the letter E. (The correct alphabetic order is indicated alongside the names in the example, and the answer should be D.)*

Example:

J. W. Martin	(2)
James E. Martin	(4)
J. Martin	(1)
George Martins	(5)
James Martin	(3)

1. Albert Brown
   James Borenstein
   Frieda Albrecht
   Samuel Brown
   George Appelman

2. Hugh F. Martenson
   A. S. Martinson
   Albert Martinsen
   Albert S. Martinson
   M. Martanson

3. James McCormack
   Ruth MacNamara
   Kathryn McGillicuddy
   Frances Mason
   Arthur MacAdams

4. James Ryn
   Francis Ryan
   Wm. Roanan
   Frances S. Ryan
   Francis P. Ryan

5. Aaron M. Michelson
   Samuel Michels
   Arthur L. Michaelson, Sr.
   John Michell
   Daniel Michelsohn

6. Dr. Francis Karell
   John Joseph Karalsen, Jr.
   John J. Karelsen, Sr.
   Mrs. Jeanette Kelly
   Estelle Karel

7. Norman Fitzgibbons
   Charles F. Franklin
   Jas. Fitzgerald
   Andrew Fitzsimmons
   James P. Fitzgerald

8. **Chas. R. Connolly**
   Frank Conlon
   Charles S. Connolly
   Abraham Cohen
   Chas. Conolly

9. **The 5th Ave. Bus. Co.**
   The Baltimore and Ohio Railroad
   3rd Ave. Elevated Co.
   Pennsylvania Railroad
   The 4th Ave. Trolley Line

Test 7

Time: 5 minutes. 10 questions.

DIRECTIONS: *Each question contains four names. For each question, choose the name that should be* first *if the four names were arranged in alphabetical order in accordance with the Rules for Alphabetical Filing. Read these rules carefully. Then, for each question, select the letter before the name that should be* first *in alphabetical order.*

Example:

  (A) Fred Town (2) (C) D. Town (1)
  (B) Jack Towne (3) (D) Jack S. Towne (4)

The numbers in parentheses indicate the proper alphabetical order in which these names should be filed. Since the name that should be filed *first* is D. Town, the answer is (C).

1. (A) Board of Elections
 (B) Board of Ethics
 (C) Board of Estimate
 (D) Board of Education

2. (A) C. Alfred Foster
 (B) Charles Alan Foster
 (C) Mrs. Carol Foster
 (D) Chas. A. Foster

3. (A) Department of Correction
 (B) Office of Collective Bargaining
 (C) Department of Commerce
 (D) Community Development Agency

4. (A) O'Donnell & Sons
 (B) Paul Brian Donnelly
 (C) Paul B. O'Donald
 (D) Donnally's Pub

5. (A) Delafield Hospital
 (B) Dr. John DeLaVega
 (C) Del Laboratories
 (D) Dolores De Lauro, R.N.

6. (A) DeHostos Apartments
 (B) Dyckman Apartments
 (C) Douglass Houses
 (D) Drew-Hamilton Houses

7. (A) Brooklyn College
 (B) Bernard M. Baruch College
 (C) Bronx Community College
 (D) Boro of Manhattan Community College

8. (A) G.E. Smith Assoc.
 (B) Geo. Edw. Smith
 (C) The Smith-Grace Ins. Agency
 (D) Geo. E. Smith

9. (A) Tom VanDerMeer
 (B) Van D. Williams, III
 (C) Wm. Vandewalle
 (D) Zelda Vanderberg

10. (A) Third of May Car Wash
 (B) Two Bros. Auto Sales, Inc.
 (C) Three Boros Service Station
 (D) 13–40 Collision Corp.

Test 8

Time: 6 minutes. 12 questions.

DIRECTIONS: *Each question consists of four names. For each question, indicate in the correspondingly numbered space on the answer sheet the capital letter preceding the name that should be* fourth *in alphabetical order.*

Example:

(A) William Brown   (2)
(B) Arthur F. Browne   (4)
(C) Arthur Browne   (3)
(D) F. Brown   (1)

The numbers in parentheses indicate the proper alphabetical order in which these names should be filed. Since the name that should be filed *fourth* is Arthur F. Browne, the answer is *B.*

1. (A) Francis Lattimore
   (B) H. Latham
   (C) G. Lattimore
   (D) Hugh Latham

2. (A) Thomas B. Morgan
   (B) Thomas Morgan
   (C) T. Morgan
   (D) Thomas Bertram Morgan

3. (A) Lawrence A. Villon
   (B) Chas. Valente
   (C) Charles M. Valent
   (D) Lawrence De Villon

4. (A) 71st Street Theater
   (B) The Seven Seas Corp.
   (C) 7th Ave. Service Co.
   (D) Walter R. Sevan and Co.

5. (A) Alfred Devance
   (B) A.R. D'Amico
   (C) Arnold De Vincent
   (D) A. De Pino

6. (A) Dr. Milton A. Bergmann
   (B) Miss Evelyn M. Bergmenn
   (C) Prof. E. N. Bergmenn
   (D) Mrs. L.B. Bergmann

7. (A) Mary Lobell Art Shop
   (B) John La Marca, Inc.
   (C) Lawyer's Guild
   (D) Frank Le Goff Studios

8. (A) William Carver
   (B) Howard Cambell
   (C) Arthur Chambers
   (D) Charles Banner

9. (A) George MacDougald
   (B) Thomas McHern
   (C) William Macholt
   (D) Frank McHenry

10. (A) Third National Bank
    (B) Robt. Tempkin Corp.
    (C) 32nd Street Carpet Co.
    (D) Wm. Templeton, Inc.

11. (A) 9th Avenue Garage
    (B) Jos. Nuren Food Co.
    (C) The New Book Store
    (D) Novelty Card Corp.

12. (A) Paul Moore
    (B) William Moore
    (C) Paul A. Moore
    (D) William Allen Moore

Test 9

Time: 4 minutes. 8 questions.

DIRECTIONS: Each question consists of three lists of three names. The three lists of three names are in separate columns marked (A), (B), and (C). Only one list of names in a question is in correct filing order, in accordance with the Rules for Alphabetical Filing. Identify in each question the list of names in correct filing order and mark in the correspondingly numbered space on your answer sheet the capital letter on top of the column in which the correct list was found.

Example:

(A)	(B)	(C)
Brown, A. J.	Browne, A.	Brownstein, A.
Browne, A.	Brown, A. J.	Brown, A. J.
Brownstein, A.	Brownstein, A.	Browne, A.

Since Arrangement A is the correct filing order, according to standard rules for alphabetic filing, the correct answer is A.

(A)	(B)	(C)
1. Nichols, C. Arnold	Nichols, Bruce	Nicholson, Arthur
Nichols, Bruce	Nichols, C. Arnold	Nichols, Bruce
Nicholson, Arthur	Nicholson, Arthur	Nichols, C. Arnold
2. Schaefer's Drug Store	Schaefer Bros.	Schaefer Bros.
Schaefer, Harry T.	Schaefer, Harry T.	Schaefer's Drug Store
Schaefer Bros.	Schaefer's Drug Store	Schaefer, Harry T.
3. Adams' Dime Store	Adami, David	Adami, David
Adami, David	Adams' Dime Store	Adams, Donald
Adams, Donald	Adams, Donald	Adams' Dime Store
4. Newton, Jas. F.	Newton-Jarvis Law Firm	Newton, Janet
Newton, Janet	Newton, Jas. F.	Newton-Jarvis Law Firm
Newton-Jarvis Law Firm	Newton, Janet	Newton, Jas. F.
5. Radford and Bigelow	Radford-Smith, Albert	Radford Transfer Co.
Radford-Smith, Albert	Radford Transfer Co.	Radford and Bigelow
Radford Transfer Co.	Radford and Bigelow	Radford-Smith, Albert
6. Trent, Inc.	20th Century Film Corp.	Trent Farm Products
Trent Farm Products	Trent Farm Products	Trent, Inc.
20th Century Film Corp.	Trent, Inc.	20th Century Film Corp.
7. Morrell, Ralph	Morrell, Ralph	M. R. B. Paper Co.
M. R. B. Paper Co.	Mt. Ranier Hospital	Morrell, Ralph
Mt. Ranier Hospital	M. R. B. Paper Co.	Mt. Ranier Hospital
8. Vanity Faire Shop	The Williams Magazine Corp.	Van Loon, Charles
Van Loon, Charles	Van Loon, Charles	Vanity Faire Shop
The Williams Magazine Corp.	Vanity Faire Shop	The Williams Magazine Corp.

Test 10

Time: 8 minutes. 10 questions.

DIRECTIONS: *Each question consists of four lists of four names. The four lists of four names are in separate columns marked (A), (B), (C), and (D). Only one list of names in a question is in correct filing order, in accordance with the Rules for Alphabetical Filing. Identify in each question the list of names in correct filing order and mark in the correspondingly numbered space on your answer sheet the capital letter on top of the column in which the correct list was found.*

Example:

(A)	(B)	(C)	(D)
Arnold Robinson	Arthur Roberts	Arnold Robinson	Arthur Roberts
Arthur Roberts	J.B. Robin	Arthur Roberts	James Robin
J.B. Robin	James Robin	James Robin	J.B. Robin
James Robin	Arnold Robinson	J.B. Robin	Arnold Robinson

Since, in this sample, column B is the only one in which the four names are correctly arranged alphabetically, the answer is B.

	(A)	(B)	(C)	(D)
1.	Alice Thompson	Eugene Thompkins	B. Thomas	Arnold G. Thomas
	Arnold G. Thomas	Alice Thompson	Arnold G. Thomas	B. Thomas
	B. Thomas	Arnold G. Thomas	Eugene Thompkins	Eugene Thompkins
	Eugene Thompkins	B. Thomas	Alice Thompson	Alice Thompson
2.	Albert Green	A.B. Green	Albert Green	A. B. Green
	A.B. Green	Albert Green	Wm. Greenfield	Frank E. Green
	Frank E. Green	Frank E. Green	A.B. Green	Albert Green
	Wm. Greenfield	Wm. Greenfield	Frank E. Green	Wm. Greenfield
3.	Steven M. Comte	Steven Le Comte	Steven M. Comte	Robt. Count
	Robt. Count	Steven M. Comte	Steven Le Comte	Robert B. Count
	Robert B. Count	Robert B. Count	Robt. Count	Steven Le Comte
	Steven Le Comte	Robt. Count	Robert B. Count	Steven M. Comte
4.	Prof. David Towner	Dr. Frank I. Tower	Miss Edna Tower	Prof. David Towner
	Miss Edna Tower	Miss Edna Tower	Dr. Frank I. Tower	Mrs. K.C. Towner
	Dr. Frank I. Tower	Mrs. K.C. Towner	Prof. David Towner	Miss Edna Tower
	Mrs. K.C. Towner	Prof. David Towner	Mrs. K.C. Towner	Dr. Frank I. Tower

5. The Jane Miller Shop   Joseph Millard Corp.   The Jane Miller Shop   Joseph Millard Corp.
    Joseph Millard Corp.   The Jane Miller Shop   Jean Mullins, Inc.   John Muller & Co.
    John Muller & Co.   John Muller & Co.   John Muller & Co.   Jean Mullins, Inc.
    Jean Mullins, Inc.   Jean Mullins, Inc.   Joseph Millard Corp.   The Jane Miller Shop

6. Anthony Delaney   Anthony Delaney   A. De Landri   A. De Landri
    A.M. D'Elia   A. De Landri   A.M. D'Elia   Anthony Delaney
    A. De Landri   A.M. D'Elia   Alfred De Monte   A.M. D'Elia
    Alfred De Monte   Alfred De Monte   Anthony Delaney   Alfred De Monte

7. D. McAllen   D. McAllen   Doris MacAllister   Doris MacAllister
    Lewis McBride   Doris MacAllister   Lewis T. MacBride   D. McAllen
    Doris MacAllister   Lewis McBride   D. McAllen   Lewis T. MacBride
    Lewis T. MacBride   Lewis T. MacBride   Lewis McBride   Lewis McBride

8. 6th Ave. Swim Shop   23rd Street Salon   6th Ave. Swim Shop   The Sky Ski School
    The Sky Ski School   The Sky Ski School   Sport Shoe Store   6th Ave. Swim Shop
    Sport Shoe Store   6th Ave. Swim Shop   The Sky Ski School   Sport Shoe Store
    23rd Street Salon   Sport Shoe Store   23rd Street Salon   23rd Street Salon

9. Charlotte Stair   C.B. Stare   Elaine La Stella   Charles B. Stare
    C.B. Stare   Charles B. Stare   Charlotte Stair   C.B. Stare
    Charles B. Stare   Charlotte Stair   C.B. Stare   Charlotte Stair
    Elaine La Stella   Elaine La Stella   Charles B. Stare   Elaine La Stella

10. John O'Farrell Corp.   Finest Glass Co.   John O'Farrell Corp.   Finest Glass Co.
    Finest Glass Co.   4th Guarantee Bank   Finest Glass Co.   George Fraser Co.
    George Fraser Co.   George Fraser Co.   4th Guarantee Bank   John O'Farrell Corp.
    4th Guarantee Bank   John O'Farrell Corp.   George Fraser Co.   4th Guarantee Bank

Answer Key For Filing Practice Tests

Test 1

1. E	7. D	13. D	19. D	25. B
2. A	8. C	14. B	20. E	26. D
3. D	9. C	15. C	21. A	27. B
4. B	10. D	16. A	22. E	28. A
5. E	11. C	17. D	23. C	29. C
6. D	12. A	18. C	24. C	30. D

Test 2

1. D	7. D	13. C	19. B	25. C
2. A	8. B	14. C	20. B	26. B
3. B	9. C	15. B	21. C	27. B
4. B	10. B	16. C	22. C	28. A
5. B	11. B	17. A	23. C	29. D
6. B	12. B	18. C	24. A	30. A

Test 3

1. B	6. D	11. D	16. A	21. A
2. B	7. A	12. C	17. D	22. C
3. C	8. D	13. C	18. B	23. B
4. A	9. C	14. A	19. D	24. B
5. C	10. A	15. D	20. C	

Test 4

1. A	6. D	11. D	16. D	21. D	26. C	31. B	36. B
2. C	7. C	12. E	17. B	22. A	27. D	32. E	37. E
3. D	8. C	13. D	18. E	23. C	28. E	33. A	38. A
4. D	9. A	14. D	19. E	24. A	29. D	34. D	39. A
5. A	10. D	15. E	20. B	25. C	30. E	35. C	40. D

Test 5

1. 30	11. 1	21. 13	31. 9	41. 10	51. 15	61. 5	71. 17
2. 11	12. 8	22. 27	32. 28	42. 6	52. 22	62. 13	72. 21
3. 26	13. 9	23. 22	33. 28	43. 29	53. 1	63. 1	73. 18
4. 15	14. 10	24. 18	34. 6	44. 9	54. 17	64. 15	74. 1
5. 22	15. 10	25. 19	35. 9	45. 25	55. 7	65. 16	75. 9
6. 8	16. 17	26. 25	36. 3	46. 7	56. 26	66. 21	
7. 21	17. 13	27. 20	37. 13	47. 8	57. 16	67. 25	
8. 29	18. 13	28. 27	38. 17	48. 25	58. 8	68. 18	
9. 10	19. 17	29. 23	39. 5	49. 11	59. 9	69. 1	
10. 8	20. 15	30. 22	40. 5	50. 16	60. 15	70. 5	

Test 6

1. E 2. E 3. C 4. D 5. D 6. D 7. A 8. C 9. B

Test 7

1. D 2. A 3. B 4. D 5. C 6. A 7. B 8. A 9. D 10. A

Test 8

1. C 2. D 3. A 4. A 5. C 6. B 7. A 8. C 9. B 10. C 11. B 12. D

Test 9

1. B 2. C 3. B 4. A 5. A 6. C 7. C 8. A

Test 10

1. D 2. B 3. A 4. C 5. B 6. D 7. C 8. A 9. C 10. B

MATHEMATICS REFRESHER COURSE

Before we begin a systematic discussion of mathematics necessary to Arithmetic Reasoning and Mathematics Knowledge, let us quickly list a few basic rules that must be mastered for speed and accuracy in performing Numerical Operations. You should memorize these rules:

Any number multiplied by 0 = 0.
   $5 \times 0 = 0.$
Zero divided by any number = 0.
   $0 \div 2 = 0$
If 0 is added to any number, that number does not change.
   $7 + 0 = 7$
If 0 is subtracted from any number, that number does not change.
   $4 - 0 = 4$
If a number is multiplied by 1, that number does not change.
   $3 \times 1 = 3$
If a number is divided by 1, that number does not change.
   $6 \div 1 = 6$
A number added to itself is doubled.
   $4 + 4 = 8$
If a number is subtracted from itself, the answer is 0.
   $9 - 9 = 0$
If a number is divided by itself, the answer is 1.
   $8 \div 8 = 1$

If you have memorized these rules, you should be able to write the answers to the questions in the following exercise as fast as you can read the questions.

Exercise 1.

1. $1 - 1 =$
2. $3 \div 1 =$
3. $6 \times 0 =$
4. $6 - 0 =$
5. $0 \div 8 =$
6. $9 \times 1 =$
7. $5 + 0 =$
8. $4 - 0 =$
9. $2 \div 1 =$
10. $7 - 7 =$
11. $8 \times 0 =$
12. $0 \div 4 =$
13. $1 + 0 =$
14. $3 - 0 =$
15. $5 \times 1 =$
16. $9 \div 1 =$
17. $6 + 6 =$
18. $4 - 4 =$
19. $5 \div 5 =$
20. $6 \times 1 =$

The more rules, procedures, and formulas you are able to memorize, the easier it will be to solve mathematical problems on your exam and throughout life. Become thoroughly familiar with the following rules and try to commit to memory as many as possible.

When multiplying a number by 10, 100, 1,000, etc., move the decimal point to the right a number of spaces equal to the number of zeros in the multiplier. If the number being multiplied is a whole number, push the decimal point to the *right* by inserting the appropriate number of zeros.

$$.36 \times 100 = 36.$$
$$1.2 \times 10 = 12.$$
$$5. \times 10 = 50.$$
$$60.423 \times 100 = 6,042.3$$

When dividing a number by 10, 100, 1,000, etc., again count the zeros, but this time move the decimal point to the *left*.

$$123. \div 100 = 1.23$$
$$352.9 \div 10 = 35.28$$
$$16. \div 100 = .16$$
$$7. \div 1,000 = .007$$

Exercise 2.

1. $18 \times 10 =$
2. $5 \div 100 =$
3. $1.3 \times 1,000 =$
4. $3.62 \times 10 =$
5. $9.86 \div 10 =$

6. $.12 \div 100 =$
7. $4.5 \times 10 =$
8. $83.28 \div 1,000 =$
9. $761 \times 100 =$
10. $68.86 \div 10 =$

When adding or subtracting decimals, it is most important to keep the decimal points in line. Once the decimal points are aligned, proceed with the problem in exactly the same way as with whole numbers, simply maintaining the location of the decimal point.

36.08	If you find it easier,	036.0800
745.	you may fill in the	745.0000
+ 4.362	spaces with zeros.	+ 004.3620
58.6	The answer will be	058.6000
.0061	unchanged.	000.0061
844.0481		844.0481

82.1	82.100
− 7.928	− 7.928
74.172	74.172

Exercise 3.

1. $1.52 + .389 + 42.9 =$
2. $.6831 + .01 + 4.26 + 98 =$
3. $84 - 1.9 =$
4. $3.25 + 5.66 + 9.1 =$
5. $17 - 12.81 =$
6. $46.33 - 12.1 =$

7. 51 + 7.86 + 42.003 =
8. 35.4 − 18.21 =
9. .85 − .16 =
10. 7.6 + .32 + 830 =

When multiplying decimals, you can ignore the decimal points until you reach the product. Then the placement of the decimal point is dependent on the sum of the places to the right of the decimal point in both the multiplier and number being multiplied.

$$
\begin{array}{r}
1.482 \text{ (3 places to right of decimal point)} \\
\times \quad .16 \text{ (2 places to right of decimal point)} \\
\hline
8892 \\
14820 \\
\hline
.23712 \text{ (5 places to right of decimal point)}
\end{array}
$$

You cannot divide by a decimal. If the divisor is a decimal, you must move the decimal point to the right until the divisor becomes a whole number, an integer. Count the number of spaces by which you moved the decimal point to the right and move the decimal point in the dividend (the number being divided) the same number of spaces to the right. The decimal point in the answer should be directly above the decimal point in the dividend.

$$
\begin{array}{r}
70.2 \text{ Decimal point moves two spaces} \\
.06\overline{)4.21\ 2} \text{ to the right.}
\end{array}
$$

Exercise 4.

1. 3.62 × 5.6 =
2. 92 × .11 =
3. 18 ÷ .3 =
4. 1.5 × .9 =
5. 7.55 ÷ 5 =

6. 6.42 ÷ 2.14 =
7. 12.01 × 3 =
8. 24.82 ÷ 7.3 =
9. .486 ÷ .2 =
10. .21 × 12 =

When fractions are to be added or subtracted they must have the same denominator, a *common denominator*. The common denominator is a number into which the denominators of all the fractions in the problem can be divided without a remainder. The common denominator of ⅜, ⅚, ¼, and ⅔ is 24. If you want to add these fractions, they must all be converted to fractions with the denominator 24. Convert each fraction by dividing 24 by the denominator and multiplying the numerator by the quotient.

$$
\frac{3}{8} = \frac{(24 \div 8) \times 3}{24} = \frac{3 \times 3}{24} = \frac{9}{24}
$$
$$
\frac{5}{6} = \frac{(24 \div 6) \times 5}{24} = \frac{4 \times 5}{24} = \frac{20}{24}
$$
$$
\frac{1}{4} = \frac{(24 \div 4) \times 1}{24} = \frac{6 \times 1}{24} = \frac{6}{24}
$$
$$
\frac{2}{3} = \frac{(24 \div 3) \times 2}{24} = \frac{8 \times 2}{24} = \frac{16}{24}
$$

Now you can add the fractions:

$$\frac{3}{8} = \frac{9}{24}$$
$$\frac{5}{6} = \frac{20}{24}$$
$$\frac{1}{4} = \frac{6}{24}$$
$$\frac{2}{3} = \frac{16}{24}$$
$$\overline{\qquad\quad \frac{51}{24}}$$

The answer, $^{51}/_{24}$, is an improper fraction; that is, its numerator is greater than its denominator. To convert the answer to a mixed number, divide the numerator by the denominator and express the remainder as a fraction.

$$\frac{51}{24} = 51 \div 24 = 2\frac{3}{24} = 2\frac{1}{8}$$

Exercise 5. Express your answers as simple mixed numbers.

1. $\dfrac{2}{3} + \dfrac{3}{5} + \dfrac{1}{2} =$ 6. $\dfrac{1}{2} + \dfrac{1}{4} + \dfrac{2}{3} =$

2. $\dfrac{6}{8} = \dfrac{2}{4} =$ 7. $\dfrac{5}{6} - \dfrac{1}{2} =$

3. $\dfrac{1}{3} + \dfrac{1}{2} =$ 8. $\dfrac{5}{8} - \dfrac{1}{3} =$

4. $\dfrac{4}{5} - \dfrac{3}{5} =$ 9. $\dfrac{5}{12} + \dfrac{3}{4} =$

5. $\dfrac{7}{8} + \dfrac{3}{4} + \dfrac{1}{3} =$ 10. $\dfrac{8}{9} - \dfrac{2}{3} =$

When multiplying fractions, multiply numerators by numerators and denominators by denominators.

$$\frac{3}{5} \bullet \frac{4}{7} \bullet \frac{1}{5} = \frac{3 \times 4 \times 1}{5 \times 7 \times 5} = \frac{12}{175}$$

In multiplying fractions, try to work with numbers that are as small as possible. You can make numbers smaller by *canceling*. Cancel by dividing the numerator of any one fraction and the denominator of any one fraction by the same number.

$$\frac{\overset{1}{\cancel{3}}}{\underset{2}{\cancel{4}}} \bullet \frac{\overset{1}{\cancel{2}}}{\underset{3}{\cancel{9}}} = \frac{1 \times 1}{2 \times 3} = \frac{1}{6}$$

In this case the numerator of the first fraction and the denominator of the other fraction were divided by 3, while the denominator of the first fraction and the numerator of the other fraction were divided by 2.

To divide by a fraction, invert the fraction following the division sign and multiply.

$$\frac{3}{16} \div \frac{1}{8} = \frac{3}{\overset{2}{\cancel{16}}} \times \frac{\overset{1}{\cancel{8}}}{1} = \frac{3}{2} = 1\frac{1}{2}$$

Exercise 6. Cancel wherever possible and express your answer in the simplest terms possible.

1. $\frac{4}{5} \cdot \frac{3}{6} =$ 6. $\frac{7}{8} \div \frac{2}{3} =$

2. $\frac{2}{4} \cdot \frac{8}{12} \cdot \frac{7}{1} =$ 7. $\frac{4}{6} \cdot \frac{8}{12} \cdot \frac{10}{3} =$

3. $\frac{3}{4} \div \frac{3}{8} =$ 8. $\frac{1}{6} \cdot \frac{7}{6} \cdot \frac{12}{3} =$

4. $\frac{5}{2} \div \frac{3}{6} =$ 9. $\frac{3}{7} \div \frac{9}{4} =$

5. $\frac{8}{9} \cdot \frac{3}{4} \cdot \frac{1}{2} =$ 10. $\frac{2}{3} \div \frac{2}{3} =$

The line in a fraction means "divided by." To change a fraction to a decimal follow through on the division.

$$\frac{4}{5} = 4 \div 5 = .8$$

To change a decimal to a percent, move the decimal point two places to the right and add a percent sign.

$$.8 = 80\%$$

Exercise 7. Change each fraction first to a decimal to three places and then to a percent.

1. $\frac{2}{4}$ 6. $\frac{2}{3}$

2. $\frac{7}{8}$ 7. $\frac{3}{5}$

3. $\frac{5}{6}$ 8. $\frac{4}{10}$

4. $\frac{6}{8}$ 9. $\frac{1}{4}$

5. $\frac{3}{4}$ 10. $\frac{2}{5}$

To find a percent of a number, change the percent to a decimal and multiply the number by it.

$$5\% \text{ of } 80 = 80 \times .05 = 4$$

To find out what a number is when a percent of it is given, change the percent to a decimal and divide the given number by it.

5 is 10% of what number?

$$5 \div .10 = 50$$

To find what percent one number is of another number, create a fraction by putting the part over the whole. Reduce the fraction if possible, then convert it to a decimal (remember: the line means *divide by,* so divide the numerator by the denominator) and change to a percent by multiplying by 100, moving the decimal point two places to the right.

4 is what percent of 80?

$$\frac{4}{80} = \frac{1}{20} = .05 = 5\%$$

Exercise 8.

1. 10% of 32 =
2. 8 is 25% of what number?
3. 12 is what percent of 24?
4. 20% of 360 is
5. 5 is what percent of 60?
6. 12 is 8% of what number?
7. 6% of 36 =
8. 25 is 5% of what number?
9. 70 is what percent of 140?
10. What percent of 100 is 19?

An equation is an equality. The values on either side of the equal sign in an equation must be equal. In order to learn the value of an unknown in an equation, do the same thing to both sides of the equation so as to leave the unknown on one side of the equal sign and its value on the other side.

$$X - 2 = 8$$

Add 2 to both sides of the equation.

$$X - 2 + 2 = 8 + 2; X = 10$$

$$5X = 25$$

Divide both sides of the equation by 5.

$$\frac{\overset{1}{\cancel{5}}X}{\underset{1}{\cancel{5}}} = \frac{25}{5}; X = 5$$

$$Y + 9 = 15$$

Subtract 9 from both sides of the equation.

$$Y + 9 - 9 = 15 - 9; Y = 6$$
$$A \div 4 = 48$$

Multiply both sides of the equation by 4.

$$\frac{\overset{1}{\cancel{4}}A}{\cancel{4}} = 48 \times 4; A = 192$$

Sometimes more than one step is required to solve an equation.

$$6A \div 4 = 48$$

First, multiply both sides of the equation by 4.

$$\frac{6A}{\underset{1}{\cancel{4}}} \times \frac{\overset{1}{\cancel{4}}}{1} = 48 \times 4; 6A = 192$$

Then divide both sides of the equation by 6.

$$\frac{\overset{1}{\cancel{6}}A}{\underset{1}{\cancel{6}}} = \frac{192}{6}; A = 32$$

Exercise 9. Solve for X.

1. X + 13 = 25
2. 4X = 84
3. X − 5 = 28
4. X ÷ 9 = 4
5. 3X + 2 = 14

6. $\frac{X}{4} - 2 = 4$
7. 10X − 27 = 73
8. 2X ÷ 4 = 13
9. 8X + 9 = 81
10. 2X ÷ 11 = 6

Answers to Math Refresher Course Exercises

Exercise 1

1. 0
2. 3
3. 0
4. 6
5. 0
6. 9
7. 5
8. 4
9. 2
10. 0

11. 0
12. 0
13. 1
14. 3
15. 5
16. 9
17. 12
18. 0
19. 1
20. 6

Exercise 2

1. 180
2. .05
3. 1,300
4. 36.2
5. .986

6. .0012
7. 45
8. .08328
9. 76,100
10. 6.886

Exercise 3

1. 44.809
2. 102.9531
3. 82.1
4. 18.01
5. 4.19

6. 34.23
7. 100.863
8. 17.19
9. .69
10. 837.92

Exercise 4

1. 20.272
2. 10.12
3. 60
4. 1.35
5. 1.51

6. 3
7. 36.03
8. 3.4
9. 2.43
10. 2.52

Exercise 5

1. $\frac{32}{20} = 1\frac{12}{20} = 1\frac{3}{5}$
2. $\frac{2}{8} = \frac{1}{4}$
3. $\frac{5}{6}$
4. $\frac{1}{5}$
5. $\frac{47}{24} = 1\frac{23}{24}$

6. $\frac{17}{12} = 1\frac{5}{12}$
7. $\frac{2}{6} = \frac{1}{3}$
8. $\frac{7}{24}$
9. $\frac{14}{12} = 1\frac{2}{12} = 1\frac{1}{6}$
10. $\frac{2}{9}$

Exercise 6

1. $\frac{2}{5}$
2. $2\frac{1}{3}$
3. 2
4. $\frac{15}{3} = 5$
5. $\frac{1}{3}$

6. $\frac{21}{16} = 1\frac{5}{16}$
7. $1\frac{13}{27}$
8. $\frac{7}{9}$
9. $\frac{4}{21}$
10. 1

Exercise 7

1. $.50 = 50\%$
2. $.875 = 87\frac{1}{2}\%$
3. $.833 = 83\frac{1}{3}\%$
4. $.75 = 75\%$
5. $.75 = 75\%$

6. $.666 = 66\frac{2}{3}\%$
7. $.60 = 60\%$
8. $.40 = 40\%$
9. $.25 = 25\%$
10. $.40 = 40\%$

Exercise 8

1. $32 \times .10 = 3.2$

2. $8 \div .25 = 32$

3. $\dfrac{12}{24} = \dfrac{1}{2} = .50 = 50\%$

4. $360 \times .20 = 72$

5. $\dfrac{5}{60} = \dfrac{1}{12} = .0833 = 8\dfrac{1}{3}\%$

6. $12 \div .08 = 150$

7. $36 \times .06 = 2.16$

8. $25 \div .05 = 500$

9. $\dfrac{70}{140} = \dfrac{1}{2} = .50 = 50\%$

10. $\dfrac{19}{100} = .19 = 19\%$

Exercise 9

1. $X = 12$
2. $X = 21$
3. $X = 33$
4. $X = 36$
5. $X = 4$

6. $X = 24$
7. $X = 10$
8. $X = 26$
9. $X = 9$
10. $X = 33$

ARITHMETIC COMPUTATIONS

To add valuable points to your exam score you must master arithmetical computations. And by this we mean doing them quickly and with absolute accuracy. The computations themselves will be simple, although the form in which they are presented may rattle you if you're not prepared. In addition to calculation, they measure your ability to interpret and act on directions. Thus this chapter provides practice through a series of tests modeled on the different question types that have actually appeared on examinations. An important tip from our years of experience with the self-tutored test-taker: Study the Directions! We have included those you are most likely to meet on your exam. Control over them will gain precious minutes for you. This doesn't mean you can skip reading directions on your actual exam. It does mean that you will be ahead of the game for knowing the language examiners use. Then you can afford to play it cool. A misunderstood direction can lead to a run of incorrect answers. Avoid this costly carelessness.

To Score High on Math Tests

1. *Schedule your study.* Set a definite time, and stick to it. Enter Arithmetic Computations on a study schedule.
2. *Plan* on taking different types of Computation Tests in each study period. Keep alert to the differences and complications. That will help keep you bright and interested.
3. *Do your best* and work fast to complete each test before looking at our Correct Answers. Keep pushing yourself.
4. *Record* time taken for each test next to your score. Your schedule may allow you to take the tests again. And you may want to see how your speed and accuracy have improved.
5. *Review your errors.* This is a must for every study session. Allow time for redoing every incorrect answer. The good self-tutor is a good self-critic. He learns most from his mistakes. And never makes them again.
6. *Don't guess at answers.* Because each practice test, like the actual examination, requires a multiple-choice answer, you might be tempted to pick up speed by approximating the answers. This is fatal. Carefully work out your answer to each question. Then choose the right answer. Any other way is certain to create confusion, slow you down, lower your score.
7. *Clarity & order.* Write all your figures clearly, in neat rows and columns. And this includes the figures you have to carry over from one column to another. Don't make mistakes because of lack of space and cramped writing. Use scratch paper wherever necessary.
8. *Skip the puzzlers.* If a single question gives you an unusual amount of trouble, go on to the next question. Come back to the tough one after you have done all the others, and still have time left.
9. *Study the sample solutions.* Note how carefully we have worked out each step. Get into this habit in doing all the practice tests. You'll quickly find that it's a time-saver . . . a high-scoring habit.

Sample Questions and Detailed Solutions

DIRECTIONS: Each question has five suggested answers lettered (A), (B), (C), (D), and (E). Suggested answer (E) is NONE OF THESE. Blacken space E only if your answer for a question does not exactly agree with any of the first four suggested answers. When you have finished the three questions, compare your answers with the correct answers.

Example 1:

Divide:

$$4.6\overline{)233.404}$$

(A) 50.74
(B) 52.24
(C) 57.30
(D) 58.24
(E) None of these

SOLUTION 1.

$$
\begin{array}{r}
50.74 \\
4.6\overline{)233.404} \\
\underline{230} \\
3\ 40 \\
\underline{3\ 22} \\
184 \\
\underline{184}
\end{array}
$$

Since the answer is clearly 50.74, blacken A on the answer sheet. Do not mark any of the other letter choices. There is only one correct answer.

Example 2:

Multiply:

$$
\begin{array}{r}
2946 \\
\times\ 7.007
\end{array}
$$

(A) 21,642.622
(B) 20,642.622
(C) 41,244.001
(D) 20,641.622
(E) None of these

SOLUTION 2.

$$
\begin{array}{r}
2946 \\
\times\ 7.007 \\
\hline
20\ 622 \\
00\ 00 \\
000\ 0 \\
20\ 622 \\
\hline
20{,}642.622
\end{array}
$$

The answer is 20,642.622, which is answer choice (B). This answer is similar to answer choices (A) and (D), but it is not the same. So you must be careful not to let the (A) and (D) choices confuse you. Blacken only B on your answer sheet.

Example 3:

A certain kind of stencil can be bought for 20 cents each or in packages of 12 for $2. How much more would it cost to buy 240 stencils singly than to buy them in the 12-stencil packages?

(A) $0.40
(B) $8
(C) $40
(D) $48
(E) none of these

SOLUTION 3.

"How *much more* would it cost to buy 240 stencils singly than to buy them in the 12-stencil packages?" asks the question, and you are given clues to work with. The first step is to figure the cost of both methods and find the difference. Buying 240 stencils singly at 20 cents each would cost $48 ($0.20 × 240 = $48). Buying the stencils in packages of 12 would mean buying 20 packages (240 ÷ 12 = 20); at $2 a package they would cost $40 ($2 × 20 = $40). The difference is $8 ($48 − $40 = $8), and the answer is B.

Answer Sheet For Arithmetic Computations Practice Tests

Test 1

1 Ⓐ Ⓑ	11 Ⓐ Ⓑ	21 Ⓐ Ⓑ	31 Ⓐ Ⓑ	41 Ⓐ Ⓑ
2 Ⓐ Ⓑ	12 Ⓐ Ⓑ	22 Ⓐ Ⓑ	32 Ⓐ Ⓑ	42 Ⓐ Ⓑ
3 Ⓐ Ⓑ	13 Ⓐ Ⓑ	23 Ⓐ Ⓑ	33 Ⓐ Ⓑ	43 Ⓐ Ⓑ
4 Ⓐ Ⓑ	14 Ⓐ Ⓑ	24 Ⓐ Ⓑ	34 Ⓐ Ⓑ	44 Ⓐ Ⓑ
5 Ⓐ Ⓑ	15 Ⓐ Ⓑ	25 Ⓐ Ⓑ	35 Ⓐ Ⓑ	45 Ⓐ Ⓑ
6 Ⓐ Ⓑ	16 Ⓐ Ⓑ	26 Ⓐ Ⓑ	36 Ⓐ Ⓑ	46 Ⓐ Ⓑ
7 Ⓐ Ⓑ	17 Ⓐ Ⓑ	27 Ⓐ Ⓑ	37 Ⓐ Ⓑ	47 Ⓐ Ⓑ
8 Ⓐ Ⓑ	18 Ⓐ Ⓑ	28 Ⓐ Ⓑ	38 Ⓐ Ⓑ	48 Ⓐ Ⓑ
9 Ⓐ Ⓑ	19 Ⓐ Ⓑ	29 Ⓐ Ⓑ	39 Ⓐ Ⓑ	49 Ⓐ Ⓑ
10 Ⓐ Ⓑ	20 Ⓐ Ⓑ	30 Ⓐ Ⓑ	40 Ⓐ Ⓑ	50 Ⓐ Ⓑ

Test 2

1 Ⓐ Ⓑ	21 Ⓐ Ⓑ	41 Ⓐ Ⓑ	61 Ⓐ Ⓑ
2 Ⓐ Ⓑ	22 Ⓐ Ⓑ	42 Ⓐ Ⓑ	62 Ⓐ Ⓑ
3 Ⓐ Ⓑ	23 Ⓐ Ⓑ	43 Ⓐ Ⓑ	63 Ⓐ Ⓑ
4 Ⓐ Ⓑ	24 Ⓐ Ⓑ	44 Ⓐ Ⓑ	64 Ⓐ Ⓑ
5 Ⓐ Ⓑ	25 Ⓐ Ⓑ	45 Ⓐ Ⓑ	65 Ⓐ Ⓑ
6 Ⓐ Ⓑ	26 Ⓐ Ⓑ	46 Ⓐ Ⓑ	66 Ⓐ Ⓑ
7 Ⓐ Ⓑ	27 Ⓐ Ⓑ	47 Ⓐ Ⓑ	67 Ⓐ Ⓑ
8 Ⓐ Ⓑ	28 Ⓐ Ⓑ	48 Ⓐ Ⓑ	68 Ⓐ Ⓑ
9 Ⓐ Ⓑ	29 Ⓐ Ⓑ	49 Ⓐ Ⓑ	69 Ⓐ Ⓑ
10 Ⓐ Ⓑ	30 Ⓐ Ⓑ	50 Ⓐ Ⓑ	70 Ⓐ Ⓑ
11 Ⓐ Ⓑ	31 Ⓐ Ⓑ	51 Ⓐ Ⓑ	71 Ⓐ Ⓑ
12 Ⓐ Ⓑ	32 Ⓐ Ⓑ	52 Ⓐ Ⓑ	72 Ⓐ Ⓑ
13 Ⓐ Ⓑ	33 Ⓐ Ⓑ	53 Ⓐ Ⓑ	73 Ⓐ Ⓑ
14 Ⓐ Ⓑ	34 Ⓐ Ⓑ	54 Ⓐ Ⓑ	74 Ⓐ Ⓑ
15 Ⓐ Ⓑ	35 Ⓐ Ⓑ	55 Ⓐ Ⓑ	75 Ⓐ Ⓑ
16 Ⓐ Ⓑ	36 Ⓐ Ⓑ	56 Ⓐ Ⓑ	76 Ⓐ Ⓑ
17 Ⓐ Ⓑ	37 Ⓐ Ⓑ	57 Ⓐ Ⓑ	77 Ⓐ Ⓑ
18 Ⓐ Ⓑ	38 Ⓐ Ⓑ	58 Ⓐ Ⓑ	78 Ⓐ Ⓑ
19 Ⓐ Ⓑ	39 Ⓐ Ⓑ	59 Ⓐ Ⓑ	79 Ⓐ Ⓑ
20 Ⓐ Ⓑ	40 Ⓐ Ⓑ	60 Ⓐ Ⓑ	80 Ⓐ Ⓑ

Test 3

1 Ⓐ Ⓑ Ⓒ Ⓓ	11 Ⓐ Ⓑ Ⓒ Ⓓ	21 Ⓐ Ⓑ Ⓒ Ⓓ
2 Ⓐ Ⓑ Ⓒ Ⓓ	12 Ⓐ Ⓑ Ⓒ Ⓓ	22 Ⓐ Ⓑ Ⓒ Ⓓ
3 Ⓐ Ⓑ Ⓒ Ⓓ	13 Ⓐ Ⓑ Ⓒ Ⓓ	23 Ⓐ Ⓑ Ⓒ Ⓓ
4 Ⓐ Ⓑ Ⓒ Ⓓ	14 Ⓐ Ⓑ Ⓒ Ⓓ	24 Ⓐ Ⓑ Ⓒ Ⓓ
5 Ⓐ Ⓑ Ⓒ Ⓓ	15 Ⓐ Ⓑ Ⓒ Ⓓ	25 Ⓐ Ⓑ Ⓒ Ⓓ
6 Ⓐ Ⓑ Ⓒ Ⓓ	16 Ⓐ Ⓑ Ⓒ Ⓓ	26 Ⓐ Ⓑ Ⓒ Ⓓ
7 Ⓐ Ⓑ Ⓒ Ⓓ	17 Ⓐ Ⓑ Ⓒ Ⓓ	27 Ⓐ Ⓑ Ⓒ Ⓓ
8 Ⓐ Ⓑ Ⓒ Ⓓ	18 Ⓐ Ⓑ Ⓒ Ⓓ	28 Ⓐ Ⓑ Ⓒ Ⓓ
9 Ⓐ Ⓑ Ⓒ Ⓓ	19 Ⓐ Ⓑ Ⓒ Ⓓ	29 Ⓐ Ⓑ Ⓒ Ⓓ
10 Ⓐ Ⓑ Ⓒ Ⓓ	20 Ⓐ Ⓑ Ⓒ Ⓓ	30 Ⓐ Ⓑ Ⓒ Ⓓ

Test 4

1 Ⓐ Ⓑ Ⓒ Ⓓ	4 Ⓐ Ⓑ Ⓒ Ⓓ	7 Ⓐ Ⓑ Ⓒ Ⓓ	10 Ⓐ Ⓑ Ⓒ Ⓓ
2 Ⓐ Ⓑ Ⓒ Ⓓ	5 Ⓐ Ⓑ Ⓒ Ⓓ	8 Ⓐ Ⓑ Ⓒ Ⓓ	11 Ⓐ Ⓑ Ⓒ Ⓓ
3 Ⓐ Ⓑ Ⓒ Ⓓ	6 Ⓐ Ⓑ Ⓒ Ⓓ	9 Ⓐ Ⓑ Ⓒ Ⓓ	12 Ⓐ Ⓑ Ⓒ Ⓓ

Test 5

1 Ⓐ Ⓑ Ⓒ Ⓓ Ⓔ	7 Ⓐ Ⓑ Ⓒ Ⓓ Ⓔ	13 Ⓐ Ⓑ Ⓒ Ⓓ Ⓔ	19 Ⓐ Ⓑ Ⓒ Ⓓ Ⓔ
2 Ⓐ Ⓑ Ⓒ Ⓓ Ⓔ	8 Ⓐ Ⓑ Ⓒ Ⓓ Ⓔ	14 Ⓐ Ⓑ Ⓒ Ⓓ Ⓔ	20 Ⓐ Ⓑ Ⓒ Ⓓ Ⓔ
3 Ⓐ Ⓑ Ⓒ Ⓓ Ⓔ	9 Ⓐ Ⓑ Ⓒ Ⓓ Ⓔ	15 Ⓐ Ⓑ Ⓒ Ⓓ Ⓔ	21 Ⓐ Ⓑ Ⓒ Ⓓ Ⓔ
4 Ⓐ Ⓑ Ⓒ Ⓓ Ⓔ	10 Ⓐ Ⓑ Ⓒ Ⓓ Ⓔ	16 Ⓐ Ⓑ Ⓒ Ⓓ Ⓔ	22 Ⓐ Ⓑ Ⓒ Ⓓ Ⓔ
5 Ⓐ Ⓑ Ⓒ Ⓓ Ⓔ	11 Ⓐ Ⓑ Ⓒ Ⓓ Ⓔ	17 Ⓐ Ⓑ Ⓒ Ⓓ Ⓔ	23 Ⓐ Ⓑ Ⓒ Ⓓ Ⓔ
6 Ⓐ Ⓑ Ⓒ Ⓓ Ⓔ	12 Ⓐ Ⓑ Ⓒ Ⓓ Ⓔ	18 Ⓐ Ⓑ Ⓒ Ⓓ Ⓔ	24 Ⓐ Ⓑ Ⓒ Ⓓ Ⓔ

Test 6

1 Ⓐ Ⓑ Ⓒ Ⓓ Ⓔ	6 Ⓐ Ⓑ Ⓒ Ⓓ Ⓔ	11 Ⓐ Ⓑ Ⓒ Ⓓ Ⓔ	16 Ⓐ Ⓑ Ⓒ Ⓓ Ⓔ
2 Ⓐ Ⓑ Ⓒ Ⓓ Ⓔ	7 Ⓐ Ⓑ Ⓒ Ⓓ Ⓔ	12 Ⓐ Ⓑ Ⓒ Ⓓ Ⓔ	17 Ⓐ Ⓑ Ⓒ Ⓓ Ⓔ
3 Ⓐ Ⓑ Ⓒ Ⓓ Ⓔ	8 Ⓐ Ⓑ Ⓒ Ⓓ Ⓔ	13 Ⓐ Ⓑ Ⓒ Ⓓ Ⓔ	18 Ⓐ Ⓑ Ⓒ Ⓓ Ⓔ
4 Ⓐ Ⓑ Ⓒ Ⓓ Ⓔ	9 Ⓐ Ⓑ Ⓒ Ⓓ Ⓔ	14 Ⓐ Ⓑ Ⓒ Ⓓ Ⓔ	19 Ⓐ Ⓑ Ⓒ Ⓓ Ⓔ
5 Ⓐ Ⓑ Ⓒ Ⓓ Ⓔ	10 Ⓐ Ⓑ Ⓒ Ⓓ Ⓔ	15 Ⓐ Ⓑ Ⓒ Ⓓ Ⓔ	20 Ⓐ Ⓑ Ⓒ Ⓓ Ⓔ

Test 1

TIME: 25 minutes. 50 questions.

DIRECTIONS: In this test you are asked to do two of the fundamental operations in arithmetic: addition and multiplication. They are closely related in that multiplication is really a succession of additions. Blacken space A if the given answer is correct. Blacken space B if the answer is incorrect.

MULTIPLICATION   **WORK SPACE**   **ADDITION**   **WORK SPACE**

1.
$$\begin{array}{r} 39 \\ \times\ 7 \\ \hline 273 \end{array}$$
2.
$$\begin{array}{r} 73 \\ \times\ 4 \\ \hline 282 \end{array}$$

3.
$$\begin{array}{r} 44 \\ \times\ 6 \\ \hline 264 \end{array}$$
4.
$$\begin{array}{r} 27 \\ \times\ 2 \\ \hline 54 \end{array}$$

5.
$$\begin{array}{r} 94 \\ \times\ 8 \\ \hline 752 \end{array}$$
6.
$$\begin{array}{r} 25 \\ \times\ 7 \\ \hline 185 \end{array}$$

7.
$$\begin{array}{r} 47 \\ \times\ 3 \\ \hline 131 \end{array}$$
8.
$$\begin{array}{r} 36 \\ \times\ 8 \\ \hline 298 \end{array}$$

9.
$$\begin{array}{r} 64 \\ \times\ 7 \\ \hline 448 \end{array}$$
10.
$$\begin{array}{r} 72 \\ \times\ 9 \\ \hline 658 \end{array}$$

11.
$$\begin{array}{r} 13 \\ 68 \\ 34 \\ +\ 25 \\ \hline 140 \end{array}$$
12.
$$\begin{array}{r} 56 \\ 88 \\ 44 \\ +\ 19 \\ \hline 207 \end{array}$$

13.
$$\begin{array}{r} 89 \\ 29 \\ 56 \\ +\ 36 \\ \hline 200 \end{array}$$
14.
$$\begin{array}{r} 48 \\ 69 \\ 42 \\ +\ 26 \\ \hline 185 \end{array}$$

15.
$$\begin{array}{r} 13 \\ 21 \\ 96 \\ +\ 47 \\ \hline 177 \end{array}$$
16.
$$\begin{array}{r} 85 \\ 64 \\ 93 \\ +\ 79 \\ \hline 331 \end{array}$$

17.
$$\begin{array}{r} 38 \\ 56 \\ 47 \\ +\ 21 \\ \hline 162 \end{array}$$
18.
$$\begin{array}{r} 75 \\ 63 \\ 78 \\ +\ 47 \\ \hline 263 \end{array}$$

19.
$$\begin{array}{r} 40 \\ 35 \\ 64 \\ +\ 68 \\ \hline 207 \end{array}$$
20.
$$\begin{array}{r} 26 \\ 62 \\ 25 \\ +\ 37 \\ \hline 160 \end{array}$$

MULTIPLICATION

21. 21   22. 16   23. 27
   × 7   × 9   × 4
   157   144   118

24. 39   25. 78   26. 44
   × 3   × 2   × 5
   107   156   220

27. 56   28. 17   29. 21
   × 7   × 8   × 5
   382   146   104

30. 24   31. 28   32. 36
   × 9   × 2   × 3
   216   56   108

33. 45   34. 52   35. 64
   × 4   × 8   × 6
   180   426   374

WORK SPACE

ADDITION

36. 17   37. 17   38. 43
     92   50   85
     11   86   24
   + 46   + 21   + 94
   166   174   256

39. 25   40. 69   41. 91
     92   23   56
     74   53   32
   + 31   + 19   + 35
   232   164   214

42. 12   43. 10   44. 12
     17   94   60
     78   29   63
   + 53   + 27   + 38
   160   170   183

45. 14   46. 31   47. 29
     57   89   56
     21   77   58
   + 13   + 55   + 95
   105   252   228

48. 45   49. 37   50. 56
     37   75   95
     97   49   53
   + 33   + 23   + 77
   222   194   281

Test 2

TIME: 40 minutes. 80 questions.

DIRECTIONS: Subtraction and division are two of the basic operations in arithmetic. This test will help you gain proficiency in both these diminution processes, and thereby in many others. Blacken Space A if the given answer is correct. Blacken space B if the answer is incorrect. We suggest that you do all the division problems before going on to subtraction. Although the processes are related, you should be able to work more accurately and quickly if you do the test this way.

SUBTRACTION		WORK SPACE	DIVISION		WORK SPACE

SUBTRACTION

1.
$$\begin{array}{r} 16 \\ -11 \\ \hline 5 \end{array}$$
2.
$$\begin{array}{r} 23 \\ -18 \\ \hline 15 \end{array}$$

3.
$$\begin{array}{r} 45 \\ -29 \\ \hline 16 \end{array}$$
4.
$$\begin{array}{r} 61 \\ -32 \\ \hline 39 \end{array}$$

5.
$$\begin{array}{r} 32 \\ -19 \\ \hline 13 \end{array}$$
6.
$$\begin{array}{r} 77 \\ -51 \\ \hline 26 \end{array}$$

7.
$$\begin{array}{r} 48 \\ -39 \\ \hline 9 \end{array}$$
8.
$$\begin{array}{r} 53 \\ -25 \\ \hline 38 \end{array}$$

9.
$$\begin{array}{r} 86 \\ -47 \\ \hline 49 \end{array}$$
10.
$$\begin{array}{r} 66 \\ -52 \\ \hline 14 \end{array}$$

11.
$$\begin{array}{r} 38 \\ -17 \\ \hline 21 \end{array}$$
12.
$$\begin{array}{r} 94 \\ -43 \\ \hline 51 \end{array}$$

13.
$$\begin{array}{r} 69 \\ -31 \\ \hline 38 \end{array}$$
14.
$$\begin{array}{r} 99 \\ -19 \\ \hline 70 \end{array}$$

15.
$$\begin{array}{r} 57 \\ -32 \\ \hline 15 \end{array}$$
16.
$$\begin{array}{r} 35 \\ -14 \\ \hline 21 \end{array}$$

DIVISION

17. $5\overline{)30}$ (6) 18. $2\overline{)18}$ (8)

19. $5\overline{)25}$ (4) 20. $7\overline{)35}$ (5)

21. $4\overline{)12}$ (4) 22. $8\overline{)24}$ (4)

23. $6\overline{)24}$ (4) 24. $7\overline{)49}$ (7)

25. $4\overline{)32}$ (9) 26. $5\overline{)35}$ (7)

27. $9\overline{)81}$ (8) 28. $7\overline{)42}$ (7)

29. $7\overline{)28}$ (4) 30. $5\overline{)40}$ (8)

31. $8\overline{)16}$ (2) 32. $4\overline{)16}$ (3)

SUBTRACTION

33.	61 − 19 = 42	34.	78 − 51 = 26	35.	64 − 28 = 26
36.	36 − 16 = 20	37.	83 − 38 = 55	38.	43 − 12 = 31
39.	87 − 79 = 8	40.	55 − 31 = 23	41.	80 − 14 = 76
42.	93 − 40 = 53	43.	79 − 64 = 5	44.	28 − 12 = 16
45.	70 − 34 = 46	46.	98 − 83 = 15	47.	69 − 37 = 42
48.	47 − 33 = 14	49.	60 − 49 = 11	50.	73 − 28 = 45
51.	21 − 16 = 4	52.	88 − 77 = 11	53.	97 − 59 = 39
54.	53 − 29 = 25	55.	31 − 19 = 12	56.	77 − 49 = 28

WORK SPACE

DIVISION

57. $7\overline{)21}$ = 4   58. $2\overline{)14}$ = 7   59. $7\overline{)56}$ = 8

60. $5\overline{)45}$ = 8   61. $9\overline{)72}$ = 9   62. $7\overline{)14}$ = 2

63. $5\overline{)20}$ = 4   64. $7\overline{)63}$ = 9   65. $3\overline{)12}$ = 4

66. $5\overline{)15}$ = 2   67. $4\overline{)20}$ = 4   68. $9\overline{)63}$ = 7

69. $8\overline{)32}$ = 3   70. $8\overline{)56}$ = 7   71. $4\overline{)24}$ = 6

72. $9\overline{)54}$ = 5   73. $8\overline{)40}$ = 6   74. $4\overline{)28}$ = 7

75. $6\overline{)54}$ = 9   76. $6\overline{)18}$ = 4   77. $8\overline{)48}$ = 7

78. $3\overline{)18}$ = 6   79. $6\overline{)36}$ = 7   80. $9\overline{)27}$ = 4

Test 3

TIME: 30 minutes. 30 questions.

DIRECTIONS The sample arithmetic questions below are similar to the questions on your test. Use the space around each question for figuring. Each question has four suggested answers lettered A, B, C, and D. In most questions, suggested answer D is none of these. Blacken space D only if your answer for such a question does not exactly agree with any of the first three suggested answers.

1. Add:
   285
   946
   + 327

   Answers
   (A) 1,448
   (B) 1,548
   (C) 1,558
   (D) none of
       these

2. Add:
   456
   973
   + 514

   (A) 1,933
   (B) 2,034
   (C) 2,039
   (D) none of
       these

3. Subtract:
   704
   − 636

   (A) 68
   (B) 78
   (C) 168
   (D) none of
       these

4. Subtract:
   685
   − 288

   (A) 307
   (B) 397
   (C) 413
   (D) none of
       these

5. Multiply:
   378
   × 607

   (A) 25,326
   (B) 169,446
   (C) 229,446
   (D) none of
       these

6. Multiply:
   587
   × 49

   (A) 28,763
   (B) 28,853
   (C) 28,963
   (D) none of
       these

7. Divide:

   73)38,544

   (A) 529
   (B) 542
   (C) 543
   (D) none of
       these

8. Divide:

$$246\overline{)16,974}$$

(A) 62.1
(B) 67.9
(C) 69.0
(D) none of these

9. Add:
$7.6 + .85 + 44.0 =$

(A) 45.61
(B) 52.45
(C) 601
(D) none of these

10. Add:
$.48 + 2.7 + .009 =$

(A) 3.189
(B) 7.59
(C) 84
(D) none of these

11. Add:
$.006 + .05 + .74 =$

(A) .7456
(B) .796
(C) 1.84
(D) none of these

12. Subtract:
$85.67 - 63.5 =$

(A) 22.62
(B) 25.32
(C) 79.32
(D) none of these

13. Subtract:
$3.64 - .236 =$

(A) 2.306
(B) 3.306
(C) 3.404
(D) none of these

14. Subtract:
$74.3 - 6.58 =$

(A) 8.5
(B) 67.72
(C) 77.88
(D) none of these

15. Multiply:
$$\begin{array}{r} 69.27 \\ \times\quad .38 \\ \hline \end{array}$$

(A) 26.3226
(B) 263.226
(C) 2,632.26
(D) none of these

16. Multiply:
$$\begin{array}{r} 70.4 \\ \times\ 4.55 \\ \hline \end{array}$$

(A) 6.336
(B) 32.032
(C) 319.320
(D) none of these

17. Multiply:
    2946
    × 7.007

    (A) 20,642.622
    (B) 22,684.200
    (C) 41,244.000
    (D) none of
        these

18. Divide:

    .87)6.438

    (A) .74
    (B) 7.4
    (C) 74.0
    (D) none of
        these

19. Divide:

    4.6)233.404

    (A) 50.74
    (B) 52.24
    (C) 57.30
    (D) none of
        these

20. Divide:

    .009).000522

    (A) .00058
    (B) .0058
    (C) .058
    (D) none of
        these

21. 39.8 increased by 3% =

    (A) 1.119
    (B) 40.994
    (C) 51.74
    (D) none of
        these

22. 24.7 decreased by 6% =

    (A) 1.482
    (B) 9.88
    (C) 20.6
    (D) none of
        these

23. What is 8% of 4.56?

    (A) .57
    (B) 3.99
    (C) 4.1952
    (D) none of
        these

24. 63% of 637 =

    (A) 10.111
    (B) 57.33
    (C) 401.31
    (D) none of
        these

25. 3.7% of 951 =

    (A) 25.703
    (B) 35.187
    (C) 257.027
    (D) none of
        these

26. $\dfrac{2.0976}{23.0}$

    expressed as a
    percent =

    (A) .0912%
    (B) .912%
    (C) 9.12%
    (D) none of
    these

27. ¹⁴/₃₂, changed to
    a decimal, =

    (A) .4375
    (B) 4.375
    (C) 43.75
    (D) none of
    these

28. What is the sum of

    .941 and 3²/₅,

    written as a
    decimal?

    (A) 4.141
    (B) 4.341
    (C) 4.441
    (D) none of
    these

29. Which of the suggested an-
    swers is the *largest* number?

    (A) ¹⁹⁵/₂₀
    (B) ¹⁹⁶/₉₈
    (C) 5.0025
    (D) .750

30. Which of the suggested an-
    swers is the *smallest*
    number?

    (A) .78
    (B) ⁴⁰/₄₅
    (C) .87%
    (D) ⅞

Test 4

Time: 12 minutes. 12 questions.

DIRECTIONS: Each problem in this test involves a certain amount of logical reasoning and thinking on your part, besides the usual simple computations, to help you in finding the solution. Read each problem carefully and choose the correct answer from choices that follow.

1. Find 5 1/2% of $2,800
   (A) $140   (B) $154   (C) $160   (D) $172

2. Add 10 1/6, 2 7/12, 7 2/3
   (A) 12 1/2   (B) 15 2/3   (C) 18 5/6   (D) 20 5/12

3. Subtract $27.95 from $50
   (A) $22.05   (B) $25.95   (C) $26.05   (D) $27.95

4. Divide 3 3/4 by 2
   (A) 1 3/16   (B) 1 3/4   (C) 1 7/8   (D) 2 5/8

5. Multiply $2.04 by 60.5
   (A) $96.20   (B) $104.40   (C) $114.80   (D) $123.42

6. Divide 768 by .32
   (A) 2.4   (B) 4.9   (C) 6.8   (D) 9.4

7. Add 6 1/2, 8 3/4, 5 1/8
   (A) 18 1/4   (B) 19 1/2   (C) 20 3/8   (D) 21 7/8

8. Subtract 14 2/3 from 56
   (A) 41 1/3   (B) 44 2/3   (C) 46 1/3   (D) 48 2/3

9. Add $124.00, $48.25, $.98, $8.09 and $9.67
   (A) $140.62   (B) $152.81   (C) $188.24   (D) $190.99

10. Find 3 1/3 ÷ 2/3
    (A) 2   (B) 3   (C) 4   (D) 5

11. Divide 2.064 by .24
    (A) 6.9   (B) 8.6   (C) 9.1   (D) 9.9

12. Multiply $1.04 by 8 1/4
    (A) $6.44   (B) $7.39   (C) $8.58   (D) $9.46

Test 5

Time: 24 minutes. 24 questions.

DIRECTIONS: The following arithmetic word problems have been devised to make you think with numbers. In each question, the arithmetic is simple, but the objective is to comprehend what you have to do with the numbers and/or quantities. Read the problem carefully and choose the correct answer from the five choices that follow each question.

1. The fraction 7/16 expressed as a decimal is

   (A) .1120   (B) .4375   (C) .2286   (D) .4850   (E) None of these

2. If .10 is divided by 50, the result is

   (A) .002   (B) .02   (C) .2   (D) 2.   (E) None of these

3. The number 60 is 40% of

   (A) 24   (B) 84   (C) 96   (D) 150   (E) None of these

4. If 3/8 of a number is 96, the number is

   (A) 132   (B) 36   (C) 256   (D) 156   (E) None of these

5. The sum of 637.894, 8352.16, 4.8673 and 301.5 is, most nearly,

   (A) 8989.5   (B) 9021.35   (C) 9294.9   (D) 9296.4   (E) None of these

6. If 30 is divided by .06, the result is

   (A) 5   (B) 50   (C) 500   (D) 5000   (E) None of these

7. The sum of the fractions 1/3, 4/6, 3/4, 1/2, and 1/12 is

   (A) 1/4   (B) 1/3   (C) 1/6   (D) 1 11/12   (E) None of these

8. If 96,934.42 is divided by 53.496, the result is most nearly

   (A) 181   (B) 552   (C) 18199   (D) 5520   (E) None of these

9. If 25% of a number is 48, the number is

   (A) 12   (B) 60   (C) 144   (D) 192   (E) None of these

10. The number 88 is 2/5 of

    (A) 123   (B) 141   (C) 221   (D) 440   (E) None of these

11. If the product of 8.3 multiplied by .42 is subtracted from the product of 156 multiplied by .09, the result is most nearly

    (A) 10.6   (B) 13.7   (C) 17.5   (D) 20.8   (E) None of these

12. Add the following lengths: 4 yards, 2 feet, 3 inches; 4 feet, 11 inches; 6 yards, 8 inches; 6 yards; and give the answer in feet and fractions thereof.

    (A) 39'   (B) 38 1/2'   (C) 38 3/4'   (D) 39 1/4'   (E) None of these

13. What is the net amount of a bill of $428 after a discount of 6% has been allowed?

    (A) $401.10
    (B) $401.23
    (C) $402.32
    (D) $402.23
    (E) None of these

14. What number decreased by 3/7 of itself is equal to 56?

    (A) 97   (B) 100   (C) 96   (D) 91   (E) None of these

15. The length of time from 8:23 A.M. to 2:53 P.M. is

    (A) 6 hours 16 minutes
    (B) 6 hours 30 minutes
    (C) 7 hours 16 minutes
    (D) 6 hours 40 minutes
    (E) None of these

16. The sum of 9/16, 11/32, 15/64 and 1 3/32 is most nearly

    (A) 2.234   (B) 2.134   (C) 2.334   (D) 2.214   (E) None of these

17. At 4 cents each, the cost of 144 fuses would be

    (A) $.48   (B) $5.76   (C) $4.00   (D) $8.00   (E) None of these

18. Milk sells at 42 1/2 cents a quart. The cost of 4 gallons of milk is

    (A) $6.50   (B) $6.60   (C) $6.70   (D) $6.80   (E) None of these

19. The sum of the numbers 38,806, 2,074, 48,761, 9,632, 7,899, 4,628, is

    (A) 111,800   (B) 112,000   (C) 14,900   (D) 111,700   (E) None of these

20. If a piece of wood measuring 4 feet 2 inches is divided into three equal parts, each part is

    (A) 1 foot 4 2/3 inches
    (B) 1 foot 4 inches
    (C) 1 foot 2 1/3 inches
    (D) 1 foot 7/18 inches
    (E) None of these

21. If gaskets are sold at the rate of 3 for 7 cents, then 21 gaskets will cost

    (A) 21 cents   (B) 50 cents   (C) 70 cents   (D) $1.41   (E) None of these

22. A worker receives $36.70 per day. After working 13 days his total earnings should be

    (A) $477.30   (B) $477.20   (C) $477.10   (D) $477.40   (E) None of these

23. 1/7 changed to a two-place decimal is

    (A) .15   (B) 14.29   (C) 15.00   (D) .14   (E) None of these

24. A square has an area of 49 sq. in. The number of inches in its perimeter is

    (A) 7   (B) 28   (C) 14   (D) 98   (E) None of these

Test 6

Time: 20 minutes. 20 questions.

DIRECTIONS: Each problem in this test involves a certain amount of logical reasoning and thinking on your part, besides the usual simple computations, to help you in finding the solution. Read each problem carefully and choose the correct answer from the five choices that follow. Mark E as your answer if none of the suggested answers agrees with your answer.

1. Find the interest on $25,800 for 144 days at 6% per annum. Base your calculations on a 360-day year.

   (A) $619.20   (B) $619.02   (C) $691.02   (D) $691.20   (E) None of these

2. A court clerk estimates that the untried cases on the docket will occupy the court for 150 trial days. If new cases are accumulating at the rate of 1.6 trial days per day (Saturday and Sunday excluded) and the court sits 5 days a week, how many days' business will remain to be heard at the end of 60 trial days?

   (A) 168 trial days
   (B) 185 trial days
   (C) 188 trial days
   (D) 186 trial days
   (E) None of these

3. The visitors section of a courtroom seats 105 people. The court is in session 6 hours of the day. On one particular day 486 people visited the court and were given seats. What is the average length of time spent by each visitor in the court? Assume that as soon as a person leaves his seat it is immediately filled and that at no time during the day is one of the 105 seats vacant. Express your answer in hours and minutes.

   (A) 1 hr. 20 min.
   (B) 1 hr. 18 min.
   (C) 1 hr. 30 min
   (D) 2 hr.
   (E) None of these

4. If paper costs $2.92 per ream and 5% discount is allowed for cash, how many reams can be purchased for $138.70 cash? Do not discard fractional part of a cent in your calculations.

   (A) 49 reams
   (B) 60 reams
   (C) 50 reams
   (D) 53 reams
   (E) None of these

5. How much time is there between 8:30 a.m. today and 3:15 a.m. tomorrow.

   (A) 17 3/4 hrs.
   (B) 18 hrs.
   (C) 18 2/3 hrs.

(D) 18 1/2 hrs.

(E) None of these

6. How many days are there between September 19th and December 25th, both inclusive?

(A) 98 days   (B) 96 days   (C) 89 days   (D) 90 days   (E) None of these

7. A clerk is requested to file 800 cards. If he can file cards at the rate of 80 cards an hour, the number of cards remaining to be filed after 7 hours of work is

(A) 40   (B) 250   (C) 140   (D) 260   (E) None of these

8. An officer's weekly salary is increased from \$200.00 to \$225.00. The percent of increase is

(A) 10%   (B) 11 1/9%   (C) 12 1/2%   (D) 14 1/7%   (E) None of these

9. If there are 245 sections in the city, the average number of sections for each of the 5 boroughs is

(A) 50 sections
(B) 49 sections
(C) 47 sections
(D) 59 sections
(E) None of these

10. If a section had 45 miles of street to plow after a snowstorm and 9 plows are used, each plow would cover an average of how many miles?

(A) 7 miles   (B) 6 miles   (C) 8 miles   (D) 5 miles   (E) None of these

11. If a crosswalk plow engine is run 5 minutes a day for 10 days in a given month, it would run how long in the course of this month?

(A) 50 min.   (B) 1 1/2 hr.   (C) 1 hrs.   (D) 30 min.   (E) None of these

12. If the department uses 1,500 men in manual street cleaning and half as many more to load and drive trucks, the total number used is

(A) 2200 men
(B) 2520 men
(C) 2050 men
(D) 2250 men
(E) None of these

13. If an inspector issued 186 summonses in the course of 7 hours, his hourly average of summonses issued was

(A) 23 summonses
(B) 26 summonses
(C) 25 summonses
(D) 28 summonses
(E) None of these

14. If, of 186 summonses issued, one hundred were issued to first offenders, then there were how many summonses issued to other than first offenders?

(A) 68   (B) 90   (C) 86   (D) 108   (E) None of these

15. A truck going at a rate of 20 miles an hour will reach a town 40 miles away in how many hours?

    (A) 3 hrs. (B) 1 hrs. (C) 4 hr. (D) 5 hrs. (E) None of these

16. If a barrel has a capacity of 100 gallons, it will contain how many gallons when it is two-fifths full?

    (A) 20 gal. (B) 60 gal. (C) 40 gal. (D) 80 gal. (E) None of these

17. If a salary of $12,000 is subject to a 20 percent deduction, the net salary is

    (A) $8,000 (B) $9,600 (C) $10,000 (D) $10,400 (E) None of these

18. If $1,000 is the cost of repairing 100 square yards of pavement, the cost of repairing one square yard is

    (A) $10 (B) $150 (C) $100 (D) $300 (E) None of these

19. If a man's base pay is $9000 and it is increased by a bonus of $1050 and a seniority increment of $750, his total salary is

    (A) $10,800 (B) $10,500 (C) $9,000 (D) $11,100 (E) None of these

20. If an annual salary of $8640 is increased by a bonus of $2880 and by a service increment of $480, the total pay rate is

    (A) $11,840 (B) $15,840 (C) $10,760 (D) $12,000 (E) None of these

Answer Key For Arithmetic Computations Practice Tests

Test 1

1. A	11. A	21. B	31. A	41. A
2. B	12. A	22. A	32. A	42. A
3. A	13. B	23. B	33. A	43. B
4. A	14. A	24. B	34. B	44. B
5. A	15. A	25. A	35. B	45. A
6. B	16. B	26. A	36. A	46. A
7. B	17. A	27. B	37. A	47. B
8. B	18. A	28. B	38. B	48. B
9. A	19. A	29. B	39. B	49. B
10. B	20. B	30. A	40. A	50. A

Test 2

1. A	21. B	41. B	61. B
2. B	22. B	42. A	62. A
3. B	23. A	43. B	63. A
4. B	24. A	44. A	64. A
5. A	25. B	45. B	65. A
6. A	26. A	46. A	66. B
7. A	27. B	47. B	67. B
8. B	28. B	48. A	68. A
9. B	29. A	49. A	69. B
10. A	30. A	50. A	70. A
11. A	31. A	51. B	71. A
12. A	32. B	52. A	72. B
13. A	33. A	53. B	73. B
14. B	34. B	54. B	74. A
15. B	35. B	55. A	75. A
16. A	36. A	56. A	76. B
17. A	37. B	57. B	77. B
18. B	38. A	58. A	78. A
19. B	39. A	59. A	79. B
20. A	40. B	60. B	80. B

Test 3

1. C	5. C	9. B	13. C	17. A	21. B	25. B	28. B
2. D	6. A	10. A	14. B	18. B	22. D	26. C	29. A
3. A	7. D	11. B	15. A	19. A	23. D	27. A	30. C
4. B	8. C	12. D	16. D	20. C	24. C		

Test 4

1. B	3. A	5. D	7. C	9. D	11. B
2. D	4. C	6. A	8. A	10. D	12. C

Test 5

1. B	4. C	7. B	10. E	13. B	16. A	19. A	22. C
2. A	5. D	8. E	11. A	14. E	17. B	20. A	23. D
3. D	6. C	9. D	12. E	15. B	18. D	21. E	24. B

Test 6

1. A	6. A	11. A	16. C
2. D	7. E	12. D	17. B
3. B	8. C	13. B	19. A
4. C	9. B	14. C	19. A
5. E	10. D	15. E	20. D

CORRECT ENGLISH USAGE

Grammar

This is not a complete review of English grammar. Only those points are covered that may likely be sources of errors in answering questions on your examination.

NOUNS are names of persons, things, places, or ideas (lawyer, chair, prairie, liberty).
PRONOUNS are words used instead of nouns (he, she, it, we, etc.). The noun for which the pronoun stands is called the antecedent. The antecedent is either before the pronoun in the same sentence or in the sentence before that sentence.

Nouns and pronouns have several properties that help them to perform various functions in sentences. These properties are as follows:

1. **NUMBER:** If a noun or pronoun stands for a single person, place or thing, it is in the singular. If it stands for more than one, it is in the plural.
2. **GENDER:** Depending on whether a noun or pronoun refers to a male, a female, or a thing, its gender is masculine, feminine, or neuter, respectively.
3. **PERSON:** Indicates whether the noun or pronoun refers to the speaker or to the person spoken to or about. Pronouns have the property of person (I, you, he, she, it, etc.). Nouns, for practical purposes, do not have the property of person. The noun in salutations in letters (such as "Dear Sir") may be considered to be in the second person singular (you).
4. **CASE:** The three cases of nouns and pronouns are nominative, objective, and possessive. In form, nouns in the nominative and objective cases are identical. Pronouns, on the other hand, differ in form in their nominative and objective cases *(I* and *me, we* and *us,* etc.).

In the **nominative** case the noun or pronoun is the subject of the sentence. It is the person, place, or thing about which an assertion is made in the sentence. For example: The boy mows the lawn.
"Boy" is the noun in the nominative because the assertion is made about the boy. If passive construction is used, the sentence reads: The lawn is mowed by the boy.
In this sentence the noun "lawn" is in the nominative because the assertion is made about the lawn.
In the **objective** case a noun or pronoun represents a person, place, or thing acted on by the subject of the sentence. The subject of the sentence is the noun in the nominative. For example: The boy mows the lawn.
"Lawn" is in the objective case because the lawn is acted on by the subject of the sentence, "boy."
The noun in the objective case may also be a person, place, or thing linked to another word in the sentence by a preposition. For example: The lawn is mowed by the boy.
"Boy" is in the objective case because it is linked to the verb "mowed" by the preposition "by."
The **possessive** case of the noun or pronoun indicates that a person, place, or thing possesses something. For example: The boy's shirt is blue.
"Boy's" is in the possessive case. It indicates that he is the owner of the shirt.

121

VERBS are words that express action or state of being (work, exist). Every sentence *must* have a verb.

The properties of verbs are voice, mood, tense, person, and number. All of the properties of a verb can be formed from its principal parts: present tense, past tense, and past participle (bake, baked, baked—a regular verb; drive, drove, driven—an irregular verb).

AGREEMENTS: As seen from the foregoing, nouns, pronouns, and verbs share some properties. It is obvious that unless related words agree in their properties, the meaning of the sentence may become unclear.

Number, person, and gender are properties shared by nouns and pronouns. Verbs share with nouns and pronouns the properties of number and person. Verbs have no gender. The rules of agreement are illustrated in the following statement: Alice drives her own car.

This statement is made about one female (Alice); the subject of the verb "drives." Accordingly, the properties of the noun and verb must agree. Therefore, the verb (drives) is in the third person singular. The pronoun (her) is properly feminine third person singular because it refers to its antecedent (Alice), which has the same property.

One must be especially careful not to overlook lack of agreement between a subject and verb separated by several words. It is a common mistake to make the verb agree with the word next to it rather than with its subject, as in the following: The nomination*s* to the Supreme Court in the last legislative session *was* approved by large majorities.

"Nominations" is the subject in the sentence (not "session"). Accordingly, the verb should be in plural, *"were* approved."

In connection with agreements between subject and verbs, the following usages should be observed:

- Collective nouns, which stand for a group of individuals or things as a unit, take a singular verb. (The committee is in session.)
- When a verb in a sentence has two or more subjects, connected by "and," a plural verb is required. (Mary and Jane are classmates.) However, if any of the subjects in the sentence are preceded by words like "a," "each," "every," etc., a singular verb is required. (Each piece of luggage and handbag is to be checked.)
- If two or more singular subjects are connected by "or" or "nor," a singular verb is required. (Neither Bill nor Tom has applied for a scholarship.)
- If two or more subjects connected by "or" or "nor" differ in number or person, the verb should agree with the subject that is nearest to it. (Neither the children nor the mother is entitled to benefits. Neither you nor I am eligible to enter the contest.)

Punctuation

The following rules cover only the most frequent uses of punctuation marks. The purpose of punctuation marks is to make clearer the intended meaning of written material and to prevent it from being misread.

A **period** is used in the following cases:

1. *After a sentence* that is not a question or exclamation. (Today is Sunday.)
2. *After most abbreviations* (Gal., N.Y., St., Inc., Jr.). Exceptions: Initials of government agencies (FBI, IRS) and abbreviations that are commonly used in

everyday speech instead of the word abbreviated (Intercom, USA, UN, IBM); abbreviated first names (Ben, Al, Tom, Will), but there are periods after Thos. and Wm.

3. *In numerals before the decimal fraction* (3.14).
4. *Between dollars and cents written in numerals* ($9.95).
5. *After the middle initial in names* (Ronald W. Reagan).

A **comma** is used in the following cases:

1. *To separate in a sentence unrelated words or figures* that if not separated, may cause confusion. (To John, Smith was very courteous. What the cause of it is, is unknown. In 1986, 235 new employees were hired by the firm.)
2. *In dates,* as follows:
   If the month, day, and year are given, there is a comma only between the day and the year (July 4, 1776).
   If the day is not given, a comma separates the month and the year. (The colonies declared their independence in July, 1776).
   If the day of the week is also indicated, it is separated by a comma from the month. (The wedding will be held Sunday, June 20, 1987, at 10 a.m.)
3. *After the name of the person followed by Jr., Sr., Esq., Ph.D.* (John W. Smith Jr.; Mary F. Baker, Ph.D.).
4. *Between the title of the position of a person and the name of the organization* (Alice W. Walker, Vice President, City Bank; Robert T. Moore, Colonel, US Army).
5. *In addresses,* between the city and the state; but there is no comma between the state and the zip code (New York, N.Y. 10013).
6. *To divide numbers of four digits or more* into groups of three, counting from right to left. (The population of the United States is 243,462,000.)
7. *To set off nonrestrictive parenthetical clauses from the rest of the sentence.*
   Nonrestrictive parenthetical clauses are merely explanatory. If such a clause is omitted from the sentence, the general sense of the sentence will not change. (Franklin Roosevelt, *then Governor of New York,* opened the George Washington Bridge in 1931. Mr. Green, *the employer of the defendant,* was the first witness. Dr. Watt, *a Harvard graduate,* is a competent surgeon.)
   On the other hand, restrictive parenthetical clauses are not set off by commas. They are not merely explanatory. If such a clause is omitted, the sentence loses its original sense. (The man *who fell* broke his arm. A thermometer that is *inaccurate* is worthless. The dam *that gave way* was poorly constructed.)
8. *To separate two or more adjectives modifying a noun.* (All of a sudden a bearded, stooped, frail old man entered the room.)
9. *To separate a series of words or phrases* in a sentence listing specific items. (The staff of the firm consisted of clerks, typists, engineers, lawyers, and accountants. Paragraphs b., d., f., and h. of the law do not apply in this case.)
   Note: The use of the comma before "and" is optional.
10. *After an introductory word or phrase at the beginning of a sentence.* (However, the law does not apply to persons over 65. Therefore, the law applies only to those under 65. To make a long story short, I have missed the train.)
11. *After the salutation in a personal letter* (Dear Mary,).

A **colon** is used in the following cases:

1. *To introduce some specific information,* such as a quotation, listing of items or questions. (The conductor shouted: "All aboard," and the train pulled out of the station. The following were called as witnesses: James Smith, Carl Weber, Jane

Cox, and John Bates. In connection with the burglary at 522 Mapes Ave., the following questions arise: At what part of the day did it take place, are there any signs of forcible entry, what items have been removed, what is the amount of loss.)

2. *After the salutation in an official or business letter* (Dear Mr. Powel:).

A **semicolon** is used as follows: *To separate phrases containing commas.* (The members of the committee were P. J. Young, Vice President, City Bank; F. R. Grant, Chairman, Security Insurance Co.; and Paul Burke, Counsel, Lambert & Co.)

Quotation marks are used in the following cases:

1. *To enclose a direct quotation.* In a direct quotation the *exact* words spoken or written by someone are reproduced. In an indirect quotation only the sense of what someone has said or written is conveyed. Only direct quotations are enclosed in quotation marks. (Direct quotation: Mr. Smith, to everyone's surprise, made the following announcement: "I shall retire as of July 1, 1987." Indirect quotation: Everyone was surprised when Mr. Smith announced that he will retire as of July 1, 1987.)
2. *For titles of short articles (not books), paintings, statues, and names of ships.* (The editorial was entitled "Looking Forward to 1987." The "Mona Lisa" and the "Venus de Milo" are in the Louvre in Paris. Before World War II the "Queen Mary" was the fastest ocean liner.)
3. *For words to which special attention is directed.* (The article "the" is disregarded in alphabetical listings of book titles. The controversy hinges on what is a "reasonable" length of time.)
4. *For colloquial words or expressions in a formal discussion.* (She quit working as a secretary five years ago, and her stenography became "rusty.")

Capitalization

The following are the most important rules for capitalization, the use of initial capital letters.

Capitalize:

1. *The first word of a sentence.*
2. *Proper nouns and adjectives derived from proper nouns* (George Washington, America, American, Texas, Texan).
3. *The word "God" and words used to refer to the deity* (the Almighty).
4. *Titles of persons when used with their names* (Senator John W. Smith) and when, in a later sentence, reference is made again to the Senator without mentioning his name. (The Senator voted against the tax increase.) But if the title does not refer to a specific person, do not capitalize it. (The majority of senators voted against the tax increase.)
5. *The names of organized bodies* (United States Navy, Department of Agriculture, New York Yankees, Consolidated Edison Co.).
6. *Titles of books, plays, movies, chapter headings*—all words in them except prepositions and connectives (Pride and Predudice, Gone with the Wind).
7. *Months of the year, days of the week, and holidays.* (The last Thursday of

November is Thanksgiving Day.) Do not capitalize the names of seasons (winter, spring, etc.).

8. *West, east, north, south*. If these words stand for a direction, they are not capitalized (The needle of the compass points to the north.) If, however, they refer to a region, they are capitalized. (The North defeated the South in the Civil War.)

Exercise 1. Grammar and Usage

DIRECTIONS: Find what, if anything, is wrong in each of the sentences that follow. If there is an error, decide which underlined part must be changed to make the sentence correct. Circle the number of the underlined portion you think is incorrect. If there is no error, circle answer choice (E). Correct and explanatory answers are provided on page 133.

1. If he <u>had had</u> the <u>forethought</u> to arrange an <u>appointment</u>, his reception
        A   B   C
   <u>would have been</u> more friendly. <u>No error.</u>
       D   E

2. The job was <u>too</u> big for <u>any one</u> of us to handle alone; so we <u>decided</u> to divide
           A   B   C
   the responsibilities <u>between</u> the three of us. <u>No error.</u>
               D   E

3. When Mr. Brown <u>inspected</u> his grounds, he <u>found</u> <u>that</u> the hurricane <u>destroyed</u>
              A   B C   D
   one of his favorite trees. <u>No error.</u>
                   E

4. The crowd, <u>subdued</u> while the home team <u>trailed</u>, <u>sung</u> with gusto when the
            A   B   C
   team <u>forged</u> ahead. <u>No error.</u>
       D   E

5. His education had filled him <u>with anger</u> against those <u>whom</u> he <u>believed</u> had
                      A   B   C
   hurt or <u>humiliated</u> him. <u>No error.</u>
          D   E

6. <u>Rather then</u> go <u>with John</u>, he <u>decided</u> to stay <u>at home</u>. <u>No error.</u>
       A   B   C   D   E

7. Fred <u>couldn't</u> scarcely see <u>to drive</u> when the fog <u>rolled</u> in <u>off</u> the water. <u>No error.</u>
         A   B   C D   E

8. The <u>victim's</u> mother, <u>besides</u> herself <u>with grief</u>, could give no <u>coherent</u> account
           A   B   C   D
   of the accident. <u>No error.</u>
             E

9. Steve <u>threw</u> the stick into the water and <u>stood</u> back <u>to watch</u> as his dog <u>swum</u>
          A   B   C   D
   furiously after it. <u>No error.</u>
               E

10. The child <u>felt</u> very <u>bad</u> when his teacher criticized him <u>before</u> the <u>entire</u> class.
             A   B   C   D
    <u>No error.</u>
     E

11. Neither tears <u>or</u> protests <u>effected</u> the <u>least</u> change in their <u>parents'</u> decision.
          A   B   C   D
<u>No error.</u>
E

12. Ms. Cleary is the <u>most</u> sympathetic, <u>most</u> understanding, and <u>most</u> kindest
                A   B   C
teacher I <u>have ever had.</u> <u>No error.</u>
        D   E

13. Mary will join <u>you</u> and <u>I</u> in <u>attempting</u> to persuade Bill not to act so <u>rashly.</u>
              A   B   C   D
<u>No error.</u>
E

14. <u>Having rescued</u> the sleeping child from the smoke-filled room, the fireman
     A
<u>descended</u> <u>down</u> the ladder to <u>safety.</u> <u>No error.</u>
   B   C   D   E

15. <u>Admirers</u> of American ballet have made the claim that <u>its</u> stars can dance
    A   B
<u>as well</u> or <u>better than</u> the best of the Russian artists. <u>No error.</u>
   C   D   E

16. As long as you <u>are going</u> to the library, please <u>bring</u> this book with you and
             A   B
<u>return</u> it to the <u>children's</u> room. <u>No error.</u>
  C   D   E

17. Never before, to the best of my <u>recollection,</u> have <u>there</u> <u>been</u> so <u>much</u> small cars
                        A   B C   D
on the highways. <u>No error.</u>
          E

18. <u>Granting</u> this <u>to be true,</u> what would you <u>imply</u> from the <u>statement</u> which he
    A   B   C   D
has made? <u>No error.</u>
      E

19. <u>Neither</u> rain <u>nor</u> snow <u>keep</u> the dedicated jogger from <u>his</u> daily exercise.
    A   B   C   D
<u>No error.</u>
E

20. <u>Each</u> of the candidates <u>had</u> ten minutes <u>to present</u> <u>their</u> views. <u>No error.</u>
  A   B   C   D   E

21. We objected to <u>him</u> scolding us for <u>our good,</u> especially when he said it <u>hurt</u> him
         A   B   C
more than <u>us.</u> <u>No error.</u>
      D   E

22. The following description, <u>together with</u> the drawings, <u>present</u> a <u>master</u> plan for
                     A   B   C
the <u>development</u> of the airport. <u>No error.</u>
   D   E

23. <u>His</u> father was <u>disturbed</u> to find that the boy <u>had lied</u> <u>rather than telling</u> the
  A   B   C   D
truth. <u>No error.</u>
    E

24. Every week Mrs. Foley buys two <u>gallons</u> of milk, three <u>loaves</u> of bread, and ten
                                 A   B

    <u>pounds</u> of meat for her <u>families</u> meals. <u>No error.</u>
     C   D   E

25. <u>Every</u> sheet of <u>ruled</u> paper and every sheet of <u>unruled</u> paper <u>is</u> carefully
   A   B   C   D

    examined before it is returned. <u>No error.</u>
                                        E

Exercise 2. Sentence Correction

DIRECTIONS: Each of the following sentences may or may not be correct as given. Below each sentence you will find five different ways of writing the underlined part. If you think the sentence is correct as given, choose answer (A), which is always the same as the underlined part. If you think one of the other choices makes a better sentence, circle the number of your choice. Correct and explanatory answers appear on page 133.

1. Flinging himself <u>at the heavy metal fire door he pounded on it</u> furiously.

   (A) at the heavy metal fire door he pounded on it
   (B) at the heavy metal fire door: he pounded on it
   (C) at the heavy metal fire door, he pounded on it
   (D) at the heavy metal fire door and pounding on it
   (E) at the heavy metal fire door; he pounded on it

2. Edna burst into the room shouting, "Why <u>was Marilyn and he</u> permitted to go?"

   (A) was Marilyn and he
   (B) was Marilyn and him
   (C) was Marilyn and his
   (D) were Marilyn and he
   (E) were Marilyn and him

3. <u>Don't worry John: we all make mistakes.</u>

   (A) Don't worry John: we all make mistakes.
   (B) Do not worry John: we all make mistakes.
   (C) Don't worry John—we all make mistakes.
   (D) Don't worry, John; we all make mistakes.
   (E) Don't worry, John, we all make mistakes.

4. How much <u>has fuel costs raised</u> during the past year?

   (A) has fuel costs raised
   (B) have fuel costs raised
   (C) has fuel costs risen
   (D) have fuel costs risen
   (E) has fuel costs rose

5. The teacher, <u>with all her students, was</u> late for the train.

    (A) with all her students, was
    (B) with all her students was
    (C) with all her students, were
    (D) with all her students; was
    (E) with all her students were

6. Vicki, the president of the class and <u>who is also captain of the girls' volley ball team,</u> will lead the pep rally.

    (A) who is also captain of the girls' volley ball team
    (B) whom is also captain of the girls' volley ball team
    (C) captain of the girls' volley ball team
    (D) also being captain of the girls' volley ball team
    (E) since she is captain of the girls' volley ball team

7. The situation was explained, and each one was allowed to <u>express their opinions</u> openly.

    (A) express their opinions
    (B) express there opinions
    (C) express themselves
    (D) express their opinion
    (E) express his opinion

8. Some gardeners put dead leaves or straw between the rows of seedlings so that the ground doesn't dry out and <u>you don't have to weed as much.</u>

    (A) you don't have to weed as much
    (B) they don't have to weed as much
    (C) they don't have weeding as much as before
    (D) your weeding is less
    (E) you don't have as much weeding to do

9. <u>Pat went to Jones Beach with his girlfriend wearing a blue and white bathing suit.</u>

    (A) Pat went to Jones Beach with his girlfriend wearing a blue and white bathing suit.
    (B) Pat went to Jones Beach, wearing a blue and white bathing suit, with his girlfriend.
    (C) Pat, wearing a blue and white bathing suit, went to Jones Beach with his girlfriend.
    (D) To Jones Beach, wearing a blue and white bathing suit, went Pat with his girlfriend.
    (E) With his girlfriend, wearing a blue and white bathing suit, Pat went to Jones Beach.

10. When the flurry of <u>angry words ended. It was evident</u> that the cool heads had not prevailed.

    (A) angry words ended. It was evident
    (B) angry words ended: it was evident
    (C) angry words ended; it was evident
    (D) angry words ended, it was evident
    (E) angry words ended it was evident

11. "You ought to be <u>ashamed of yourselves</u>" I blurted out just as I began to realize how distorted their actions really were.

    (A) ashamed of yourselves" I blurted out
    (B) ashamed of yourselfs," I blurted out
    (C) ashamed of yourselves." I blurted out
    (D) ashamed of yourselves!" I blurted out
    (E) ashamed of yourselves"! I blurted out

12. Watching the takeoff, the small boy waved his arms <u>as if he were a plane himself.</u>

    (A) as if he were a plane himself
    (B) as he was a plane himself
    (C) like he was a plane hisself
    (D) like he was a plane himself
    (E) as if he were to be a plane himself

13. His film is beautifully photographed but very violent; I don't like <u>that kind of a movie.</u>

    (A) that kind of a movie
    (B) those kind of movies
    (C) that kind of movie
    (D) those type of movies
    (E) that sort of movie

14. <u>It was all so different than I had expected.</u>

    (A) It was all so different than I had expected.
    (B) It was all so different from what I had expected.
    (C) It was all different and not expected.
    (D) It was all different that what I had expected.
    (E) It was all different than I had expected.

15. The three main characters in the story <u>are Neal King, a teenager, his father a widower, and the local pharmacist.</u>

    (A) are Neal King, a teenager, his father a widower, and the local pharmacist.
    (B) are Neal King, a teenager, his father, a widower, and the local pharmacist.
    (C) are Neal King a teenager, his father a widower, and the local pharmacist.
    (D) are Neal King a teenager, his father a widower and the local pharmacist.
    (E) are Neal King, a teenager; his father, a widower; and the local pharmacist.

16. Joan was the only one of the applicants <u>whom as you know was</u> declared eligible for the beauty pageant.

    (A) whom as you know was
    (B) whom, as you know, was
    (C) who as you know were
    (D) whom, as you know, were
    (E) who as you know was

17. There should be no objection <u>to him winning the most valuable player</u> award since all the coaches in the league voted for him.

    (A) to him winning the most valuable player
    (B) to his winning the most valuable player

(C) to his having had won the most valuable player
(D) of him winning the most valuable player
(E) at him winning the most valuable player

18. Neither Marty or his parents knows how to speak French.

    (A) Neither Marty or his parents knows
    (B) Neither Marty or his parents can know
    (C) Neither Marty nor his parents knows
    (D) Neither Marty nor his parents know
    (E) Neither Marty or his parents know

19. To keep up one's grades and hold a job at the same time it require good organizations.

    (A) it require good organization
    (B) it require that one be well organized
    (C) require that you be well organized
    (D) require good organization
    (E) good organizaion is required

20. I do not know of no more worthy motive than that expressed by the congressman.

    (A) I do not know of no more worthy motive
    (B) I don't know of no more worthy motive
    (C) I do not know of anymore worthy motive
    (D) I do not know of a more worthy motive
    (E) I can't know of no more worthy motive

21. Perched on the roof like a fantastic mechanical bird, electricity is generated by the windmill to light the building.

    (A) electricity is generated by the windmill to light the building
    (B) the building is lit by electricity generated by the windmill
    (C) the windmill's electricity is generated to light the building
    (D) the windmill generates electricity and lights the building
    (E) the windmill generates electricity to light the building

22. The examiner told us that the instructions were to be read by us carefully.

    (A) that the instructions were to be read by us carefully
    (B) that the instructions were read by us carefully
    (C) that careful reading of the instructions was required of us
    (D) to read the instructions carefully
    (E) carefully to read the instructions

23. David told the story carefully and in a lucid manner.

    (A) in a lucid manner
    (B) lucid
    (C) lucidly
    (D) luminously
    (E) in a lucid way

24. The exhausted animal lay there, not moving a single muscle.

    (A) The exhausted animal lay there,
    (B) The exhausted animal lie there,

(C) The exhausted animal lied there,
(D) The exhausted animal laid there,
(E) The exhausted animal layed there,

25. The world seems to grow smaller as they devise faster means of communication.

(A) they devise faster means of communication
(B) they device faster means of communication
(C) means of communication are devised faster
(D) they devise faster communication means
(E) faster means of communication are devised

Answer Key for Correct English Usage Practice Exercises

Exercise 1.   Grammar and Usage

1. E	6. A	11. A	16. B	21. A
2. D	7. A	12. C	17. D	22. B
3. D	8. B	13. B	18. C	23. D
4. C	9. D	14. C	19. C	24. D
5. B	10. E	15. C	20. D	25. E

Exercise 2.   Sentence Correction

1. C	6. C	11. D	16. E	21. E
2. D	7. E	12. A	17. B	22. D
3. D	8. B	13. C	18. D	23. C
4. D	9. C	14. B	19. D	24. A
5. A	10. D	15. E	20. D	25. E

Explanatory Answers

Exercise 1.   Grammar and Usage

1. **(E)** There is no error in this sentence.

2. **(D)** "The job was too big for any one of us to handle alone; so we decided to divide the responsibilities *among* the three of us." "Between" is used for two persons or things; "among," for three or more.

3. **(D)** "When Mr. Brown inspected his grounds, he found that the hurricane *had destroyed* one of his favorite trees." Use the past perfect tense to place one past action before another past action. (The destruction took place before the inspection.)

4. **(C)** "The crowd, subdued while the home team trailed, *sang* with gusto when the team forged ahead." The past tense of the verb "to sing" is "sang."

5. **(B)** "His education had filled him with anger against those *who* he believed had hurt or humiliated him." The case of a relative pronoun is determined by its use within the clause. In this sentence, "who" acts as the subject of the verb "had hurt" and therefore must be in the nominative case.

6. **(A)** "Rather *than* go with John, he decided to stay at home." "Than" is used for comparisons. "Then" is an adverb meaning "at that time" or "next."

7. **(A)** "Fred *could* scarcely see to drive when the fog rolled in off the water." Do not use a negative, "couldn't," with a half-negative, "scarcely."

8. **(B)** "The victim's mother, *beside* herself with grief, could give no coherent account of the accident." The meaning of this sentence requires the idiom "beside oneself," which means to be wild or upset with fear, rage, etc.

9. **(D)** "Steve threw the stick into the water and stood back to watch as his dog *swam* furiously after it." The past tense of the verb "to swim" is "swam."

10. **(E)** This sentence is correct.

11. **(A)** "Neither tears *nor* protests effected the least change in their parents' decision." "Neither" must be accompanied by "nor."

12. **(C)** "Ms. Cleary is the most sympathetic, most understanding, and *kindest* teacher I have ever had." Avoid the double comparison "most kindest"; "kindest" alone will do.

13. **(B)** "Mary will join you and *me* in attempting to persuade Bill not to act so rashly." The direct objects of the verb "join" are "you" and "me"(not "I").

14. **(C)** "Having rescued the sleeping child from the smoke-filled room, the fireman descended the ladder to safety." The word "down" is redundant when used with "descended."

15. **(C)** "Admirers of American ballet have made the claim that its stars can dance *as well as* or better than the best of the Russian artists." The addition of the second "as" is necessary to complete the comparison, "as well as or better than."

16. **(B)** "As long as you are going to the library, please *take* this book with you and return it to the children's room." "Bring" means to convey toward the speaker; "take" means to convey away from the speaker.

17. **(D)** "Never before, to the best of my recollection, have there been so *many* small cars on the highways." "Many" refers to a number. "Much" refers to a quantity in bulk.

18. **(C)** "Granting this to be true, what would you *infer* from the statement which he had made?" The speaker "implies," meaning suggests; the listener "infers," meaning deduces.

19. **(C)** "Neither rain nor snow *keeps* the dedicated jogger from his daily exercise." Use a singular verb after two singular subjects connected by "or" or "nor."

20. **(D)** "Each of the candidates had ten minutes to present *his* (or *her*) views." A pronoun must agree with its antecedent in number. Since "each" is singular, it must be followed by a singular pronoun (either "his" or "her").

21. **(A)** "We objected to *his* scolding us for our good, especially when he said it hurt him more than us." The gerund "scolding" takes a possessive pronoun "his."

22. **(B)** "The following description, together with the drawings, *presents* a master plan for the development of the airport." The singular verb "presents" is needed to agree with the singular subject "description."

23. **(D)** "His father was disturbed to find that the boy had lied rather than *told* the truth." The past tense "told" is required after the past perfect "had lied" for proper sequence of tenses in this sentence.

24. **(D)** "Every week Mrs. Foley buys two gallons of milk, three loaves of bread, and ten pounds of meat for her *family's* meals." The possessive "family's" is needed, not the plural "families."

25. **(E)** There is no error in this sentence.

Exercise 2. Sentence Correction

1. **(C)** "Flinging himself at the heavy metal fire door" is an introductory participle phrase. Such phrases are separated from the rest of the sentence by a comma and not by a colon, answer choice **(B)**, or a semicolon, answer choice **(E)**. Answer choice **(D)** is a sentence fragment.

2. **(D)** "Marilyn and he" are the subjects of the verb "to be permitted"; therefore, the nominative form "he" is required and the verb must be the third person plural "were permitted."

3. **(D)** Two complete ideas are expressed. Of the choices offered, only the semicolon correctly joins two separate but closely related thoughts.

4. **(D)** The subject of this sentence is "costs," a plural noun, which requires a plural verb form. This eliminates answer choices **(A)**, **(C)**, and **(E)**. The verb "raise" takes an object, while the verb "rise" describes a state and does not take an object. Since "costs" did not raise anything and a condition is being described, "risen" is correct, not "raised."

5. **(A)** The subject of the sentence is "teacher," a singular noun. The word "teacher" is modified by the prepositional phrase "with all her students." The verb must agree with the subject; therefore, answer choices **(C)** and **(E)** are incorrect. Because "with all her students" is a nonrestrictive phrase, it must be set off by commas; therefore, answer choices **(B)** and **(D)** are incorrect.

6. **(C)** Parallel ideas should be expressed in similar grammatical form. In this sentence, the subject "Vicki" is modified by both an appositive clause, "the president of the class," and a relative clause, "who is also captain of the girls' volley ball team." Since the appositive clause cannot be changed, the correct answer is the one that changes the relative clause to an appositive clause.

7. **(E)** "Each one" is singular and requires a singular pronoun. "Their," answer choices **(A)** and **(D)**, is a plural pronoun. "There," answer choice **(B)**, is not a pronoun. Answer choice **(C)** changes the meaning of the sentence.

8. **(B)** A sentence that starts in the third person, "gardeners," should stay in the third person, "they." It is incorrect to switch from the third person to the second person ("you") in the middle of a sentence.

9. **(C)** In answer choices **(A)** and **(E)**, the girlfriend could be wearing the blue and white bathing suit and both choices are therefore incorrect. In answer choices **(B)** and **(D)**, Jones Beach could be wearing the blue and white bathing suit and both choices are therefore incorrect. Only answer choice **(C)** makes it clear that Pat went to the beach and Pat wore the bathing suit.

10. **(D)** The introductory adverbial clause "When the flurry of angry words ended" must be followed by a comma. It cannot stand alone as a complete sentence.

11. **(D)** The exclamation mark is included before the quotation marks and takes the place of a comma. There is no such word as "yourselfs" as in answer choice **(B)**.

12. **(A)** This sentence is correct. "Were" is used to describe a condition that is contrary to fact (the boy is not a plane).

13. **(C)** The expression is "kind of," not "kind of a." "Kind" is singular and must be modified by "that," not "those."

14. **(B)** The correct idiom is "different from." Answer choice **(C)** changes the meaning of the sentence.

15. **(E)** As the sentence stands, it is impossible to tell whether there are three or five characters in the story. When a sentence contains internal commas for a series, then semicolons must be used to separate the elements of the series.

16. **(E)** "Who" is used as a subject, while "whom" is used as an object. This sentence requires "who" as the subject of the relative clause, thus eliminating answer choices **(A)**, **(B)**, and **(D)**. The singular subject requires the singular verb "was declared."

17. **(B)** The word "winning" is a gerund, and therefore must be modified by the possessive pronoun "his."

18. **(D)** The correlative form is "neither . . . nor," not "neither . . . or." In a neither . . . nor construction, the number of the verb is determined by the number of the subject following "nor"; in this case, "parents." Since "parents" is plural, the verb must be "know."

19. **(D)** The use of "it" in the original sentence is awkward and unnecessary.

20. **(D)** Answer choices **(A)**, **(B)**, and **(E)** contain double negatives, "don't know—no more," "can't know—no more," and are therefore incorrect. "Anymore" is incorrectly used in answer choice **(C)**.

21. **(E)** The original sentence contains a dangling phrase. Since "perched" must refer to "windmill," windmill should be made the subject of the sentence, which eliminates answer choices **(A)**, **(B)**, and **(C)**. The windmill does not light the building as in answer choice **(D)**; therefore, answer choice **(E)** is correct.

22. **(D)** The use of the passive "were to be read" makes this an awkward sentence. It is more direct and less wordy in the active voice.

23. **(C)** Items linked by "and" should be grammatically parallel. Since the first item is the adverb "carefully," the second item should be the adverb "lucidly."

24. **(A)** The other choices have incorrectly used the verb "to lie," instead of "to lay."

25. **(E)** Avoid using "they" without a clear antecedent, as in answer choices **(A)**, **(B)**, and **(D)**. "Faster" modifies "means of communication," not "devised"; therefore, answer choice **(E)** is correct.

Answer Sheet for Correct English Usage Practice Tests

Test 1

1 Ⓐ Ⓑ Ⓒ Ⓓ
2 Ⓐ Ⓑ Ⓒ Ⓓ
3 Ⓐ Ⓑ Ⓒ Ⓓ
4 Ⓐ Ⓑ Ⓒ Ⓓ

5 Ⓐ Ⓑ Ⓒ Ⓓ
6 Ⓐ Ⓑ Ⓒ Ⓓ
7 Ⓐ Ⓑ Ⓒ Ⓓ

8 Ⓐ Ⓑ Ⓒ Ⓓ
9 Ⓐ Ⓑ Ⓒ Ⓓ
10 Ⓐ Ⓑ Ⓒ Ⓓ

11 Ⓐ Ⓑ Ⓒ Ⓓ
12 Ⓐ Ⓑ Ⓒ Ⓓ
13 Ⓐ Ⓑ Ⓒ Ⓓ

Test 2

1 Ⓐ Ⓑ Ⓒ Ⓓ
2 Ⓐ Ⓑ Ⓒ Ⓓ
3 Ⓐ Ⓑ Ⓒ Ⓓ
4 Ⓐ Ⓑ Ⓒ Ⓓ

5 Ⓐ Ⓑ Ⓒ Ⓓ
6 Ⓐ Ⓑ Ⓒ Ⓓ
7 Ⓐ Ⓑ Ⓒ Ⓓ
8 Ⓐ Ⓑ Ⓒ Ⓓ

9 Ⓐ Ⓑ Ⓒ Ⓓ
10 Ⓐ Ⓑ Ⓒ Ⓓ
11 Ⓐ Ⓑ Ⓒ Ⓓ

12 Ⓐ Ⓑ Ⓒ Ⓓ
13 Ⓐ Ⓑ Ⓒ Ⓓ
14 Ⓐ Ⓑ Ⓒ Ⓓ

Test 3

1 Ⓐ Ⓑ Ⓒ Ⓓ
2 Ⓐ Ⓑ Ⓒ Ⓓ
3 Ⓐ Ⓑ Ⓒ Ⓓ
4 Ⓐ Ⓑ Ⓒ Ⓓ

5 Ⓐ Ⓑ Ⓒ Ⓓ
6 Ⓐ Ⓑ Ⓒ Ⓓ
7 Ⓐ Ⓑ Ⓒ Ⓓ

8 Ⓐ Ⓑ Ⓒ Ⓓ
9 Ⓐ Ⓑ Ⓒ Ⓓ
10 Ⓐ Ⓑ Ⓒ Ⓓ

11 Ⓐ Ⓑ Ⓒ Ⓓ
12 Ⓐ Ⓑ Ⓒ Ⓓ
13 Ⓐ Ⓑ Ⓒ Ⓓ

Test 4

1 Ⓐ Ⓑ Ⓒ Ⓓ
2 Ⓐ Ⓑ Ⓒ Ⓓ
3 Ⓐ Ⓑ Ⓒ Ⓓ

4 Ⓐ Ⓑ Ⓒ Ⓓ
5 Ⓐ Ⓑ Ⓒ Ⓓ
6 Ⓐ Ⓑ Ⓒ Ⓓ

7 Ⓐ Ⓑ Ⓒ Ⓓ
8 Ⓐ Ⓑ Ⓒ Ⓓ
9 Ⓐ Ⓑ Ⓒ Ⓓ

10 Ⓐ Ⓑ Ⓒ Ⓓ
11 Ⓐ Ⓑ Ⓒ Ⓓ

Test 1

TIME: 13 minutes. 13 questions.

DIRECTIONS: In each of the following groups of sentences, select the one sentence that is grammatically INCORRECT. Mark the answer sheet with the letter of that incorrect sentence.

1. (A) Everyone at camp must have his or her medical certificate on file before participating in competitive sports.
   (B) A crate of oranges were sent from Florida for all the children in Cabin Six.
   (C) John and Danny's room looks as if they were prepared for inspection.
   (D) Three miles is too far for a young child to walk.

2. (A) The game over, the spectators rushed out on the field and tore down the goalposts.
   (B) The situation was aggravated by disputes over the captaincy of the team.
   (C) Yesterday they lay their uniforms aside with the usual end-of-the-season regret.
   (D) It is sometimes thought that politics is not for the high-minded.

3. (A) Sandburg's autobiography, as well as his poems, are familiar to many readers.
   (B) A series of authentic records of the American Indian tribes is being published.
   (C) The Smokies is the home of the descendants of this brave tribe.
   (D) Five dollars is really not too much to pay for a book of this type.

4. (A) Being tired, I stretched out on a grassy knoll.
   (B) While we were rowing on the lake, a sudden squall almost capsized the boat.
   (C) Entering the room, a strange mark on the floor attracted my attention.
   (D) Mounting the curb, the empty car crossed the sidewalk and came to rest against a building.

5. (A) The text makes the process of developing and sustaining a successful home zoo appear to be a pleasant and profitable one.
   (B) The warmth and humor, the clear characterization of the Walmsey family, which includes three children, two dogs and two cats, is such fun to read that this reviewer found herself reading it all over again.
   (C) You will be glad, I am sure, to give the book to whoever among your young friends has displayed an interest in animals.
   (D) The consensus among critics of children's literature is that the book is well worth the purchase price.

6. (A) Not one in a thousand readers take the matter seriously.
   (B) Let it lie there.
   (C) You are not so tall as he.
   (D) The people began to realize how much she had done.

7. (A) In the case of members who are absent, a special letter will be sent.
   (B) The visitors were all ready to see it.
   (C) I like Burns's poem "To a Mountain Daisy."
   (D) John told William that he was sure he had seen it.

8. (A) B. Nelson & Co. has a sale of dacron shirts today.
   (B) Venetian blinds—called that although they probably did not originate in Venice—are no longer used as extensively as they were at one time.
   (C) He determined to be guided by the opinion of whoever spoke first.
   (D) There is often disagreement as to whom is the better Shakespearean actor, Evans or Gielgud.

9. (A) It did not take him long to develop an interest in the great American pastime—baseball.
   (B) If you had made your way to the Whipsnade Zoo, you would have had an opportunity of seeing wild animals in more or less natural habitats.
   (C) How I should have liked to have spent a few more days in Paris!
   (D) Neither baseball pools nor any other form of gambling is allowed in or near the school.

10. (A) If the bill were introduced, it would provoke endless debate.
    (B) Since George, with his two dogs, is to be with us, it might be better to rent a cabin.
    (C) He, not I, is the one to decide.
    (D) He is, however, one of those restless people who never seems content in his present environment.

11. (A) Everyone can have a wonderful time in New York if they will just not try to see the entire city in one week.
    (B) Being a stranger in town myself, I know how you feel.
    (C) New York is a city of man-made wonders, as awe-inspiring as those found in nature.
    (D) He felt deep despair (as who has not?) at the evidence of man's inhumanity to man.

12. (A) A clerk should be careful as well as punctual, even though he or she are otherwise efficient.
    (B) Regardless of whether it may be true, some students are not very studious.
    (C) Not every writer can say that his opinion is always the best.
    (D) We often think of people who assume airs as being affected.

13. (A) We were not entirely dissatisfied with the conditions.
    (B) There is a chair and a table in the room.
    (C) He was among the few writers who do not experience difficulty with words.
    (D) Remember that the man to whom you are speaking is my friend.

Test 2

Time: 14 minutes. 14 questions.

DIRECTIONS: In each of the following groups of sentences, select the one sentence that is grammatically INCORRECT. Mark the answer sheet with the letter of that incorrect sentence.

1. (A) This is the woman whom I saw.
   (B) She could solve even this problem.
   (C) She divided the money among the three of us.
   (D) Either she or I are guilty.

2. (A) Consider that the person which is always idle can never be happy.
   (B) Because a man understands a woman does not mean they are necessarily compatible.
   (C) He said that accuracy and speed are both essential.
   (D) Can it be said that the better of the two books is less expensive?

3. (A) Neither the critics nor the author were right about the reaction of the public.
   (B) The senator depended upon whoever was willing to assist him.
   (C) I don't recall any time when Edgar has broken his word.
   (D) Every one of the campers but John and me is going on the hike.

4. (A) Everyone entered promptly but her.
   (B) Each of the messengers were busily occupied.
   (C) At which exit did you leave him?
   (D) The work was not done well.

5. (A) Never before have I seen anyone who has the skill John has when he repairs engines.
   (B) If anyone can be wholly just in his decisions, it is he.
   (C) Because of his friendliness, the new neighbor was immediately accepted by the community.
   (D) Imagine our embarrassment when us girls saw Miss Maltinge sitting with her beau in the front row.

6. (A) I wondered why it was that the Mayor objected to the Governor's reference to the new tax law.
   (B) I have never read *Les Miserables,* but I plan to do so this summer.
   (C) After much talk and haranguing, the workers received an increase in wages.
   (D) The author and myself were the only cheerful ones at the macabre gathering.

7. (A) The doctor had carelessly left all the instruments on the operating table.
   (B) Was it them whom the professor regarded with such contempt?
   (C) Despite all the power he has, I should still hate to be in his shoes.
   (D) I feel bad because I gave such a poor performance in the play tonight.

8. (A) It seems to me that every one of the waiters is well able to do his share of the work.

(B) His parents told him to wait at the station for his uncle and to bring him home in the car.

(C) Who did you think was going to win the tennis match?

(D) If he would have answered the detective honestly, he would not have been arrested.

9. (A) The general regarded whomever the colonel honored with disdain.

(B) Everyone who reads this book will think themselves knights errant on missions of heroism.

(C) The reason the new leader was so unsuccessful was that he had fewer responsibilities.

(D) All the new mechanical devices we have today have made our daily living a great deal simpler, it is said.

10. (A) The town consists of three distinct sections, of which the western one is by far the larger.

(B) Of London and Paris, the former is the wealthier.

(C) Chicago is larger than any other city in Illinois.

(D) America is the greatest nation, and of all other nations England is the greatest.

11. (A) I can but do my best.

(B) I cannot help comparing him with his predecessor.

(C) I wish that I was in Florida now.

(D) I like this kind of grape better than any other.

12. (A) Neither Tom nor John was present for the rehearsal.

(B) The happiness or misery of men's lives depends on their early training.

(C) Honor as well as profit are to be gained by these studies.

(D) The egg business is only incidental to the regular business of the general store.

13. (A) It was superior in every way to the book previously used.

(B) His testimony today is different from that of yesterday.

(C) If you would have studied the problem carefully you would have found the solution more quickly.

(D) The flowers smelled so sweet that the whole house was perfumed.

14. (A) When either or both habits become fixed, the student improves.

(B) Neither his words nor his action was justifiable.

(C) A calm almost always comes before a storm.

(D) The gallery with all its pictures were destroyed.

Test 3

Time: 13 minutes. 13 questions.

DIRECTIONS: In each of the following groups of sentences, select the one sentence that is grammatically INCORRECT. Mark the answer sheet with the letter of that incorrect sentence.

1. (A) Who did they say won?
   (B) The man whom I thought was my friend deceived me.
   (C) Send whoever will do the work.
   (D) The question of who should be leader arose.

2. (A) A box of choice figs was sent him for Christmas.
   (B) Neither Charles nor his brother finished his assignment.
   (C) There goes the last piece of cake and the last spoonful of ice cream.
   (D) Diamonds are more desired than any other precious stones.

3. (A) As long as you are ready, you may as well start promptly.
   (B) My younger brother insists that he is as tall as me.
   (C) We walked as long as there was any light to guide us.
   (D) Realizing I had forgotten my gloves, I returned to the theatre.

4. (A) The supervisor has given you and me difficult assignments.
   (B) This is just between you and I.
   (C) That question is not for you and me to answer.
   (D) He acted as a loyal employee should.

5. (A) His knowledge of methods and procedures enable him to assist the director in many ways.
   (B) A new set of rules and regulations has been made.
   (C) Reports that the strike has been settled were circulated yesterday.
   (D) The blame is shared equally between you and him.

6. (A) The Credit Bureau rates you as high as him.
   (B) He is no better than you or me.
   (C) You will be notified as soon as I.
   (D) The unopened mail was lying on the desk of the boss.

7. (A) Neither the stenographer nor the typist has returned from lunch.
   (B) Either the operators or the machines are at fault.
   (C) One or the other of those clerks are responsible for these errors.
   (D) To whom should we give the new assignment?

8. (A) The Board of Directors has prepared a manual for their own use.
   (B) The company has announced its new policy of advertising.
   (C) The jury were out about thirty minutes when they returned a verdict.
   (D) The salary of stenographers is higher than the salary of typists.

9. (A) Who does he think he is?
   (B) Whom does he consider in making a decision?
   (C) Whom did they say is to be appointed?
   (D) Each office employee in the firm works 35 hours a week.

10. (A) Who shall I say called?
    (B) The water has frozen the pipes.
    (C) Everyone has left except them.
    (D) Everyone of the salesmen must supply their own car.

11. (A) Two-thirds of the building is finished.
    (B) Where are Mr. Keene and Mr. Herbert?
    (C) Neither the salesladies nor the floor-walker want to work overtime.
    (D) The committee was agreed.

12. (A) Amends have been made for the damage to one of our cars.
    (B) Neither the customer nor the clerk were aware of the fire in the store.
    (C) A box of spare pencils is on the desk.
    (D) There is the total number of missing pens.

13. (A) The company insist on everyone's being prompt.
    (B) Each one of our salesmen takes an aptitude test.
    (C) It is the location that appeals to me.
    (D) Most of the men have left the building.

Test 4

Time: 11 minutes. 11 questions.

DIRECTIONS: *In each of the following groups of sentences, select the one sentence that is grammatically INCORRECT. Mark the answer sheet with the letter of that incorrect sentence.*

1. (A) The students in the dormitories were forbidden, unless they had special passes, from staying out after 11:30 p.m.
   (B) The Student Court rendered a decision satisfactory to both the defendant and the accuser.
   (C) Margarine is being substituted for butter to a considerable extent.
   (D) In this school there are at least fifteen minor accidents a year that are due to this traffic violation.

2. (A) Sailing along New England's craggy coastline, you will relive a bygone era of far-roving whalers and graceful clipper ships.
   (B) The march of history is reenacted in folk festivals, outdoor pageants, and fiestas—local in theme, but national in import.
   (C) Visiting the scenes of the past, our interest in American history is renewed and enlivened.
   (D) What remained was a few unrecognizable fragments.

3. (A) I knew it to be he by the style of his clothes.
   (B) No one saw him doing it.
   (C) Her going away is a loss to the community.
   (D) Illness prevented him graduating in June.

4. (A) No one but her could have recognized him.
   (B) She knew the stranger to be he whom she had given up as lost.
   (C) He looked like he had been in some strange land where age advanced at a double pace.
   (D) It is impossible to include that item; the agenda has already been mimeographed.

5. (A) You have probably heard of the new innovation in the regular morning broadcast.
   (B) During the broadcast you are expected to stand, to salute, and to sing the fourth stanza of "America."
   (C) None of the rocks that form the solid crust of our planet is more than two billion years old.
   (D) "I have finished my assignment," said the pupil. "May I go home now?"

6. (A) The coming of peace effected a change in her way of life.
   (B) Spain is as weak, if not weaker than, she was in 1900.
   (C) In regard to that, I am not certain what my attitude will be.
   (D) That unfortunate family faces the problem of adjusting itself to a new way of life.

7. (A) Participation in active sports produces both release from tension as well as physical well-being.
   (B) The problem of taxes is still with them.
   (C) Every boy and every girl in the auditorium was thrilled when the color guard appeared.
   (D) At length our club decided to send two representatives to the meeting, you and me.

8. (A) Remains of an ancient civilization were found near Mexico City.
   (B) It is interesting to compare the interior of one of the pyramids in Mexico to the interior of one of the pyramids in Egypt.
   (C) In two days' journey you will be reminded of political upheavals comparable to the volcanic eruptions still visible and audible in parts of Mexico.
   (D) There is little danger of the laws being broken, so drastic is the penalty.

9. (A) Instead of looking disdainfully at London grime, think of it as a mantle of tradition.
   (B) Nobody but the pilot and the co-pilot was permitted to handle the mysterious package.
   (C) Not only is industry anxious to hire all available engineers, but they are being offered commissions by the armed forces.
   (D) For immediate service go direct to the store manager.

10. (A) The delegates alighted and started off in a taxi, their baggage having been taken care of.
    (B) That kind of potato is grown in Idaho.
    (C) Besides Alan Stevens, there were eight officers of the organization on the dais.
    (D) As the delegates reached the convention hall late, they blamed their tardiness on the taxi driver.

11. (A) The new system is superior from every point of view to the inefficient system in use until now.
    (B) The reason for the strike, you may recall, was because the union demanded a closed shop.
    (C) Who's to decide whether it is to be installed?
    (D) To suit Mr. Knolls, the new device will have to save time, money, and the dispositions of the employees.

Answer Key for Correct English Usage Practice Tests

Test 1

1. B	4. C	7. D	10. D	13. B
2. C	5. B	8. D	11. A	
3. A	6. A	9. C	12. A	

Test 2

1. D	4. B	7. B	10. A	13. C
2. A	5. D	8. D	11. C	14. D
3. A	6. D	9. B	12. C	

Test 3

1. B	4. B	7. C	10. D	13. A
2. C	5. A	8. A	11. C	
3. B	6. B	9. C	12. B	

Test 4

1. A	4. C	7. A	10. D
2. C	5. A	8. B	11. B
3. D	6. B	9. C	

TOP SCORES IN SPELLING

The material in this chapter has appeared repeatedly on past examinations. It's all quite relevant and well worth every minute of your valuable study time. Beginning with basic rules, it proceeds to an illuminating presentation of a wide variety of questions and answers that will strengthen your ability to answer actual test questions quickly and accurately.

The importance of spelling cannot be overestimated. Bad spelling is a principal cause of failure among examinees.

It is impossible in this brief résumé to supply a set of easy rules for all cases and all exceptions. However, we can give you some guidance that will almost certainly raise your test score.

We offer here a set of rules and a word list based on our study of many tests. After working through the sample test questions with these rules in mind, we suggest that you make a list of any words that you have misspelled. Further study of this list should then give you a big boost.

We also suggest that you find in your local library such books as "Words Frequently Misspelled," and "Spelling Word Lists," for supplementary work.

A Few Rules That Really Help

1. EI or IE

I comes before *E*   *Examples:* friend, belief, niece, grieve

except after *C*   *Examples:* deceit, ceiling, conceive, receipt

or when sounded like *AY*   *Examples:* vein, neighbor, feign, heinous

Exceptions: either, neither, height, foreign, sovereign, forfeit, seize, counterfeit, financier

2. S or ES

Add *ES* to words ending in *S, SH, X,* or *Z*
Examples: rush, rushes; success, successes; bench, benches; fox, foxes

And to words ending in *Y* after a consonant, but first change *Y* to *I*
Examples: try, tries; artery, arteries; community, communities

Add *S* alone to any other words where *S* is needed
Examples: boy, boys; chair, chairs; friend, friends; want, wants; decide, decides

3. L or LL

Final *L* is doubled following a single vowel in words of one syllable
Examples: fall, bell, sill, doll, hull

And following a single vowel in words of more than one syllable, when the stress falls on the last syllable
Examples: recall, fortell, distill

Final *L* is single following more than one vowel in words of one syllable
Examples: bail, real, soul, feel

And following more than one vowel in words of more than one syllable when the stress falls on the last syllable
Examples: conceal, ideal, detail

Also following a single vowel in words of more than one syllable, when the stress falls *before* the last syllable
Examples: marginal, alcohol, dismal

4. Suffixes

These are syllables that are added to a base word to make a new word.

Some common suffixes:

able	er	ing	ly	ness
ed	ful	less	ment	ous

You can add these suffixes to some base words without changing the spelling of either the base word or the suffix.

Base Word	Suffix	New Word
expend	able	expendable
roar	ed	roared
read	er	reader
use	ful	useful
sink	ing	sinking
count	less	countless
love	ly	lovely
arrange	ment	arrangement
glad	ness	gladness
peril	ous	perilous

However, some base words must be changed slightly before you can add the suffix. Here are some rules for these changes.

In words ending in *E* drop the *E* when the suffix begins with a vowel
Examples: like, likable; love, loved; trace, tracer

Or after *DG*   *Examples:* judge, judgment; acknowledge, acknowledging

In words ending in *Y,* change *Y* to *I* after a consonant in words of more than one syllable
Examples: lovely, lovelier; accompany, accompaniment; tardy, tardiness; levy, levied

But keep the *Y* when you add *ING*
Examples: rally, rallying; fry, frying; reply, replying; destroy, destroying

And when you add *LY* or *NESS* to words of one syllable
Examples: sly, slyly, slyness; shy, shyly, shyness; dry, dryly, dryness
Exceptions: day, daily; lay, laid; say, said; slay, slain; pay, paid

In words ending in a consonant double the final consonant if it follows a single vowel In words of one syllable, and if the suffix begins with a vowel
Examples: fat, fatter; hop, hopping; wed, wedding

Or if it follows a single vowel in words of more than one syllable and the stress remains on the same syllable
Examples: refer, referred; control, controlled

5. Prefixes

These are syllables that go in front of a base word to make a new word.
Some common prefixes:

ab	com	en	ir	per
ac	con	il	mal	pro
ad	de	im	mis	re
bi	dis	in	over	under

You can add any prefix to a base word without changing the spelling of either the prefix or the base word.

Examples:

Prefix	Base Word	New Word
ab	normal	abnormal
ac	company	accompany
ad	join	adjoin
bi	lateral	bilateral
com	mission	commission
con	dense	condense
de	centralize	decentralize
dis	organize	disorganize
en	lace	enlace
il	legible	illegible
im	possible	impossible
in	sincere	insincere
ir	rational	irrational
mis	spell	misspell
mal	formed	malformed
over	do	overdo
per	form	perform
pre	text	pretext
pro	noun	pronoun
re	flex	reflex
under	go	undergo

We listed the foregoing rules in the order of their importance for you. Should they seem more than you can handle, we suggest that you memorize *at least* the following: all three points of (1); the first two points of (2) (the third point is practically self-evident); and the first two points of (3) (because if you know when to double the final *l,* you can leave it single for all the words that do not fit into these rules).

If you memorize these eight short statements, you will have taken a big step toward success in any spelling examination. Then study (4) carefully, and try to think of additional words you can make by using a base word and a suffix. Check your result, and if you have made mistakes, study it again until getting the right answer comes naturally. Go over (5), too, but you needn't put so much effort into it. The important thing here is to be able to recognize a prefix when you see it.

Words Frequently Misspelled

aberration	capitol	diocese	illegitimate	nickel	resilience
abeyance	carburetor	diphtheria	imminent	ninth	resonance
abscess	category	disappearance	impartiality		responsibility
abundance	cemetery	dissatisfied	impeccable	occur	rheostat
accessible	chamois	distinguished	impromptu	official	rhetorical
accumulation	character		incongruity	ordinance	rhythm
acquaint	chauffeur	ecstasy	indictment		routine
across	circumstantial	eczema	individual	pacifist	
actually	citation	effects	ingenuous	pamphlet	sacrilegious
adage	clamorous	elaborate	inimitable	panicky	salable
addressee	clique	electrolysis	innocuous	parliament	salient
adjunct	colossal	embarrass	integrity	patient	sandwich
adoption	column	eminently	intelligence	patronize	scissors
advise	commandant	emolument	intercede	peculiar	scripture
aggravate	commemorate	emphasis	interruption	permissible	secretary
allege	committal	emphatically	irreparably	picnicking	senior
amendment	community	ephemeral		piquancy	similar
amplify	compel	equilibrium	jeopardy	plagiarism	sobriquet
ancient	complacency	equinoctial	journal	pneumonia	sophomore
anecdote	conciliatory	equipped	judgment	policy	source
anemia	confectionery	essential	judiciary	possession	sovereign
angle	connoisseur	exaggerate		prairie	specialized
annoyance	consummation	exceed	laboratory	preceding	specifically
antipathy	controller	exercise	labyrinth	precious	staunch
apologetic	conversant	exhortation	lacquer	predatory	stretch
apparatus	coroner	existence	liquidate	predilection	subversive
appellate	corporal	extraordinary	loose	preferably	succeed
appetite	correlation		lucrative	preparation	summarize
aquatic	correspondence	facilitation	mackerel	presumptuous	surfeit
arouse	corrugated	fallibility	maintenance	previous	surgeon
arraignment	criticism	fascinated	maneuver	principal	symmetrical
ascertain	crucial	feudal	marital	proletarian	
assessment	crystallized	financier	masquerade	promissory	tariff
aversion	currency	foreign	matinee	propaganda	temperament
		forfeit	mechanical	psychology	thorough
baccalaureate	dearth	function	medallion	publicity	transaction
bankruptcy	deceive		medieval	punctilious	transient
beatitude	deferred	gelatin	mediocrity		tremendous
beleaguered	deliberate	grandeur	memoir	queue	vacillate
belligerent	demurrage		midget		vacuum
biased	denunciatory	harass	mischievous	realize	vengeance
biscuit	derogatory	hearth	moribund	reasonable	
blamable	description	heinous	murmuring	recognizable	warrant
bookkeeping	desecration	heritage	myriad	regrettable	whether
bounteous	detrimental	hindrance		rehearsal	wholly
bureau	dilapidated	histrionic	negligible	relevant	wield
		hygienic	nevertheless	renascence	
				repetitious	yacht

The verb endings *"sede," "ceed," and "cede"* are pronounced the same. Only one verb ends in "sede": *supersede;* only three end in "ceed": *exceed, proceed,* and *succeed;* all other verb endings pronounced the same are spelled "cede," as *accede, concede, precede, secede,* etc.

Answer Sheet for Spelling Practice Tests

Test 1

1 Ⓐ Ⓑ Ⓒ Ⓓ	31 Ⓐ Ⓑ Ⓒ Ⓓ	61 Ⓐ Ⓑ Ⓒ Ⓓ
2 Ⓐ Ⓑ Ⓒ Ⓓ	32 Ⓐ Ⓑ Ⓒ Ⓓ	62 Ⓐ Ⓑ Ⓒ Ⓓ
3 Ⓐ Ⓑ Ⓒ Ⓓ	33 Ⓐ Ⓑ Ⓒ Ⓓ	63 Ⓐ Ⓑ Ⓒ Ⓓ
4 Ⓐ Ⓑ Ⓒ Ⓓ	34 Ⓐ Ⓑ Ⓒ Ⓓ	64 Ⓐ Ⓑ Ⓒ Ⓓ
5 Ⓐ Ⓑ Ⓒ Ⓓ	35 Ⓐ Ⓑ Ⓒ Ⓓ	65 Ⓐ Ⓑ Ⓒ Ⓓ
6 Ⓐ Ⓑ Ⓒ Ⓓ	36 Ⓐ Ⓑ Ⓒ Ⓓ	66 Ⓐ Ⓑ Ⓒ Ⓓ
7 Ⓐ Ⓑ Ⓒ Ⓓ	37 Ⓐ Ⓑ Ⓒ Ⓓ	67 Ⓐ Ⓑ Ⓒ Ⓓ
8 Ⓐ Ⓑ Ⓒ Ⓓ	38 Ⓐ Ⓑ Ⓒ Ⓓ	68 Ⓐ Ⓑ Ⓒ Ⓓ
9 Ⓐ Ⓑ Ⓒ Ⓓ	39 Ⓐ Ⓑ Ⓒ Ⓓ	69 Ⓐ Ⓑ Ⓒ Ⓓ
10 Ⓐ Ⓑ Ⓒ Ⓓ	40 Ⓐ Ⓑ Ⓒ Ⓓ	70 Ⓐ Ⓑ Ⓒ Ⓓ
11 Ⓐ Ⓑ Ⓒ Ⓓ	41 Ⓐ Ⓑ Ⓒ Ⓓ	71 Ⓐ Ⓑ Ⓒ Ⓓ
12 Ⓐ Ⓑ Ⓒ Ⓓ	42 Ⓐ Ⓑ Ⓒ Ⓓ	72 Ⓐ Ⓑ Ⓒ Ⓓ
13 Ⓐ Ⓑ Ⓒ Ⓓ	43 Ⓐ Ⓑ Ⓒ Ⓓ	73 Ⓐ Ⓑ Ⓒ Ⓓ
14 Ⓐ Ⓑ Ⓒ Ⓓ	44 Ⓐ Ⓑ Ⓒ Ⓓ	74 Ⓐ Ⓑ Ⓒ Ⓓ
15 Ⓐ Ⓑ Ⓒ Ⓓ	45 Ⓐ Ⓑ Ⓒ Ⓓ	75 Ⓐ Ⓑ Ⓒ Ⓓ
16 Ⓐ Ⓑ Ⓒ Ⓓ	46 Ⓐ Ⓑ Ⓒ Ⓓ	76 Ⓐ Ⓑ Ⓒ Ⓓ
17 Ⓐ Ⓑ Ⓒ Ⓓ	47 Ⓐ Ⓑ Ⓒ Ⓓ	77 Ⓐ Ⓑ Ⓒ Ⓓ
18 Ⓐ Ⓑ Ⓒ Ⓓ	48 Ⓐ Ⓑ Ⓒ Ⓓ	78 Ⓐ Ⓑ Ⓒ Ⓓ
19 Ⓐ Ⓑ Ⓒ Ⓓ	49 Ⓐ Ⓑ Ⓒ Ⓓ	79 Ⓐ Ⓑ Ⓒ Ⓓ
20 Ⓐ Ⓑ Ⓒ Ⓓ	50 Ⓐ Ⓑ Ⓒ Ⓓ	80 Ⓐ Ⓑ Ⓒ Ⓓ
21 Ⓐ Ⓑ Ⓒ Ⓓ	51 Ⓐ Ⓑ Ⓒ Ⓓ	81 Ⓐ Ⓑ Ⓒ Ⓓ
22 Ⓐ Ⓑ Ⓒ Ⓓ	52 Ⓐ Ⓑ Ⓒ Ⓓ	82 Ⓐ Ⓑ Ⓒ Ⓓ
23 Ⓐ Ⓑ Ⓒ Ⓓ	53 Ⓐ Ⓑ Ⓒ Ⓓ	83 Ⓐ Ⓑ Ⓒ Ⓓ
24 Ⓐ Ⓑ Ⓒ Ⓓ	54 Ⓐ Ⓑ Ⓒ Ⓓ	84 Ⓐ Ⓑ Ⓒ Ⓓ
25 Ⓐ Ⓑ Ⓒ Ⓓ	55 Ⓐ Ⓑ Ⓒ Ⓓ	85 Ⓐ Ⓑ Ⓒ Ⓓ
26 Ⓐ Ⓑ Ⓒ Ⓓ	56 Ⓐ Ⓑ Ⓒ Ⓓ	86 Ⓐ Ⓑ Ⓒ Ⓓ
27 Ⓐ Ⓑ Ⓒ Ⓓ	57 Ⓐ Ⓑ Ⓒ Ⓓ	87 Ⓐ Ⓑ Ⓒ Ⓓ
28 Ⓐ Ⓑ Ⓒ Ⓓ	58 Ⓐ Ⓑ Ⓒ Ⓓ	88 Ⓐ Ⓑ Ⓒ Ⓓ
29 Ⓐ Ⓑ Ⓒ Ⓓ	59 Ⓐ Ⓑ Ⓒ Ⓓ	89 Ⓐ Ⓑ Ⓒ Ⓓ
30 Ⓐ Ⓑ Ⓒ Ⓓ	60 Ⓐ Ⓑ Ⓒ Ⓓ	

Test 2

1 Ⓐ Ⓑ Ⓒ Ⓓ	10 Ⓐ Ⓑ Ⓒ Ⓓ	19 Ⓐ Ⓑ Ⓒ Ⓓ	28 Ⓐ Ⓑ Ⓒ Ⓓ
2 Ⓐ Ⓑ Ⓒ Ⓓ	11 Ⓐ Ⓑ Ⓒ Ⓓ	20 Ⓐ Ⓑ Ⓒ Ⓓ	29 Ⓐ Ⓑ Ⓒ Ⓓ
3 Ⓐ Ⓑ Ⓒ Ⓓ	12 Ⓐ Ⓑ Ⓒ Ⓓ	21 Ⓐ Ⓑ Ⓒ Ⓓ	30 Ⓐ Ⓑ Ⓒ Ⓓ
4 Ⓐ Ⓑ Ⓒ Ⓓ	13 Ⓐ Ⓑ Ⓒ Ⓓ	22 Ⓐ Ⓑ Ⓒ Ⓓ	31 Ⓐ Ⓑ Ⓒ Ⓓ
5 Ⓐ Ⓑ Ⓒ Ⓓ	14 Ⓐ Ⓑ Ⓒ Ⓓ	23 Ⓐ Ⓑ Ⓒ Ⓓ	32 Ⓐ Ⓑ Ⓒ Ⓓ
6 Ⓐ Ⓑ Ⓒ Ⓓ	15 Ⓐ Ⓑ Ⓒ Ⓓ	24 Ⓐ Ⓑ Ⓒ Ⓓ	33 Ⓐ Ⓑ Ⓒ Ⓓ
7 Ⓐ Ⓑ Ⓒ Ⓓ	16 Ⓐ Ⓑ Ⓒ Ⓓ	25 Ⓐ Ⓑ Ⓒ Ⓓ	34 Ⓐ Ⓑ Ⓒ Ⓓ
8 Ⓐ Ⓑ Ⓒ Ⓓ	17 Ⓐ Ⓑ Ⓒ Ⓓ	26 Ⓐ Ⓑ Ⓒ Ⓓ	35 Ⓐ Ⓑ Ⓒ Ⓓ
9 Ⓐ Ⓑ Ⓒ Ⓓ	18 Ⓐ Ⓑ Ⓒ Ⓓ	27 Ⓐ Ⓑ Ⓒ Ⓓ	

Test 3

1 Ⓐ Ⓑ Ⓒ Ⓓ	10 Ⓐ Ⓑ Ⓒ Ⓓ	19 Ⓐ Ⓑ Ⓒ Ⓓ	28 Ⓐ Ⓑ Ⓒ Ⓓ
2 Ⓐ Ⓑ Ⓒ Ⓓ	11 Ⓐ Ⓑ Ⓒ Ⓓ	20 Ⓐ Ⓑ Ⓒ Ⓓ	29 Ⓐ Ⓑ Ⓒ Ⓓ
3 Ⓐ Ⓑ Ⓒ Ⓓ	12 Ⓐ Ⓑ Ⓒ Ⓓ	21 Ⓐ Ⓑ Ⓒ Ⓓ	30 Ⓐ Ⓑ Ⓒ Ⓓ
4 Ⓐ Ⓑ Ⓒ Ⓓ	13 Ⓐ Ⓑ Ⓒ Ⓓ	22 Ⓐ Ⓑ Ⓒ Ⓓ	31 Ⓐ Ⓑ Ⓒ Ⓓ
5 Ⓐ Ⓑ Ⓒ Ⓓ	14 Ⓐ Ⓑ Ⓒ Ⓓ	23 Ⓐ Ⓑ Ⓒ Ⓓ	32 Ⓐ Ⓑ Ⓒ Ⓓ
6 Ⓐ Ⓑ Ⓒ Ⓓ	15 Ⓐ Ⓑ Ⓒ Ⓓ	24 Ⓐ Ⓑ Ⓒ Ⓓ	33 Ⓐ Ⓑ Ⓒ Ⓓ
7 Ⓐ Ⓑ Ⓒ Ⓓ	16 Ⓐ Ⓑ Ⓒ Ⓓ	25 Ⓐ Ⓑ Ⓒ Ⓓ	34 Ⓐ Ⓑ Ⓒ Ⓓ
8 Ⓐ Ⓑ Ⓒ Ⓓ	17 Ⓐ Ⓑ Ⓒ Ⓓ	26 Ⓐ Ⓑ Ⓒ Ⓓ	
9 Ⓐ Ⓑ Ⓒ Ⓓ	18 Ⓐ Ⓑ Ⓒ Ⓓ	27 Ⓐ Ⓑ Ⓒ Ⓓ	

Test 4

1 Ⓐ Ⓑ Ⓒ Ⓓ	7 Ⓐ Ⓑ Ⓒ Ⓓ	13 Ⓐ Ⓑ Ⓒ Ⓓ
2 Ⓐ Ⓑ Ⓒ Ⓓ	8 Ⓐ Ⓑ Ⓒ Ⓓ	14 Ⓐ Ⓑ Ⓒ Ⓓ
3 Ⓐ Ⓑ Ⓒ Ⓓ	9 Ⓐ Ⓑ Ⓒ Ⓓ	15 Ⓐ Ⓑ Ⓒ Ⓓ
4 Ⓐ Ⓑ Ⓒ Ⓓ	10 Ⓐ Ⓑ Ⓒ Ⓓ	16 Ⓐ Ⓑ Ⓒ Ⓓ
5 Ⓐ Ⓑ Ⓒ Ⓓ	11 Ⓐ Ⓑ Ⓒ Ⓓ	17 Ⓐ Ⓑ Ⓒ Ⓓ
6 Ⓐ Ⓑ Ⓒ Ⓓ	12 Ⓐ Ⓑ Ⓒ Ⓓ	18 Ⓐ Ⓑ Ⓒ Ⓓ

Test 5

1. Ⓐ Ⓑ _____	21. Ⓐ Ⓑ _____
2. Ⓐ Ⓑ _____	22. Ⓐ Ⓑ _____
3. Ⓐ Ⓑ _____	23. Ⓐ Ⓑ _____
4. Ⓐ Ⓑ _____	24. Ⓐ Ⓑ _____
5. Ⓐ Ⓑ _____	25. Ⓐ Ⓑ _____
6. Ⓐ Ⓑ _____	26. Ⓐ Ⓑ _____
7. Ⓐ Ⓑ _____	27. Ⓐ Ⓑ _____
8. Ⓐ Ⓑ _____	28. Ⓐ Ⓑ _____
9. Ⓐ Ⓑ _____	29. Ⓐ Ⓑ _____
10. Ⓐ Ⓑ _____	30. Ⓐ Ⓑ _____
11. Ⓐ Ⓑ _____	31. Ⓐ Ⓑ _____
12. Ⓐ Ⓑ _____	32. Ⓐ Ⓑ _____
13. Ⓐ Ⓑ _____	33. Ⓐ Ⓑ _____
14. Ⓐ Ⓑ _____	34. Ⓐ Ⓑ _____
15. Ⓐ Ⓑ _____	35. Ⓐ Ⓑ _____
16. Ⓐ Ⓑ _____	36. Ⓐ Ⓑ _____
17. Ⓐ Ⓑ _____	37. Ⓐ Ⓑ _____
18. Ⓐ Ⓑ _____	38. Ⓐ Ⓑ _____
19. Ⓐ Ⓑ _____	39. Ⓐ Ⓑ _____
20. Ⓐ Ⓑ _____	40. Ⓐ Ⓑ _____

41. Ⓐ Ⓑ _____
42. Ⓐ Ⓑ _____
43. Ⓐ Ⓑ _____
44. Ⓐ Ⓑ _____
45. Ⓐ Ⓑ _____
46. Ⓐ Ⓑ _____
47. Ⓐ Ⓑ _____
48. Ⓐ Ⓑ _____
49. Ⓐ Ⓑ _____
50. Ⓐ Ⓑ _____
51. Ⓐ Ⓑ _____
52. Ⓐ Ⓑ _____
53. Ⓐ Ⓑ _____
54. Ⓐ Ⓑ _____
55. Ⓐ Ⓑ _____
56. Ⓐ Ⓑ _____
57. Ⓐ Ⓑ _____
58. Ⓐ Ⓑ _____
59. Ⓐ Ⓑ _____
60. Ⓐ Ⓑ _____
61. Ⓐ Ⓑ _____
62. Ⓐ Ⓑ _____
63. Ⓐ Ⓑ _____
64. Ⓐ Ⓑ _____
65. Ⓐ Ⓑ _____
66. Ⓐ Ⓑ _____
67. Ⓐ Ⓑ _____
68. Ⓐ Ⓑ _____
69. Ⓐ Ⓑ _____
70. Ⓐ Ⓑ _____

71. Ⓐ Ⓑ _____
72. Ⓐ Ⓑ _____
73. Ⓐ Ⓑ _____
74. Ⓐ Ⓑ _____
75. Ⓐ Ⓑ _____
76. Ⓐ Ⓑ _____
77. Ⓐ Ⓑ _____
78. Ⓐ Ⓑ _____
79. Ⓐ Ⓑ _____
80. Ⓐ Ⓑ _____
81. Ⓐ Ⓑ _____
82. Ⓐ Ⓑ _____
83. Ⓐ Ⓑ _____
84. Ⓐ Ⓑ _____
85. Ⓐ Ⓑ _____
86. Ⓐ Ⓑ _____
87. Ⓐ Ⓑ _____
88. Ⓐ Ⓑ _____
89. Ⓐ Ⓑ _____
90. Ⓐ Ⓑ _____
91. Ⓐ Ⓑ _____
92. Ⓐ Ⓑ _____
93. Ⓐ Ⓑ _____
94. Ⓐ Ⓑ _____
95. Ⓐ Ⓑ _____
96. Ⓐ Ⓑ _____
97. Ⓐ Ⓑ _____
98. Ⓐ Ⓑ _____
99. Ⓐ Ⓑ _____
100. Ⓐ Ⓑ _____

Test 1

Time: 60 minutes. 89 questions.

DIRECTIONS: This test gives four suggested spellings for each word listed. Choose the spelling you know to be correct and mark your answer accordingly.

1. (A) transeint   (B) transient   (C) transcient   (D) transent

2. (A) heratage   (B) heritage   (C) heiritage   (D) heretage

3. (A) exibition   (B) exhibition   (C) exabition   (D) exhebition

4. (A) intiative   (B) enitiative   (C) initative   (D) initiative

5. (A) similiar   (B) simmilar   (C) similar   (D) simuler

6. (A) sufficiantly   (B) sufisiently   (C) sufficiently   (D) suficeintly

7. (A) anticipate   (B) antisipate   (C) anticapate   (D) antisapate

8. (A) intelligence   (B) inteligence   (C) intellegence   (D) intelegence

9. (A) referance   (B) referrence   (C) referense   (D) reference

10. (A) conscious   (B) consious   (C) conscius   (D) consceous

11. (A) paralell   (B) parellel   (C) parellell   (D) parallel

12. (A) abundence   (B) abundance   (C) abundants   (D) abundents

13. (A) spesifically   (B) specificaly   (C) specifically   (D) specefically

14. (A) elemanate   (B) elimenate   (C) elliminate   (D) eliminate

15. (A) resonance   (B) resonnance   (C) resonence   (D) reasonance

16. (A) benaficial   (B) beneficial   (C) benefitial   (D) bennaficial

17. (A) retrievable   (B) retreivable   (C) retrievible   (D) retreavable

18. (A) collosal   (B) colossal   (C) colosal   (D) collossal

19. (A) inflameable   (B) inflamable   (C) enflamabel   (D) inflammable

20. (A) auxillary   (B) auxilliary   (C) auxilary   (D) auxiliary

21. (A) corregated   (B) corrigated   (C) corrugated   (D) coregated

22. (A) accumalation   (B) accumulation   (C) acumulation   (D) accumullation

23. (A) consumation   (B) consummation   (C) consumeation   (D) consomation

24. (A) retorical   (B) rhetorical   (C) rhetorrical   (D) retorrical

25. (A) inimitable   (B) iminitable   (C) innimitable   (D) inimitible

26. (A) proletarian   (B) prolletarian   (C) prolatarian   (D) proleterian

27. (A) appelate   (B) apellate   (C) appellate   (D) apelate

28. (A) esential   (B) essencial   (C) essential   (D) essantial

29. (A) assessment   (B) assesment   (C) asessment   (D) assesmant

30. (A) ordinence   (B) ordinnance   (C) ordinanse   (D) ordinance

31. (A) disapearance   (B) disappearance   (C) disappearense   (D) disappearence

32. (A) attendence   (B) attendanse   (C) attendance   (D) atendance

33. (A) acertain   (B) assertain   (C) ascertain   (D) asertain

34. (A) specimen   (B) speciman   (C) spesimen   (D) speceman

35. (A) relevant   (B) relevent   (C) rellevent   (D) relavant

36. (A) anesthetic   (B) aenesthetic   (C) anestitic   (D) annesthetic

37. (A) foriegn   (B) foreign   (C) forriegn   (D) forreign

38. (A) interuption   (B) interruption   (C) interrupsion   (D) interrupcion

39. (A) acquiesence   (B) acquiescence   (C) aquiescense   (D) acquiesance

40. (A) exceed   (B) exsede   (C) exseed   (D) excede

41. (A) maneuver   (B) manuver   (C) maneuvere   (D) manneuver

42. (A) correlation   (B) corrolation   (C) corellation   (D) corralation

43. (A) hinderence   (B) hindranse   (C) hindrance   (D) hindrence

44. (A) existence   (B) existance   (C) existense   (D) existince

45. (A) bankrupcy   (B) bankruptcy   (C) bankruptsy   (D) bankrupsy

46. (A) receipts   (B) receits   (C) reciepts   (D) recieps

47. (A) impromtu   (B) inpromtu   (C) impromptu   (D) impromptue

48. (A) pronounciation   (B) pronunciatun   (C) pronunciation   (D) pronounciatun

49. (A) entirly   (B) entirely   (C) entirley   (D) entireley

50. (A) complecation (B) complicasion (C) complication (D) complacation

51. (A) condem (B) condemn (C) condemm (D) condenm

52. (A) ocassion (B) occassion (C) ocasion (D) occasion

53. (A) contagious (B) contageous (C) contagous (D) contagiose

54. (A) perminent (B) permenant (C) permanent (D) permanant

55. (A) proceed (B) procede (C) prosede (D) proseed

56. (A) embarassment (B) embarrasment (C) embarasment (D) embarrassment

57. (A) cematery (B) cemetary (C) cemitery (D) cemetery

58. (A) believable (B) believeable (C) believeable (D) believible

59. (A) council (B) counsil (C) counsle (D) councel

60. (A) achievement (B) acheivment (C) achievment (D) acheivement

61. (A) Wendesday (B) Wensday (C) Wednesday (D) Wendnesday

62. (A) classify (B) classafy (C) classefy (D) classifey

63. (A) concensus (B) concencus (C) consencus (D) consensus

64. (A) suffiscent (B) sufficient (C) sufficiant (D) suffiscient

65. (A) responsable (B) responseable (C) responsibil (D) responsible

66. (A) remittence (B) remmittence (C) remmittance (D) remittance

67. (A) probible (B) probable (C) probbable (D) probabil

68. (A) weigt (B) wieght (C) weight (D) waight

69. (A) argument (B) argumint (C) argumant (D) arguement

70. (A) priceing (B) prising (C) priseing (D) pricing

71. (A) ballanced (B) balanced (C) balansed (D) balanct

72. (A) operateing (B) oparating (C) oparrating (D) operating

73. (A) privelege (B) privilege (C) privelige (D) privilige

74. (A) expenses (B) expences (C) expensses (D) expensces

75. (A) mispell (B) misspell (C) misspel (D) mispel

76. (A) occurrance (B) occurence (C) occurrence (D) ocurrence

77. (A) receit   (B) receipt   (C) reciept   (D) reciet

78. (A) conscience   (B) conscence   (C) consciense   (D) conscense

79. (A) deterent   (B) deterrant   (C) deterant   (D) deterrent

80. (A) responsable   (B) responsceable   (C) responsible   (D) responcible

81. (A) noticable   (B) noticible   (C) noticeable   (D) noticeble

82. (A) passable   (B) passible   (C) passeble   (D) passeable

83. (A) dissplaid   (B) displayed   (C) dissplayed   (D) displaid

84. (A) tryeing   (B) trieing   (C) trying   (D) triing

85. (A) imaterial   (B) immaterial   (C) imaterrial   (D) imatterial

86. (A) balancing   (B) balanceing   (C) balansing   (D) balanseing

87. (A) conceed   (B) consede   (C) concede   (D) conseed

88. (A) innumerible   (B) innumerable   (C) inumerable   (D) inumerible

89. (A) maintainance   (B) maintenance   (C) maintenence   (D) maintanance

Test 2

Time: 30 minutes. 35 questions.

DIRECTIONS: Each of the following four word groups contains one word that is spelled correctly. Choose the correctly spelled word.

1. (A) authority   (B) similiar   (C) refering   (D) preferebly

2. (A) suficient   (B) wheather   (C) actueally   (D) minimum

3. (A) volentary   (B) syllabus   (C) embodyeing   (D) pertanent

4. (A) simplified   (B) comunity   (C) emfasis   (D) advant

5. (A) approppriate   (B) expedient   (C) adopshun   (D) satisfactarily

6. (A) unconsiously   (B) pamflet   (C) asess   (D) adjacent

7. (A) mortgages   (B) infalible   (C) eradecated   (D) sourse

8. (A) predescessor   (B) obsolete   (C) unimpared   (D) sporadicaly

9. (A) impenitrable   (B) recognisable   (C) paresite   (D) vigilance

10. (A) emfatically   (B) manefold   (C) anxieties   (D) expence

11. (A) emfatically   (B) inculcate   (C) skilfel   (D) indigense

12. (A) indespensable   (B) encumbrance   (C) intolerible   (D) desication

13. (A) exibit   (B) critisism   (C) recieved   (D) conspicuous

14. (A) biennial   (B) monatary   (C) beninant   (D) complacensy

15. (A) propriaty   (B) legalety   (C) acquiesce   (D) conversent

16. (A) ajusted   (B) porportionate   (C) inaugurated   (D) dubeous

17. (A) responsability   (B) soceity   (C) individuel   (D) increments

18. (A) subordonate   (B) transaction   (C) buisness   (D) effitiency

19. (A) condemnation   (B) exsees   (C) ordinerily   (D) capasity

20. (A) discuscion   (B) statistics   (C) producktion   (D) disguissed

21. (A) constrictive   (B) proposel   (C) partisipated   (D) desision

22. (A) comtroller   (B) inadequasy   (C) resolusion   (D) promotion

23. (A) progresive   (B) reciepts   (C) dependent   (D) secsion

24. (A) seperate   (B) speciallized   (C) funshions   (D) publicity

25. (A) instrament   (B) vicinity   (C) offical   (D) journale

26. (A) unecessary   (B) responsebility   (C) suprintendent   (D) recommendation

27. (A) resonable   (B) curency   (C) occur   (D) critisise

28. (A) apetite   (B) preliminary   (C) concilatory   (D) cruseal

29. (A) afilliation   (B) amendement   (C) ansient   (D) patient

30. (A) recipeint   (B) pretious   (C) uncertainty   (D) marital

31. (A) illigetimate   (B) peciular   (C) addressee   (D) consintrated

32. (A) convalescent   (B) detramental   (C) elaberate   (D) accessable

33. (A) accomodate   (B) prejudise   (C) preveous   (D) exaggerate

34. (A) corroner   (B) inditment   (C) seized   (D) scissers

35. (A) araignment   (B) emolument   (C) faciletation   (D) ordanence

Test 3

Time: 30 minutes. 34 questions.

DIRECTIONS: In this test all words but one of each group are spelled correctly. Indicate the misspelled word in each group.

1. (A) extraordinary   (B) statesmen   (C) array   (D) financeer

2. (A) materialism   (B) indefatigible   (C) moribund   (D) rebellious

3. (A) queue   (B) equillibrium   (C) contemporary   (D) structure

4. (A) acquatic   (B) fascinated   (C) bogged   (D) accommodations

5. (A) embarrassment   (B) sosialization   (C) imposition   (D) incredulous

6. (A) politisians   (B) psychology   (C) susceptible   (D) antipathy

7. (A) convincing   (B) vicissetudes   (C) negligible   (D) foreign

8. (A) characters   (B) veracity   (C) testimony   (D) apolagetic

9. (A) shriek   (B) carelogue   (C) impeccable   (D) ruthless

10. (A) ocassions   (B) accomplishment   (C) assumed   (D) distinguished

11. (A) servicable   (B) preparation   (C) exceptional   (D) initiative

12. (A) primarely   (B) available   (C) paragraph   (D) routine

13. (A) ligament   (B) preseding   (C) mechanical   (D) anecdote

14. (A) judgment   (B) conclusion   (C) circumlocution   (D) breifly

15. (A) censor   (B) personel   (C) counterfeit   (D) advantageous

16. (A) liquified   (B) adage   (C) ancient   (D) imitation

17. (A) lapse   (B) questionnaire   (C) concieve   (D) staunch

18. (A) calendar   (B) typographical   (C) inexcusable   (D) sallient

19. (A) carreer   (B) eminently   (C) nevertheless   (D) fourth

20. (A) corperal   (B) sergeant   (C) lieutenant   (D) commandant

21. (A) partial   (B) business   (C) through   (D) comission

22. (A) accounts   (B) financial   (C) reciept   (D) answer

23. (A) except   (B) conection   (C) altogether   (D) credentials

24. (A) whose   (B) written   (C) strenth   (D) therefore

25. (A) catalogue   (B) familiar   (C) formerly   (D) secretery

26. (A) debtor   (B) shipment   (C) fileing   (D) correspond

27. (A) courtesy   (B) dictionery   (C) extremely   (D) exactly

28. (A) probaly   (B) directory   (C) acquired   (D) hurriedly

29. (A) hauled   (B) freight   (C) hankerchief   (D) millionaire

30. (A) goverment   (B) mileage   (C) scene   (D) ninety

31. (A) written   (B) permenent   (C) similar   (D) convenient

32. (A) cooperation   (B) duplicate   (C) negotiable   (D) Febuary

33. (A) experience   (B) interupt   (C) cylinder   (D) campaign

34. (A) cordialy   (B) completely   (C) sandwich   (D) respectfully

Test 5

Time: 60 minutes. 100 questions.

DIRECTIONS: In the following list, some words are spelled correctly, some misspelled. On your practice sheet, mark A for those words properly spelled; mark B and spell out the word correctly for those misspelled.

1. unparalleled
2. gastliness
3. mediocrity
4. exibition
5. posessing
6. lucritive
7. corresspondence
8. accellerated
9. labirynth
10. duplisity
11. repitious
12. jepardy
13. impartiallity
14. sobriquet
15. accesable
16. incredible
17. connoisseurs
18. fallibility
19. litagation
20. piquansy
21. fuedal
22. predetory
23. desparado
24. incongruity
25. delibarate
26. competetive
27. beleaguered
28. leiutenant
29. equinoxial
30. derogatory
31. denuncietory
32. panickey
33. calendar
34. belligerents

35. abolition
36. predjudice
37. propoganda
38. adolesents
39. irresistible
40. exortation
41. renascence
42. counsil
43. bullitin
44. aberation
45. integraty
46. cristallized
47. irrepairably
48. punctillious
49. catagory
50. parlament
51. medalion
52. bountious
53. aggrevate
54. midgit
55. wierd
56. elliminate
57. murmering
58. hystrionic
59. goverment
60. clamerous
61. garantee
62. presumptious
63. comemmerate
64. indispensible
65. bookeeping
66. disatisfied
67. tremendious
68. interseed

69. inaugerate
70. rehersel
71. nucleous
72. benefiting
73. wholy
74. discription
75. alright
76. representitive
77. mischievious
78. ingenuous
79. accidently
80. exilerate
81. pronounciation
82. fourty
83. mackeral
84. rescind
85. kleptomania
86. summerize
87. resillience
88. regretable
89. questionaire
90. privelege
91. judgment
92. plagiarism
93. vengence
94. subpoena
95. rythm
96. derth
97. impromtue
98. incumbant
99. forfiet
100. maintainance

Answer Key for Spelling Practice Tests

Test 1

1. B	13. C	24. B	35. A	46. A	57. D	68. C	79. D
2. B	14. D	25. A	36. A	47. C	58. A	69. A	80. C
3. B	15. A	26. A	37. B	48. C	59. A	70. D	81. C
4. D	16. B	27. C	38. B	49. B	60. A	71. B	82. A
5. C	17. A	28. C	39. B	50. C	61. C	72. D	83. B
6. C	18. B	29. A	40. A	51. B	62. A	73. B	84. C
7. A	19. D	30. D	41. A	52. D	63. D	74. A	85. B
8. A	20. D	31. B	42. A	53. A	64. B	75. B	86. A
9. D	21. C	32. C	43. C	54. C	65. D	76. C	87. C
10. A	22. B	33. C	44. A	55. A	66. D	77. B	88. B
11. D	23. B	34. A	45. B	56. D	67. B	78. A	89. B
12. B							

Test 2

1. A	8. B	15. C	22. D	29. D
2. D	9. D	16. C	23. C	30. C
3. B	10. C	17. D	24. D	31. C
4. A	11. B	18. B	25. B	32. A
5. B	12. B	19. A	26. D	33. D
6. D	13. D	20. B	27. C	34. C
7. A	14. A	21. A	28. B	35. B

Test 3

1. D	10. A	18. D	26. C
2. B	11. A	19. A	27. B
3. B	12. A	20. A	28. A
4. A	13. B	21. D	29. C
5. B	14. D	22. C	30. A
6. A	15. B	23. B	31. B
7. B	16. A	24. C	32. D
8. D	17. C	25. D	33. B
9. B			34. A

Test 4

1. A	7. A	13. B
2. B	8. B	14. A
3. A	9. C	15. A
4. A	10. C	16. B
5. A	11. B	17. C
6. A	12. B	18. A

Test 5

1. A
2. B ghastliness
3. A
4. B exhibition
5. B possessing
6. B lucrative
7. B correspondence
8. B accelerated
9. B labyrinth
10. B duplicity
11. B repetitious
12. B jeopardy
13. B impartiality
14. A
15. B accessible
16. A
17. A
18. A
19. B litigation
20. B piquancy
21. B feudal
22. B predatory
23. B desperado
24. A
25. B deliberate
26. B competitive
27. A
28. B lieutenant
29. B equinoctial
30. A
31. B denunciatory
32. B panicky
33. A
34. A
35. A
36. B prejudice
37. B propaganda
38. B adolescents
39. A
40. B exhortation
41. A
42. B counsel
43. B bulletin
44. B aberration
45. B integrity
46. B crystallized
47. B irreparably
48. B punctilious
49. B category
50. B parliament

51. B medallion
52. B bounteous
53. B aggravate
54. B midget
55. B weird
56. B eliminate
57. B murmuring
58. B histrionic
59. B government
60. B clamorous
61. B guarantee
62. B presumptuous
63. B commemorate
64. B indispensable
65. B bookkeeping
66. B dissatisfied
67. B tremendous
68. B intercede
69. B inaugurate
70. B rehearsal
71. B nucleus
72. A
73. B wholly
74. B description
75. A
76. B representative
77. B mischievous
78. A
79. B accidentally
80. B exhilarate
81. B pronunciation
82. B forty
83. B mackerel
84. A
85. A
86. B summarize
87. B resilience
88. B regrettable
89. B questionnaire
90. B privilege
91. A
92. A
93. B vengeance
94. A
95. B rhythm
96. B dearth
97. B impromptu
98. B incumbent
99. B forfeit
100. B maintenance

READING COMPREHENSION

The key to success with reading questions is not speed but comprehension. Civil Service exams are not, as a rule, heavily speeded. There is ample time in which to complete the exam, provided that you do not spend excessive time struggling with one or two "impossible" questions. If you are reading with comprehension, your mind will not wander, and your speed will be adequate.

Between now and the test day, you must work to improve your reading concentration and comprehension. Your daily newspaper provides excellent material to improve your reading. Make a point of reading all the way through any article that you begin. Do not be satisfied with the first paragraph or two. Read with a pencil in hand. Underscore details and ideas that seem to be crucial to the meaning of the article. Notice points of view, arguments, and supporting information. When you have finished the article, summarize it for yourself. Do you know the purpose of the article? The main idea presented? The attitude of the writer? The points over which there is controversy? Did you find certain information lacking? As you answer these questions, skim back over your underlinings. Did you focus on important words and ideas? Did you read with comprehension?

As you repeat this process day after day, you will find that your reading will become more efficient. You will read with greater understanding and will "get more" from your newspaper.

One aspect of your daily reading that deserves special attention is vocabulary building. The most effective reader has a rich, extensive vocabulary. As you read, make a list of unfamiliar words. Include in your list words that you understand within the context of the article but that you cannot really define. In addition, mark words that you do not understand at all. When you put aside your newspaper, go to the dictionary and look up *every* new and unfamiliar word. Write the word and its definition in a special notebook. Writing the words and their definitions helps seal them in your memory far better than just reading them, and the notebook serves as a handy reference for your own use. A sensitivity to the meanings of words and an understanding of more words will make reading easier and more enjoyable even if none of the words you learn in this way crops up on your exam. In fact, the habit of vocabulary building is a good lifetime habit to develop.

Success with reading questions depends on more than reading comprehension. You must also know how to draw the answers from the reading selection and be able to distinguish the *best* answer from a number of answers that all seem to be good ones, or from a number of answers that all seem to be wrong.

Strange as it may seem, it's a good idea to approach reading comprehension questions by reading the questions—not the answer choices, just the questions themselves—before you read the selection. The questions will alert you to look for certain details, ideas, and points of view. Use your pencil. Underscore key words in the questions. These will help you direct your attention as you read.

Next skim the selection very rapidly to get an idea of its subject matter and its organization. If key words or ideas pop out at you, underline them, but do not consciously search out details in the preliminary skimming.

Now read the selection carefully with comprehension as your main goal. Underscore the important words as you have been doing in your newspaper reading.

Finally, return to the questions. Read each question carefully. Be sure you know what it asks. Misreading of questions is a major cause of error on reading comprehension tests. Read *all* of the answer choices. Eliminate the obviously incorrect answers. You may be left with only one possible answer. If you find yourself with more than one possible answer, reread the question. Then skim the passage once more, focusing on the underlined segments. By now you should be able to conclude which answer is *best*.

Reading comprehension questions may take a number of different forms. In general, some of the most common forms are as follows:

1. **Question of fact or detail.** You may have to mentally rephrase or rearrange, but you should find the answer stated in the body of the selection.
2. **Best title or main idea.** The answer may be obvious, but the incorrect choices to the "main idea" question are often half-truths that are easily confused with the main idea. They may misstate the idea, omit part of the idea or even offer a supporting idea quoted directly from the text. The correct answer is the one that covers the largest part of the selection.
3. **Interpretation.** This type of question asks you what the question *means,* not just what it says.
4. **Inference.** This is the most difficult type of reading comprehension question. It asks you to go beyond what the selection says and to predict what might happen next. Your answer must be based on the information in the selection and your own common sense but not on any other information you may have about the subject. A variation of the inference question might be stated as "The author would expect that. . . ." To answer this question, you must understand the author's point of view and then make an inference from that viewpoint based on the information in the selection.
5. **Vocabulary.** Some Civil Service reading sections, directly or indirectly, ask the meanings of certain words as used in the selection.

Let's now work together on some typical reading comprehension selections and questions.

Selection for Practice Questions 1 to 4

The recipient gains an impression of a typewritten letter before beginning to read the message. Factors that give a good first impression include margins and spacing that are visually pleasing, formal parts of the letter that are correctly placed according to the style of the letter, copy that is free of obvious erasures and overstrikes, and transcript that is even and clear. The problem for the typist is how to produce that first, positive impression of his/her work.

There are several general rules that a typist can follow when he/she wishes to prepare a properly spaced letter on a sheet of letterhead. The width of a letter should ordinarily not be less than four inches, nor more than six inches. The side margins should also have a desirable relation to the bottom margin, as well as the space between the letterhead and the body of the letter. Usually the most appealing arrangement is when the side margins are even and the bottom margin is slightly wider than the side margins. In some offices, however, a standard line length is used for all business letters, and the secretary then varies the spacing between the date line and the inside address according to the length of the letter.

1. The best title for the preceding paragraphs is   1. Ⓐ Ⓑ Ⓒ Ⓓ
   (A) "Writing Office Letters"
   (B) "Making Good First Impressions"
   (C) "Judging Well-Typed Letters"
   (D) "Good Placing and Spacing for Office Letters"

2. According to the preceding paragraphs, which of the following might be considered the way that people quickly judge the quality of work that has been typed?
   2. Ⓐ Ⓑ Ⓒ Ⓓ
   (A) Measuring the margins to see if they are correct
   (B) Looking at the spacing and cleanliness of the typescript
   (C) Scanning the body of the letter for meaning
   (D) Reading the date line and address for errors

3. According to the preceding paragraphs, what would be definitely undesirable as the average line length of a typed letter?
   3. Ⓐ Ⓑ Ⓒ Ⓓ
   (A) 4″
   (B) 5″
   (C) 6″
   (D) 7″

4. According to the preceding paragraphs, when the line length is kept standard, the secretary
   4. Ⓐ Ⓑ Ⓒ Ⓓ
   (A) does not have to vary the spacing at all because this also is standard
   (B) adjusts the spacing between the date line and inside address for different lengths of letters
   (C) uses the longest line as a guideline for spacing between the date line and inside address
   (D) varies the number of spaces between the lines

Begin by skimming the questions and underscoring key words. Your underscored questions should look more or less like this:

1. What is the best title for the preceding paragraphs?
2. According to the preceding paragraphs, which of the following might be considered the way that people quickly judge the quality of work that has been typed?
3. According to the preceding paragraphs, what would be definitely undesirable as the average line length of a typed letter?
4. According to the preceding paragraphs, when the line length is kept standard, the secretary

Now skim the selection. This quick reading should give you an idea of the structure of the selection and of its overall meaning.

Next read the selection carefully and underscore words that seem important or that you think hold keys to the question answers. Your underscored selection should look something like this:

The recipient gains an impression of a typewritten letter before beginning to read the message. Factors that give a good first impression include margins and spacing that are visually pleasing, formal parts of the letter that are correctly placed according to the style of the letter, copy that is free of obvious erasures and overstrikes, and transcript that is even and clear. The problem for the typist is how to produce that first, positive impression of his/her work.

There are several general rules that a typist can follow when he/she wishes to prepare a properly spaced letter on a sheet of letterhead. The width of a letter should ordinarily not be less than four inches, nor more than six inches. The side margins should also have a desirable relation to the bottom margin as well as the space between the letterhead and the body of the letter. Usually the most appealing arrangement is when the side margins are even and the bottom margin is slightly wider than the side margins. In some offices, however, a standard line length is used for all business letters, and the secretary then varies the spacing between the date line and the inside address according to the length of the letter.

Finally, read the questions and answer choices, and try to choose the correct answer for each question.

The correct answers are: 1. **(D)**, 2. **(B)**, 3. **(D)**, 4. **(B)**. Did you get them all right? Whether you made any errors or not, read these explanations.

1. **(D)** The best title for any selection is the one that takes in all of the ideas presented without being too broad or too narrow. Choice (D) provides the most inclusive title for this passage. A look at the other choices shows you why. Choice (A) can be eliminated because the passage discusses typing a letter, not writing one. Although the first paragraph states that a letter should make a good first impression, the passage is clearly devoted to the letter, not the first impression, so choice (B) can be eliminated. Choice (C) puts the emphasis on the wrong aspect of the typewritten letter. The passage concerns how to type a properly spaced letter, not how to judge one.

2. **(B)** Both spacing and cleanliness are mentioned in paragraph 1 as ways to judge the quality of a typed letter. The first paragraph states that the margins should be "visually pleasing" in relation to the body of the letter, but that does not imply margins of a particular measure, so choice (A) is incorrect. Meaning is not discussed in the passage, only the look of the finished letter, so choice (C) is incorrect. The passage makes no mention of errors, only the avoidance of erasures and overstrikes, so choice (D) is incorrect.

3. **(D)** This answer comes from the information provided in paragraph 2, that the width of a letter "should not be less than four inches nor more than six inches." According to this rule, seven inches is an undesirable line length.

4. **(B)** The answer to this question is stated in the last sentence of the reading passage. When a standard line length is used, the secretary "varies the spacing between the date line and the inside address according to the length of the letter." The passage offers no support for any other choice.

Answer Sheet for Reading Comprehension Tests

Test 1

1 Ⓐ Ⓑ Ⓒ Ⓓ Ⓔ
2 Ⓐ Ⓑ Ⓒ Ⓓ
3 Ⓐ Ⓑ Ⓒ Ⓓ Ⓔ
4 Ⓐ Ⓑ Ⓒ Ⓓ Ⓔ
5 Ⓐ Ⓑ Ⓒ Ⓓ Ⓔ

6 Ⓐ Ⓑ Ⓒ Ⓓ Ⓔ
7 Ⓐ Ⓑ Ⓒ Ⓓ Ⓔ
8 Ⓐ Ⓑ Ⓒ Ⓓ
9 Ⓐ Ⓑ Ⓒ Ⓓ
10 Ⓐ Ⓑ Ⓒ Ⓓ

11 Ⓐ Ⓑ Ⓒ Ⓓ
12 Ⓐ Ⓑ Ⓒ Ⓓ Ⓔ
13 Ⓐ Ⓑ Ⓒ Ⓓ
14 Ⓐ Ⓑ Ⓒ Ⓓ Ⓔ
15 Ⓐ Ⓑ Ⓒ Ⓓ

Test 2

1 Ⓐ Ⓑ Ⓒ Ⓓ
2 Ⓐ Ⓑ Ⓒ Ⓓ
3 Ⓐ Ⓑ Ⓒ Ⓓ
4 Ⓐ Ⓑ Ⓒ Ⓓ

5 Ⓐ Ⓑ Ⓒ Ⓓ
6 Ⓐ Ⓑ Ⓒ Ⓓ
7 Ⓐ Ⓑ Ⓒ Ⓓ

8 Ⓐ Ⓑ Ⓒ Ⓓ
9 Ⓐ Ⓑ Ⓒ Ⓓ
10 Ⓐ Ⓑ Ⓒ Ⓓ

Test 3

1 Ⓐ Ⓑ Ⓒ Ⓓ
2 Ⓐ Ⓑ Ⓒ Ⓓ
3 Ⓐ Ⓑ Ⓒ Ⓓ
4 Ⓐ Ⓑ Ⓒ Ⓓ
5 Ⓐ Ⓑ Ⓒ Ⓓ

6 Ⓐ Ⓑ Ⓒ Ⓓ
7 Ⓐ Ⓑ Ⓒ Ⓓ
8 Ⓐ Ⓑ Ⓒ Ⓓ
9 Ⓐ Ⓑ Ⓒ Ⓓ
10 Ⓐ Ⓑ Ⓒ Ⓓ

11 Ⓐ Ⓑ Ⓒ Ⓓ
12 Ⓐ Ⓑ Ⓒ Ⓓ
13 Ⓐ Ⓑ Ⓒ Ⓓ
14 Ⓐ Ⓑ Ⓒ Ⓓ
15 Ⓐ Ⓑ Ⓒ Ⓓ

Test 1

Time: 20 minutes. 15 questions.

DIRECTIONS: *Carefully read each selection and the question that follows it. Then answer the question on the basis of the information given in the selection.*

Selection for Question 1

"Alertness and attentiveness are qualities essential for success as a telephone operator. The work the operator performs often takes careful attention under conditions of stress."

1. The selection best supports the statement that a telephone operator

(A) always works under great strain
(B) cannot be successful unless he/she memorizes many telephone numbers
(C) must be trained before he/she can render good service
(D) must be able to work under difficulties
(E) performs more difficult work than do office machine operators

Selection for Question 2

Rule: In foggy weather or at any time when motormen's vision is obstructed by snow, rain, sleet, smoke, etc., they must run trains so that they can stop within range of vision in order to ensure the safety of the train and passengers.

2. This rule means most nearly that

(A) the braking distance required in snow or sleet storms is about equal to the motorman's range of vision
(B) a motorman's vision is obstructed by fog about as much as it is by smoke
(C) when a motorman's range of vision is reduced, it is generally restricted by fog, snow, rain, sleet, or smoke
(D) if a motorman's view ahead is obstructed he should operate his train slowly

Selection for Question 3

"The prevention of accidents makes it necessary not only that safety devices be used to guard exposed machinery, but also that mechanics be instructed in safety rules that they must follow for their own protection and that the light in the plant be adequate."

3. The paragraph best supports the statement that industrial accidents

(A) are always avoidable
(B) may be due to ignorance

(C) usually result from inadequate machinery
(D) cannot be entirely overcome
(E) result in damage to machinery

Selection for Question 4

"Probably few people realize, as they drive on a concrete road, that steel is used to keep the surface flat in spite of the weight of buses and trucks. Steel bars, deeply embedded in the concrete, are sinews to take the stresses so that the stresses cannot crack the slab or make it wavy."

4. The paragraph best supports the statement that a concrete road

(A) is expensive to build
(B) usually cracks under heavy weights
(C) looks like any other road
(D) is used only for heavy traffic
(E) is reinforced with other material

Selection for Question 5

"Post office clerks assigned to stamp windows are directly responsible financially in the selling of postage. In addition, they are expected to have a thorough knowledge as to the acceptability of matter offered for mailing. Any information they give out to the public must be accurate."

5. The paragraph best supports the statement that clerks assigned to stamp-window duty

(A) must account for stamps issued to them for sale
(B) have had long training in other post office work
(C) advise the public only on matters of official business
(D) must refer continuously to the sources of postal regulations
(E) inspect the contents of every package offered for mailing

Selection for Question 6

"The leader of an industrial enterprise has two principal functions. He/she must manufacture and distribute a product at a profit, and he/she must keep individuals and groups of individuals working effectively together."

6. The paragraph best supports the statement that an industrial leader should be able to

(A) increase the distribution of his/her plant's products
(B) introduce large-scale production methods
(C) coordinate the activities of employees
(D) profit by the experience of other leaders
(E) expand the business rapidly

Selection for Question 7

"Numerous benefits to the employer as well as to the worker have resulted from physical examinations of employees. Such examinations are intended primarily as a means of increasing efficiency and production, and they have been found to accomplish these ends."

7. The paragraph best supports the statement that physical examinations

(A) may serve to increase output
(B) are a source of greater gain to employers than to employees
(C) are required in some plants
(D) often reveal serious defects previously unknown
(E) always are worth more than they cost

Selection for Question 8

"The forms and methods of discipline used in public agencies are as varied as the offenses that prompt disciplinary action, and range in severity from a frown of disapproval to dismissal from the service and even to prosecution in the courts."

8. On the basis of this quotation, the most accurate of the following statements is that

(A) the severity of disciplinary measures varies directly with the seriousness of the offenses
(B) dismissal from the service is the severest action that can be taken by a public agency
(C) public agencies use a variety of disciplinary measures to cope with offenses
(D) public agencies sometimes administer excessive punishments

Selection for Question 9

"A supervisor of a unit who is not specific when making assignments creates a dangerous source of friction, misunderstanding, and inefficiency."

9. The most valid implication of this statement is that

(A) supervisors are usually unaware that they are creating sources of friction
(B) it is often difficult to remove sources of friction and misunderstanding
(C) a competent supervisor attempts to find a solution to each problem facing him/her
(D) employees will perform more efficiently if their duties are defined clearly

Selection for Question 10

"Trained employees work most efficiently and with a minimum expenditure of time and energy. Suitable equipment and definite, well-developed procedures are effective only when employees know how to use the equipment and procedures."

10. This quotation means most nearly that

(A) employees can be trained most efficiently when suitable equipment and definite procedures are used
(B) training of employees is a costly but worthwhile investment

(C) suitable equipment and definite procedures are of greatest value when employees have been properly trained to use them

(D) the cost of suitable equipment and definite procedures is negligible when the saving in time and energy that they bring is considered

Selection for Question 11

"The nature of the experience and education that are made a prerequisite to employment determines in large degree the training job to be done after employment begins."

11. On the basis of this quotation, it is more accurate to state that

(A) the more comprehensive the experience and education require for employment, the more extensive the training that is usually given after appointment

(B) the training that is given to employees depends on the experience and education required of them before appointment

(C) employees who possess the experience and education required for employment should need little additional training after appointment

(D) the nature of the work that employees are expected to perform determines the training that they will need

Selection for Question 12

"There exists a false but popular idea that a clue is some mysterious fact that most people overlook but that some very keen investigator easily discovers and recognizes as having, in itself, a remarkable meaning. The clue is most often an ordinary fact that an observant person picks up—something that gains its significance when, after a long series of careful investigations, it is connected with a network of other clues."

12. According to the selection, to be of value, clues must be

(A) discovered by skilled investigators

(B) found under mysterious circumstances

(C) discovered soon after the crime

(D) observed many times

(E) connected with other facts

Selection for Question 13

"A member of the department shall not indulge in intoxicating liquor while in uniform. A member of the department not required to wear a uniform and a uniformed member while out of uniform shall not indulge in intoxicants to an extent unfitting him/her for duty."

13. Of the following, the most correct interpretation of this rule is that a (an)

(A) off-duty member, not in uniform, may drink intoxicating liquor

(B) member not on duty, but in uniform, may drink intoxicating liquor

(C) on-duty member, in uniform, may drink intoxicants

(D) uniformed member in civilian clothes may not drink intoxicants

Selection for Question 14

"Postmasters may authorize their assistants to sign their names to such reports, letters, and papers that are not specially required to be signed by the postmaster himself/herself. The signature should be: 'John Doe, post-master, by Richard Roe, assistant postmaster.' The name of the postmaster may be written or stamped, but the signature of the assistant shall be in ink."

14. According to the selection

    (A) an assistant postmaster who signs for the postmaster should include his/her own title in the signature
    (B) any postmaster's assistant has authority to sign official papers for him/her
    (C) no authority delegated to the assistant postmaster can be redelegated by him/her
    (D) requisitions must bear the personal signature of the postmaster
    (E) the assistant postmaster must write the postmaster's signature with pen and ink when he/she signs for the postmaster.

Selection for Question 15

    Rule: Accident reports, facts and conditions connected with accidents, and names of witnesses are confidential information. Employees must not communicate either orally or in writing to any person with reference to accidents except to proper officials of the System or except, with knowledge of the Authority, to the proper authorities entitled to such information.

15. The most nearly correct statement based on this rule is that

    (A) an employee witnessing an accident may give information to System officials only
    (B) an employee witnessing an accident should not make any written notes on the accident
    (C) the names of witnesses of accidents are confidential information
    (D) all accident reports must be given either orally or in writing

Test 2

Time: 15 minutes. 10 questions.

DIRECTIONS: Each selection is followed by a number of questions based on the information given in the selection. Read the selection carefully; then read each question carefully before marking your answer.

Selection for Questions 1 to 6

Basic to every office is the need for proper lighting. Inadequate lighting is a familiar cause of fatigue and serves to create a somewhat dismal atmosphere in the office. One requirement of proper lighting is that it be of an appropriate intensity. Intensity is measured in foot-candles. According to the Illuminating Engineering Society of New York, for casual seeing tasks such as in reception room, inactive file rooms, and other service areas, it is recommended that the amount of light be 30 foot-candles. For ordinary seeing tasks such as reading and work in active file rooms and in mail rooms, the recommended lighting is 100 foot-candles. For very difficult seeing tasks such as accounting, transcribing, and business machine use, the recommended lighting is 150 foot-candles.

Lighting intensity is only one requirement. Shadows and glare are to be avoided. For example, the larger the proportion of a ceiling filled with lighting units, the more glare-free and comfortable the lighting will be. Natural lighting from windows is not too dependable because on dark wintry days windows yield little usable light, and on sunny summer afternoons the glare from windows may be very distracting. Desks should not face the windows. Finally, the main lighting source ought to be overhead and to the left of the user.

1. According to the preceding passage, insufficient light in the office may cause

   (A) glare   (B) shadows   (C) tiredness   (D) distraction

2. Based on the preceding passage, which of the following must be considered when planning lighting arrangements?

   (A) The amount of natural light present
   (B) The amount of work to be done
   (C) The level of difficulty of work to be done
   (D) The type of activity to be carried out

3. It can be inferred from the preceding passage that a well-coordinated lighting scheme is likely to result in

   (A) greater employee productivity
   (B) elimination of light reflection
   (C) lower lighting cost
   (D) more use of natural light

4. Of the following, the best title for the preceding passage is

   (A) "Characteristics of Light"
   (B) "Light Measurement Devices"
   (C) "Factors to Consider When Planning Lighting Systems"
   (D) "Comfort vs. Cost When Devising Lighting Arrangements"

5. According to the preceding passage, a foot-candle is a measurement of the

   (A) number of bulbs used
   (B) strength of the light
   (C) contrast between glare and shadow
   (D) proportion of the ceiling filled with lighting units.

6. According to the prededing passage, the number of foot-candles of light that would be needed to copy figures onto a payroll is

   (A) less than 30 foot-candles
   (B) 30 foot-candles
   (C) 100 foot-candles
   (D) 150 foot-candles

Selection for Questions 7 to 10

The speed at which an elevator should run depends on several considerations: the height of the building, the size of the building, the purpose for which the elevator will be used, and how the elevator will be used. Elevators with extremely high speeds are of little advantage unless an express run can be established to make use of the speed. On local runs, by the time an elevator accelerates and then decelerates for landing, there is little time to take advantage of speed. It should also be noted that the higher the elevator speed, the larger the machine, and hence the greater the cost. Therefore, the situation must be studied before each installation and the proper speed selected to avoid the purchase of unnecessary equipment.

7. According to the preceding paragraph, extremely high-speed elevators are of little advantage unless

   (A) the building is small
   (B) there are only two elevators in a large building
   (C) they are used on express runs
   (D) they accelerate and decelerate slowly on local runs

8. Which one of the following is *not* mentioned in the preceding paragraph as a consideration in selecting the speed at which an elevator should run?

   (A) height of the building
   (B) age of the building
   (C) size of the building
   (D) purpose of the elevator

9. Based on the paragraph, it would be most correct to say that a high-speed elevator

   (A) accelerates more slowly than a low-speed elevator
   (B) uses less equipment than a low-speed elevator

(C) breaks down more often than a low-speed elevator

(D) costs more than a low-speed elevator

10. According to the preceding paragraph, one of the ways to avoid the purchase of unnecessary elevator equipment is to

(A) study the situation before each installation

(B) buy only low-speed elevators

(C) use smaller machines for high-speed elevators

(D) select low-speed elevators for express runs

Test 3

Time: 20 minutes. 15 questions.

DIRECTIONS: Each selection is followed by a number of questions based on the information given in the selection. Read the selection carefully; then read each question carefully before marking your answer.

Selection for Questions 1 to 3

Telephone service in a government agency should be adequate and complete with respect to information given or action taken. It must be remembered that telephone contacts should receive special consideration since the caller cannot see the operator. People like to feel that they are receiving personal attention and that their requests or criticisms are receiving individual rather than routine consideration. All of this contributes to what has come to be known as Tone of Service. The aim is to use standards that are very good or superior. The factors to be considered in determining what makes good Tone of Service are speech, courtesy, understanding, and explanations. A caller's impression of Tone of Service will affect the general public attitude toward the agency and city services in general.

1. The preceding passage states that people who telephone a government agency like to feel that they are

   (A) creating a positive image of themselves
   (B) being given routine consideration
   (C) receiving individual attention
   (D) setting standards for telephone service

2. Which of the following is *not* mentioned in the preceding passage as a factor in determining good Tone of Service?

   (A) courtesy   (B) education   (C) speech   (D) understanding

3. The preceding passage implies that failure to handle telephone calls properly is most likely to result in

   (A) a poor impression of city agencies by the public
   (B) a deterioration of courtesy toward operators
   (C) an effort by operators to improve the Tone of Service
   (D) special consideration by the public of operator difficulties

Selection for Questions 4 to 13

Employees required to work on or adjacent to tracks must not begin work without first displaying the proper temporary signals.

The signals to be used are as follows:

Stop Signal: A red light or a red flag swung to and from across the track

Caution Signal: A yellow light or a yellow flag fixed at the side of the track on motorman's right, preferably at a height of three to six feet above the rail

Proceed Signal: A green light or a green flag fixed at the side of the track on motorman's right, preferably at a height of three to six feet above the rail; or a white light or flag moved up and down at least two feet vertically.

The signals are to be displayed as follows:

Two yellow lights or flags, approximately 500 feet in advance of the point of work
A red light or flag not less than 50 feet in advance of the work
A green light or flag at a safe distance beyond the work.

Flags must be used for signaling during the daytime on elevated and surface lines. Lights must be used at night on elevated and surface lines and at all times in subways.

A motorman passing a point where yellow lights or flags are displayed must proceed with train under control, prepared to stop before reaching the red light or flag, and will sound four short blasts of the whistle when passing the yellow lights or flags so as to warn men at the point of work.

Workmen must immediately, upon hearing the four short blasts of the whistle, if track is clear and passable, remove the red light or flag and give motorman a proceed hand signal.

4. The proper number of signal lights to be displayed when a track gang is at work in the subway is

(A) one light   (B) two lights   (C) three lights   (D) four lights

5. Before beginning work on the tracks, it is necessary to display the proper signals

(A) only at the point of work
(B) at the point of work and in advance of it
(C) only in advance of the point of work
(D) in advance of the point of work and beyond it

6. The proper caution signals to be used on elevated lines during the daytime are

(A) white flags   (B) yellow lights   (C) red lights   (D) yellow flags

7. The distance between the caution signals and the point of work of a track gang should be about

(A) 50 feet   (B) 250 feet   (C) 500 feet   (D) 750 feet

8. The proper position for a yellow caution signal is at the side of the track on motorman's

(A) right and five feet above the track
(B) left and level with the track

(C) right and level with the track
(D) left and five feet above the track

9. A motorman should warn a track gang of the approach of his train by

(A) turning on a yellow light
(B) turning on a red light
(C) sounding the train whistle
(D) applying the brakes

10. The proper stop signal to be used in subways during the daytime is
(A) a red light
(B) two yellow lights
(C) a white flag moved up and down
(D) a yellow light

11. When signaled by the motorman of an approaching train, trackmen must first

(A) leave the track
(B) make the track clear and passable
(C) remove all caution signals
(D) remove the proceed signals

12. A hand signal is

(A) never to be used
(B) used to caution the motorman
(C) always the best type of signal to use
(D) sometimes used as a proceed signal

13. The proper signal to inform the motorman to proceed is a

(A) white light moved up and down
(B) white light swung to and fro across the track
(C) green light placed between the rails of the track
(D) yellow light swung to and fro across the track

Selection for Questions 14 and 15

"Proper firearms training is one phase of law enforcement that cannot be ignored. No part of the training of a police officer is more important or more valuable. The officer's life and often the lives of fellow officers depend directly on his/her skill with the weapon he/she is carrying. Proficiency with the revolver is not attained exclusively by the volume of ammunition used and the number of hours spent on the firing line. Supervised practice and the use of training aids and techniques help make the shooter. It is essential to have a good firing range where new officers are trained and older personnel practice in scheduled firearms sessions. The fundamental points to be stressed are grip, stance, breathing, sight alignment, and trigger squeeze. Coordination of thought, vision, and motion must be achieved before the officer gains confidence in his/her shooting ability. Attaining this ability will make the student a better officer and enhance his/her value to the force."

14. A police officer will gain confidence in his/her shooting ability only after he/she has

  (A) spent the required number of hours on the firing line
  (B) been given sufficient supervised practice
  (C) learned the five fundamental points
  (D) learned to coordinate revolver movement with sight and thought

15. Proper training in the use of firearms is one aspect of law enforcement that must be given serious consideration chiefly because it is the

  (A) most useful and essential single factor in the training of a police officer
  (B) one phase of police officer training that stresses mental and physical coordination
  (C) costliest aspect of police officer training, involving considerable expense for the ammunition used in target practice
  (D) most difficult part of police officer training, involving the expenditure of many hours on the firing line

Answer Key for Reading Comprehension Tests

Test 1

1. D	4. E	7. A	10. C	13. A
2. D	5. A	8. C	11. B	14. A
3. B	6. C	9. D	12. E	15. C

Test 2

1. C	3. A	5. B	7. D	9. D
2. D	4. C	6. D	8. B	10. B

Test 3

1. C	4. D	7. C	10. A	13. A
2. B	5. D	8. A	11. B	14. D
3. A	6. D	9. C	12. D	15. A

Part Three

PRACTICE TESTS FOR CLERICAL ABILITY

APTITUDE TESTS FOR CLERICAL OFFICE WORK

Aptitude tests do not test you for what you know in a subject area but for certain aptitudes required in an occupation. Questions measuring aptitudes required for clerical office work are usually part of the exams given for office worker positions. Scores on aptitude tests indicate how well and how fast you can perform tasks regardless of what you learned in the past. In other words, these tests are designed to test your abilities useful in clerical work, such as powers of observation, attention to detail, speed, and ability to understand what a task is about.

Aptitude tests are based on the application of certain abilities to a task. How well you can apply your abilities can be improved significantly by practice. The practice tests provided will confront you with various tasks requiring the application of abilities useful in clerical work. The practice tests will familiarize you with various tasks found in questions on actual exams. By practicing on these tests you will increase your self-confidence; you will be able to recognize quickly what is required by the tasks and do them with increasing speed and accuracy.

Your score on aptitude tests will depend on the number of questions you can complete within the time limit set. Although you will be penalized for errors, it is important to concentrate on speed. By proceeding very carefully you can reduce your errors. However, if you complete only a small number of questions, your score will be low even if you have avoided all errors. Therefore, it is suggested that you should concentrate on completing as many questions as possible but should not neglect accuracy entirely.

The practice tests which follow consist of various types of test questions for clerical aptitude. Since it is unlikely that you can recall the correct answers to aptitude test questions, you can do these tests several times over again for practice.

Answer Sheet for Name and Number Comparison Practice Tests

Test 1

1 Ⓐ Ⓑ Ⓒ Ⓓ Ⓔ   6 Ⓐ Ⓑ Ⓒ Ⓓ Ⓔ   11 Ⓐ Ⓑ Ⓒ Ⓓ Ⓔ   16 Ⓐ Ⓑ Ⓒ Ⓓ Ⓔ
2 Ⓐ Ⓑ Ⓒ Ⓓ Ⓔ   7 Ⓐ Ⓑ Ⓒ Ⓓ Ⓔ   12 Ⓐ Ⓑ Ⓒ Ⓓ Ⓔ   17 Ⓐ Ⓑ Ⓒ Ⓓ Ⓔ
3 Ⓐ Ⓑ Ⓒ Ⓓ Ⓔ   8 Ⓐ Ⓑ Ⓒ Ⓓ Ⓔ   13 Ⓐ Ⓑ Ⓒ Ⓓ Ⓔ   18 Ⓐ Ⓑ Ⓒ Ⓓ Ⓔ
4 Ⓐ Ⓑ Ⓒ Ⓓ Ⓔ   9 Ⓐ Ⓑ Ⓒ Ⓓ Ⓔ   14 Ⓐ Ⓑ Ⓒ Ⓓ Ⓔ   19 Ⓐ Ⓑ Ⓒ Ⓓ Ⓔ
5 Ⓐ Ⓑ Ⓒ Ⓓ Ⓔ   10 Ⓐ Ⓑ Ⓒ Ⓓ Ⓔ   15 Ⓐ Ⓑ Ⓒ Ⓓ Ⓔ   20 Ⓐ Ⓑ Ⓒ Ⓓ Ⓔ

Test 2

1 Ⓐ Ⓑ Ⓒ Ⓓ Ⓔ   6 Ⓐ Ⓑ Ⓒ Ⓓ Ⓔ   11 Ⓐ Ⓑ Ⓒ Ⓓ Ⓔ   16 Ⓐ Ⓑ Ⓒ Ⓓ Ⓔ
2 Ⓐ Ⓑ Ⓒ Ⓓ Ⓔ   7 Ⓐ Ⓑ Ⓒ Ⓓ Ⓔ   12 Ⓐ Ⓑ Ⓒ Ⓓ Ⓔ   17 Ⓐ Ⓑ Ⓒ Ⓓ Ⓔ
3 Ⓐ Ⓑ Ⓒ Ⓓ Ⓔ   8 Ⓐ Ⓑ Ⓒ Ⓓ Ⓔ   13 Ⓐ Ⓑ Ⓒ Ⓓ Ⓔ   18 Ⓐ Ⓑ Ⓒ Ⓓ Ⓔ
4 Ⓐ Ⓑ Ⓒ Ⓓ Ⓔ   9 Ⓐ Ⓑ Ⓒ Ⓓ Ⓔ   14 Ⓐ Ⓑ Ⓒ Ⓓ Ⓔ   19 Ⓐ Ⓑ Ⓒ Ⓓ Ⓔ
5 Ⓐ Ⓑ Ⓒ Ⓓ Ⓔ   10 Ⓐ Ⓑ Ⓒ Ⓓ Ⓔ   15 Ⓐ Ⓑ Ⓒ Ⓓ Ⓔ   20 Ⓐ Ⓑ Ⓒ Ⓓ Ⓔ

Test 3

1 Ⓐ Ⓑ Ⓒ Ⓓ Ⓔ   5 Ⓐ Ⓑ Ⓒ Ⓓ Ⓔ   8 Ⓐ Ⓑ Ⓒ Ⓓ Ⓔ
2 Ⓐ Ⓑ Ⓒ Ⓓ Ⓔ   6 Ⓐ Ⓑ Ⓒ Ⓓ Ⓔ   9 Ⓐ Ⓑ Ⓒ Ⓓ Ⓔ
3 Ⓐ Ⓑ Ⓒ Ⓓ Ⓔ   7 Ⓐ Ⓑ Ⓒ Ⓓ Ⓔ   10 Ⓐ Ⓑ Ⓒ Ⓓ Ⓔ
4 Ⓐ Ⓑ Ⓒ Ⓓ Ⓔ

Test 4

1 Ⓐ Ⓑ Ⓒ Ⓓ Ⓔ   6 Ⓐ Ⓑ Ⓒ Ⓓ Ⓔ   11 Ⓐ Ⓑ Ⓒ Ⓓ Ⓔ   16 Ⓐ Ⓑ Ⓒ Ⓓ Ⓔ
2 Ⓐ Ⓑ Ⓒ Ⓓ Ⓔ   7 Ⓐ Ⓑ Ⓒ Ⓓ Ⓔ   12 Ⓐ Ⓑ Ⓒ Ⓓ Ⓔ   17 Ⓐ Ⓑ Ⓒ Ⓓ Ⓔ
3 Ⓐ Ⓑ Ⓒ Ⓓ Ⓔ   8 Ⓐ Ⓑ Ⓒ Ⓓ Ⓔ   13 Ⓐ Ⓑ Ⓒ Ⓓ Ⓔ   18 Ⓐ Ⓑ Ⓒ Ⓓ Ⓔ
4 Ⓐ Ⓑ Ⓒ Ⓓ Ⓔ   9 Ⓐ Ⓑ Ⓒ Ⓓ Ⓔ   14 Ⓐ Ⓑ Ⓒ Ⓓ Ⓔ   19 Ⓐ Ⓑ Ⓒ Ⓓ Ⓔ
5 Ⓐ Ⓑ Ⓒ Ⓓ Ⓔ   10 Ⓐ Ⓑ Ⓒ Ⓓ Ⓔ   15 Ⓐ Ⓑ Ⓒ Ⓓ Ⓔ   20 Ⓐ Ⓑ Ⓒ Ⓓ Ⓔ

Test 5

1 Ⓐ Ⓑ Ⓒ Ⓓ Ⓔ   5 Ⓐ Ⓑ Ⓒ Ⓓ Ⓔ   9 Ⓐ Ⓑ Ⓒ Ⓓ Ⓔ   13 Ⓐ Ⓑ Ⓒ Ⓓ Ⓔ
2 Ⓐ Ⓑ Ⓒ Ⓓ Ⓔ   6 Ⓐ Ⓑ Ⓒ Ⓓ Ⓔ   10 Ⓐ Ⓑ Ⓒ Ⓓ Ⓔ   14 Ⓐ Ⓑ Ⓒ Ⓓ Ⓔ
3 Ⓐ Ⓑ Ⓒ Ⓓ Ⓔ   7 Ⓐ Ⓑ Ⓒ Ⓓ Ⓔ   11 Ⓐ Ⓑ Ⓒ Ⓓ Ⓔ   15 Ⓐ Ⓑ Ⓒ Ⓓ Ⓔ
4 Ⓐ Ⓑ Ⓒ Ⓓ Ⓔ   8 Ⓐ Ⓑ Ⓒ Ⓓ Ⓔ   12 Ⓐ Ⓑ Ⓒ Ⓓ Ⓔ   16 Ⓐ Ⓑ Ⓒ Ⓓ Ⓔ

Name and Number Comparison Practice Tests

Test 1

Time: 20 minutes. 20 questions.

DIRECTIONS: Each of the questions in this test consists of three similar names. For each question, compare the three names and decide which ones, if any, are exactly alike. Mark your Answer Sheet as follows:

> *Blacken A if all three are exactly alike*
> *Blacken B if only the first and second are exactly alike*
> *Blacken C if only the first and third are exactly alike*
> *Blacken D if only the second and third are exactly alike*
> *Blacken E if all three are different*

1. Lee Berlin Lea Berlin Les Berlin	6. Thomas O'Neill Thomas O'Neil Thomas O'Neal	11. John Finn John Fin John Finn	16. Frank Gershaw Frank Gershaw Frank Gerchaw
2. Webster Cayne Webster Cayne Wester Cain	7. Jess M. Olsen Jess N. Olson Jess M. Olsen	12. Ray Finkelstein Ray Finklestein Ray Finkelstien	17. Nancy Gerlach Nancy Gerlach Nancy Gerlach
3. Charles Danis Charles Donis Charles Danis	8. Irene Crawford Irene Crowford Irene Crawford	13. Sam Freedman Sam Friedman Sam Freedman	18. Dorothy Goldberg Dorothy Goldburg Dorothy Goldberg
4. Frank Collyer Frank Collyer Frank Collyer	9. Charles Duggan Charles Duggan Charles Dugan	14. Harold Friedberg Harold Friedberg Harold Freedberg	19. Philip Green Philip Greene Philip Greene
5. Sylvia Gross Sylvia Grohs Sylvia Grohs	10. Frank Dudley Frank Dudlee Frank Dudley	15. Trude Friedl Trude Freidl Trude Freidl	20. George Hampton George Hamton George Hamptun

Test 2

Time: 20 minutes. 20 questions.

DIRECTIONS: *Each of the questions in this test consists of three similar numbers. For each question, compare the three numbers and decide which ones, if any, are exactly alike. Mark your Answer Sheet as follows:*

Blacken A if all three are exactly alike
Blacken B if only the first and second are exactly alike
Blacken C if only the first and third are exactly alike
Blacken D if only the second and third are exactly alike
Blacken E if all three are different

1. 78541	5. 97338	9. 55149	13. 29522	17. 92889
78514	93378	55419	25922	92889
75814	98337	55419	25922	98289

2. 36395	6. 37050	10. 22037	14. 50090	18. 24892
36395	35070	22037	50090	24892
36395	37050	22037	50900	28492

3. 89612	7. 62324	11. 93476	15. 25816	19. 46648
86912	62324	94376	25816	44648
89621	62324	94376	25816	46648

4. 78111	8. 25622	12. 90731	16. 71555	20. 57048
71118	26522	90731	75111	57084
71118	22256	90731	75155	57084

Test 3

Time: 10 minutes. 10 questions.

DIRECTIONS: Each of the questions in this test consists of three similar names or numbers. For each question, compare the three names or three numbers and decide which ones, if any, are exactly alike. Mark your Answer Sheet as follows:

Blacken A if all three are exactly alike
Blacken B if only the first and second are exactly alike
Blacken C if only the first and third are exactly alike
Blacken D if only the second and third are exactly alike
Blacken E if all three are different

1. James McKiernan	James McKiernen	James McKiernan
2. Marya Mannes	Mayra Mannes	Marya Mannis
3. Henry Rauch	Henry Rauch	Henry Raush
4. Jeanne Sorrels	Jeanne Sorells	Jeanne Sorrells
5. John H. Griscom	John H. Griscom	John H. Griscom
6. 7314916	7314961	7314961
7. 4258701	4258071	4258701
8. 1869572	1869572	1896572
9. 6371485	6374185	6371845
10. 5926374	5926374	5926374

Test 4

Time: 20 minutes. 20 questions.

DIRECTIONS: *Each of the questions in this test consists of three similar names or numbers. For each question, compare the three names or three numbers and decide which ones, if any, are exactly alike. Mark your Answer Sheet as follows:*

Blacken A if all three are exactly alike
Blacken B if only the first and second are exactly alike
Blacken C if only the first and third are exactly alike
Blacken D if only the second and third are exactly alike
Blacken E if all three are different

1. Vincent Imperial
   Vincent Impirial
   Vincent Imperail

2. Robert Innes
   Robert Innes
   Robert Innes

3. Patrick Keane
   Patrick Keene
   Patrick Keen

4. Dora Krigsmann
   Dora Krigsman
   Dora Krigsman

5. Albert Lentz
   Albert Lentz
   Albet Lents

6. Seymour Lindell
   Seymour Lindel
   Seymour Lindell

7. Hugh Lunny
   Hugh Luny
   Hugh Lunny

8. Mal Mallin
   Mal Mallin
   Mal Malin

9. May Marshall
   May Marshall
   May Marshall

10. Walter Mattson
    Walter Mattson
    Walter Matson

11. 63381
    63381
    63318

12. 81585
    85185
    85185

13. 90463
    90426
    90463

14. 22249
    22249
    22294

15. 57422
    52742
    57224

16. 36264
    36264
    36264

17. 20637
    26037
    26037

18. 56299
    52699
    52996

19. 22804
    22804
    22804

20. 33266
    33266
    36623

Test 5

Time: 16 minutes. 16 questions.

DIRECTIONS: Each of the questions in this test consists of three similar names or numbers. For each question, compare the three names or three numbers and decide which ones, if any, are exactly alike. Mark your Answer Sheet as follows:

    Blacken A if all three are exactly alike
    Blacken B if only the first and second are exactly alike
    Blacken C if only the first and third are exactly alike
    Blacken D if only the second and third are exactly alike
    Blacken E if all three are different

1.	Cornelius Detwiler	Cornelius Detwiler	Cornelius Detwiler
2.	6452054	6452654	6452054
3.	8501268	8501268	8501286
4.	Ella Burk Newham	Ella Burk Newnham	Elena Burk Newnham
5.	Jno. K. Ravencroft	Jno. H. Ravencroft	Jno. H. Ravencoft
6.	Martin Wills Pullen	Martin Wills Pulen	Martin Wills Pullen
7.	3457988	3457986	3457986
8.	4695682	4695862	4695682
9.	Stricklund Kanedy	Stricklund Kanedy	Stricklund Kanedy
10.	Joy Harlor Witner	Joy Harloe Witner	Joy Harloe Witner
11.	R. M. O. Uberroth	R. M. O. Uberroth	R. N. O. Uberroth
12.	1592514	1592574	1592574
13.	2010202	2010202	2010220
14.	6177396	6177936	6177396
15.	Drusilla S. Ridgeley	Drusilla S. Ridgeley	Drusilla S. Ridgeley
16.	Andrei I. Toumantzev	Andrei I. Tourmantzev	Andrei I. Toumantzov

Answer Key for Name and Number Comparison Practice Tests

Test 1

1. E	4. A	7. C	10. C	13. C	16. B	19. D
2. B	5. D	8. C	11. C	14. B	17. A	20. E
3. C	6. E	9. B	12. E	15. D	18. C	

Test 2

1. E	5. E	9. D	13. D	17. B
2. A	6. C	10. A	14. B	18. B
3. E	7. A	11. D	15. A	19. C
4. D	8. E	12. A	16. E	20. D

Test 3

1. C	3. B	5. A	7. C	9. E
2. E	4. E	6. D	8. B	10. A

Test 4

1. E	5. B	9. A	13. C	17 D
2. A	6. C	10. B	14. B	18. E
3. E	7. C	11. B	15. E	19. A
4. D	8. B	12. D	16. A	20. B

Test 5

1. A	5. E	9. A	13. B
2. C	6. C	10. D	14. C
3. B	7. D	11. B	15. A
4. E	8. C	12. D	16. E

Answer Sheet for Matching Letters and Numbers Practice Tests

Test 1

1 Ⓐ Ⓑ Ⓒ Ⓓ Ⓔ	6 Ⓐ Ⓑ Ⓒ Ⓓ Ⓔ	11 Ⓐ Ⓑ Ⓒ Ⓓ Ⓔ	16 Ⓐ Ⓑ Ⓒ Ⓓ Ⓔ
2 Ⓐ Ⓑ Ⓒ Ⓓ Ⓔ	7 Ⓐ Ⓑ Ⓒ Ⓓ Ⓔ	12 Ⓐ Ⓑ Ⓒ Ⓓ Ⓔ	17 Ⓐ Ⓑ Ⓒ Ⓓ Ⓔ
3 Ⓐ Ⓑ Ⓒ Ⓓ Ⓔ	8 Ⓐ Ⓑ Ⓒ Ⓓ Ⓔ	13 Ⓐ Ⓑ Ⓒ Ⓓ Ⓔ	18 Ⓐ Ⓑ Ⓒ Ⓓ Ⓔ
4 Ⓐ Ⓑ Ⓒ Ⓓ Ⓔ	9 Ⓐ Ⓑ Ⓒ Ⓓ Ⓔ	14 Ⓐ Ⓑ Ⓒ Ⓓ Ⓔ	19 Ⓐ Ⓑ Ⓒ Ⓓ Ⓔ
5 Ⓐ Ⓑ Ⓒ Ⓓ Ⓔ	10 Ⓐ Ⓑ Ⓒ Ⓓ Ⓔ	15 Ⓐ Ⓑ Ⓒ Ⓓ Ⓔ	20 Ⓐ Ⓑ Ⓒ Ⓓ Ⓔ

Test 2

1 Ⓐ Ⓑ Ⓒ Ⓓ Ⓔ	6 Ⓐ Ⓑ Ⓒ Ⓓ Ⓔ	11 Ⓐ Ⓑ Ⓒ Ⓓ Ⓔ	16 Ⓐ Ⓑ Ⓒ Ⓓ Ⓔ
2 Ⓐ Ⓑ Ⓒ Ⓓ Ⓔ	7 Ⓐ Ⓑ Ⓒ Ⓓ Ⓔ	12 Ⓐ Ⓑ Ⓒ Ⓓ Ⓔ	17 Ⓐ Ⓑ Ⓒ Ⓓ Ⓔ
3 Ⓐ Ⓑ Ⓒ Ⓓ Ⓔ	8 Ⓐ Ⓑ Ⓒ Ⓓ Ⓔ	13 Ⓐ Ⓑ Ⓒ Ⓓ Ⓔ	18 Ⓐ Ⓑ Ⓒ Ⓓ Ⓔ
4 Ⓐ Ⓑ Ⓒ Ⓓ Ⓔ	9 Ⓐ Ⓑ Ⓒ Ⓓ Ⓔ	14 Ⓐ Ⓑ Ⓒ Ⓓ Ⓔ	19 Ⓐ Ⓑ Ⓒ Ⓓ Ⓔ
5 Ⓐ Ⓑ Ⓒ Ⓓ Ⓔ	10 Ⓐ Ⓑ Ⓒ Ⓓ Ⓔ	15 Ⓐ Ⓑ Ⓒ Ⓓ Ⓔ	20 Ⓐ Ⓑ Ⓒ Ⓓ Ⓔ

Test 3

1 Ⓐ Ⓑ Ⓒ Ⓓ	5 Ⓐ Ⓑ Ⓒ Ⓓ	8 Ⓐ Ⓑ Ⓒ Ⓓ	11 Ⓐ Ⓑ Ⓒ Ⓓ
2 Ⓐ Ⓑ Ⓒ Ⓓ	6 Ⓐ Ⓑ Ⓒ Ⓓ	9 Ⓐ Ⓑ Ⓒ Ⓓ	12 Ⓐ Ⓑ Ⓒ Ⓓ
3 Ⓐ Ⓑ Ⓒ Ⓓ	7 Ⓐ Ⓑ Ⓒ Ⓓ	10 Ⓐ Ⓑ Ⓒ Ⓓ	13 Ⓐ Ⓑ Ⓒ Ⓓ
4 Ⓐ Ⓑ Ⓒ Ⓓ			

Test 4

1 Ⓐ Ⓑ Ⓒ Ⓓ	5 Ⓐ Ⓑ Ⓒ Ⓓ	8 Ⓐ Ⓑ Ⓒ Ⓓ
2 Ⓐ Ⓑ Ⓒ Ⓓ	6 Ⓐ Ⓑ Ⓒ Ⓓ	9 Ⓐ Ⓑ Ⓒ Ⓓ
3 Ⓐ Ⓑ Ⓒ Ⓓ	7 Ⓐ Ⓑ Ⓒ Ⓓ	10 Ⓐ Ⓑ Ⓒ Ⓓ
4 Ⓐ Ⓑ Ⓒ Ⓓ		

Test 5

1 Ⓐ Ⓑ Ⓒ Ⓓ	5 Ⓐ Ⓑ Ⓒ Ⓓ	8 Ⓐ Ⓑ Ⓒ Ⓓ
2 Ⓐ Ⓑ Ⓒ Ⓓ	6 Ⓐ Ⓑ Ⓒ Ⓓ	9 Ⓐ Ⓑ Ⓒ Ⓓ
3 Ⓐ Ⓑ Ⓒ Ⓓ	7 Ⓐ Ⓑ Ⓒ Ⓓ	10 Ⓐ Ⓑ Ⓒ Ⓓ
4 Ⓐ Ⓑ Ⓒ Ⓓ		

Test 6

1 Ⓐ Ⓑ Ⓒ Ⓓ	5 Ⓐ Ⓑ Ⓒ Ⓓ	8 Ⓐ Ⓑ Ⓒ Ⓓ
2 Ⓐ Ⓑ Ⓒ Ⓓ	6 Ⓐ Ⓑ Ⓒ Ⓓ	9 Ⓐ Ⓑ Ⓒ Ⓓ
3 Ⓐ Ⓑ Ⓒ Ⓓ	7 Ⓐ Ⓑ Ⓒ Ⓓ	10 Ⓐ Ⓑ Ⓒ Ⓓ
4 Ⓐ Ⓑ Ⓒ Ⓓ		

Matching Letters and Numbers
Practice Tests

DIRECTIONS: In these tests of clerical ability, Column I consists of sets of numbered questions that you are to answer one at a time. Column II consists of possible answers to the set of questions in Column I. Select from Column II the one answer that contains only the numbers and letters, regardless of their order, that appear in the question in Column I. If none of the four possible answers is correct, blacken "E" on your answer sheet.

A Sample Question Explained

COLUMN I: Set of Questions	COLUMN II: Possible Answers
1. 2-Q-P-5-T-G-4-7	(A) 5-G-8-P-4-Q
	(B) P-R-7-Q-4-2
	(C) Q-5-P-9-G-2
	(D) 4-2-5-P-7-Q
	(E) None of these.

The Correct Answer to the Sample Question is (D). How did we arrive at that solution? First, remember that the instructions tell you to select as your answer the choice that contains only the numbers and letters, regardless of their order, that appear in the question. The answer choice in Column II does not have to contain *all* of the letters and numbers that appear in the question. But the answer cannot contain a number or letter that does not appear in the question. Thus, begin by checking the numbers and letters that appear in Answer (A). You will note that while 5-G-P-4-Q all appear in the Sample Question, the number 8, which is included in Answer (A), does *not* appear in the question. Answer (A) is thus incorrect. Likewise, Answer (B) is incorrect as the letter R does not appear in the Sample Question; Answer (C) is incorrect, as the number 9 does not appear in the question. In checking Answer (D), however, one notes that 4-2-5-P-7-Q all appear in the Sample Question. (D) is therefore the correct choice. Answer (E) is obviously eliminated.

Now proceed to answer the following test questions on the basis of the instructions given above.

Test 1

Time: 20 minutes. 20 questions.

The following are representative examination-type questions. They should be carefully studied and completely understood.

DIRECTIONS: In this test of clerical ability, Column 1 consists of sets of numbered questions that you are to answer one at a time. Column II consists of possible answers to the set of questions in Column I. Select from Column II the one answer that contains only the numbers and letters, regardless of their order, that appear in the question in Column I. If none of the four possible answers is correct, blacken "E" on your answer sheet.

COLUMN I: Set of Questions	COLUMN II: Possible Answers
1. 6-4-T-G-9-K-N-8	(A) Z-8-K-G-9-7
2. K-3-L-6-Z-7-9-T	(B) 7-N-Z-T-9-8
3. N-8-9-3-K-G-7-Z	(C) L-3-Z-K-7-6
4. L-Z-G-6-4-9-K-3	(D) 4-K-T-G-8-6
5. 9-T-K-8-3-7-N-Z	(E) None of these

Set of Questions	Possible Answers
6. 2-3-P-6-V-Z-4-L	(A) 3-6-G-P-7-N
7. T-7-4-3-P-Z-9-G	(B) 3-7-P-V-4-T
8. 6-N-G-Z-3-9-P-7	(C) 4-6-V-Z-2-L
9. 9-6-P-4-N-G-Z-2	(D) 4-7-G-Z-T-3
10. 4-9-7-T-L-P-3-V	(E) None of these

COLUMN I: Set of Questions	COLUMN II: Possible Answers
11. Q-1-6-R-L-9-7-V	(A) F-3-N-K-J-4
12. 8-W-2-Z-P-4-H-0	(B) Q-H-4-0-5-M
13. N-J-3-T-K-5-F-M	(C) O-W-2-Z-4-8
14. 5-T-H-M-0-4-Q-J	(D) R-9-V-1-Q-6
15. 4-Z-X-8-W-0-2-L	(E) None of these

Set of Questions	Possible Answers
16. S-2-L-8-U-Q-7-P	(A) 9-Q-T-K-2-7
17. 4-M-0-6-T-F-W-1	(B) F-0-1-4-W-M
18. J-M-4-X-W-Z-5-8	(C) U-2-8-P-Q-S
19. H-Q-2-9-T-I-K-7	(D) Z-M-4-5-8-Q
20. 8-M-Z-V-4-P-5-Q	(E) None of these

Test 2

Time: 20 minutes. 20 questions.

The following are representative examination-type questions. They should be carefully studied and completely understood.

DIRECTIONS: In this test of clerical ability, Column 1 consists of sets of numbered questions, which you are to answer one at a time. Column II consists of possible answers to the set of questions in Column I. Select from Column II the one answer that contains only the numbers and letters, regardless of their order, that appear in the question in Column I. If none of the four possible answers is correct, blacken "E" on your answer sheet.

COLUMN I: Set of Questions	**COLUMN II:** Possible Answers
1. Z-5-3-L-7-K-4-G	(A) T-4-K-5-G-2
2. K-V-6-T-2-7-4-L	(B) 7-K-4-G-Z-5
3. G-T-V-9-L-4-5-3	(C) L-5-2-G-K-7
4. G-T-5-N-9-2-K-4	(D) T-2-7-L-6-V
5. K-4-5-T-G-2-6-P	(E) None of these

Set of Questions	Possible Answers
6. V-K-Z-5-2-L-8-9	(A) N-K-8-3-5-7
7. N-Z-2-L-V-3-5-8	(B) V-N-5-8-2-L
8. N-P-3-9-V-5-6-Z	(C) 9-Z-3-V-P-6
9. Z-3-K-T-7-4-5-N	(D) K-5-Z-9-V-8
10. V-L-K-9-N-5-2-7	(E) None of these

COLUMN I: Set of Questions	**COLUMN II:** Possible Answers
11. 7-8-L-5-Z-9-P-V	(A) 9-V-4-L-N-3
12. N-6-4-L-3-Z-G-9	(B) N-4-5-Z-3-9
13. V-9-3-4-K-N-5-L	(C) 8-5-Z-L-9-P
14. L-V-9-2-N-8-T-5	(D) N-9-8-V-L-T
15. 5-Z-L-9-P-V-2-8	(E) None of these

Set of Questions	Possible Answers
16. L-2-4-8-V-P-7-N	(A) N-2-7-L-8-V
17. V-4-7-8-N-T-Z-6	(B) 2-V-T-8-G-7
18. T-L-5-N-6-8-7-V	(C) 8-6-T-L-N-4
19. L-6-N-T-2-G-8-4	(D) V-7-6-N-T-8
20. T-L-V-3-4-G-8-7	(E) None of these

Test 3

Time: 15 minutes. 13 questions.

The following are representative examination-type questions. They should be carefully studied and completely understood.

DIRECTIONS: *The codes given in Column I below begin and end with a capital letter and have an eight-digit number in between. You are to arrange the codes in Column I according to the following rules.*
1. *Arrange the codes in alphabetical order, according to the first letter.*
2. *When two or more codes have the same first letter, arrange the codes in alphabetical order according to the last letter.*
3. *When two or more of the codes have the same first and last letters, arrange the codes in numerical order, beginning with the lowest number.*
The codes in Column I are numbered (1) through (5). Column II gives you a selection of four possible answers. You are to choose from Column II the lettered choice that gives the correct listing of the codes in Column I arranged according to the above rules.

COLUMN I: Set of Codes	COLUMN II: Possible Answers
1. (1) S55126179E (2) R55136177Q (3) P55126177R (4) S55126178R (5) R55126180P	(A) 1, 5, 2, 3, 4 (B) 3, 4, 1, 5, 2 (C) 3, 5, 2, 1, 4 (D) 4, 3, 1, 5, 2
2. (1) T64217813Q (2) I642178170 (3) T642178180 (4) I64217811Q (5) T64217816Q	(A) 4, 1, 3, 2, 5 (B) 2, 4, 3, 1, 5 (C) 4, 1, 5, 2, 3 (D) 2, 3, 4, 1, 5
3. (1) C83261824G (2) C78361833C (3) G83261732G (4) C88261823C (5) G83261743C	(A) 2, 4, 1, 5, 3 (B) 4, 2, 1, 3, 5 (C) 3, 1, 5, 2, 4 (D) 2, 3, 5, 1, 4
4. (1) A11710107H (2) H17110017A (3) A11170707A (4) H17170171H (5) A11710177A	(A) 2, 1, 4, 3, 5 (B) 3, 1, 5, 2, 4 (C) 3, 4, 1, 5, 2 (D) 3, 5, 1, 2, 4
5. (1) R26794821S (2) O26794821T (3) M26794827Z (4) Q26794821R (5) S26794821P	(A) 3, 2, 4, 1, 5 (B) 3, 4, 2, 1, 5 (C) 4, 2, 1, 3, 5 (D) 5, 4, 1, 2, 3

COLUMN I: Set of Codes	COLUMN II: Possible Answers
6. (1) D89143888P (2) D98143838B (3) D89113883B (4) D89148338P (5) D89148388B	(A) 3, 5, 2, 1, 4 (B) 3, 1, 4, 5, 2 (C) 4, 2, 3, 1, 5 (D) 4, 1, 3, 5, 2
7. (1) W62455599E (2) W62455090F (3) W62405099E (4) V62455097F (5) V62405979E	(A) 2, 4, 3, 1, 5 (B) 3, 1, 5, 2, 4 (C) 5, 3, 1, 4, 2 (D) 5, 4, 3, 1, 2
8. (1) N74663826M (2) M74633286M (3) N76633228N (4) M76483686N (5) M74636688M	(A) 2, 4, 5, 3, 1 (B) 2, 5, 4, 1, 3 (C) 1, 2, 5, 3, 4 (D) 2, 5, 1, 4, 3
9. (1) P97560324B (2) R97663024B (3) P97503024E (4) R97563240E (5) P97652304B	(A) 1, 5, 2, 3, 4 (B) 3, 1, 4, 5, 2 (C) 1, 5, 3, 2, 4 (D) 1, 5, 2, 3, 4
10. (1) H92411165G (2) A92141465G (3) H92141165C (4) H92444165C (5) A92411465G	(A) 2, 5, 3, 4, 1 (B) 3, 4, 2, 5, 1 (C) 3, 2, 1, 5, 4 (D) 3, 1, 2, 5, 4
11. (1) X90637799S (2) N90037696S (3) Y90677369B (4) X09677693B (5) M09673699S	(A) 4, 3, 5, 2, 1 (B) 5, 4, 2, 1, 3 (C) 5, 2, 4, 1, 3 (D) 5, 2, 3, 4, 1
12. (1) K78425174L (2) K78452714C (3) K78547214N (4) K78442774C (5) K78547724M	(A) 4, 2, 1, 3, 5 (B) 2, 3, 5, 4, 1 (C) 1, 4, 2, 3, 5 (D) 4, 2, 1, 5, 3
13. (1) P18736652U (2) P18766352V (3) T17686532U (4) T17865523U (5) P18675332V	(A) 1, 3, 4, 5, 2 (B) 1, 5, 2, 3, 4 (C) 3, 4, 5, 1, 2 (D) 5, 2, 1, 3, 4

Test 4

Time: 12 minutes. 10 questions.

Code Table

Code letters:	Y	E	N	C	H	I	O	L	J	A
Corresponding numbers:	1	2	3	4	5	6	7	8	9	0

DIRECTIONS: The Table above provides a corresponding number for each of the 10 letters used as codes in the questions. On the first line there are 10 selected letters. On the second line there are the 10 numerals, including zero. Directly under each letter on the first line there is a corresponding number on the second line. Every question consists of three pairs of letter and number codes. Each pair of codes is on a separate line. Referring to the Code Table above, determine whether each pair of letter and number codes is made up of corresponding letters and numbers. In answering each question, compare all *three* pairs of letter and number codes. Then mark your answers as follows:

A. *if in* none *of the three pairs of codes do* all *letters and numbers correspond*
B. *if in only* one *pair of codes do* all *letters and numbers correspond*
C. *if in only* two *pairs of codes do* all *letters and numbers correspond*
D. *if in* all three *pairs of codes do* all *letters and numbers correspond*

1. JOHALI   975486
   YECOHN   124753
   ACJYLO   049187

2. NJYHEL   391528
   IOCEAY   674201
   CLYNHJ   481359

3. HOLIJA   578690
   ECILAY   246801
   LYJEAN   819203

4. ONHYAI   735106
   JILCHE   978452
   IYOAEC   617924

5. HOLYNC   578934
   JOYNHE   970352
   LECAOJ   824179

6. NYEILA   312680
   LHONJY   857391
   ENIACO   236045

7. JENOYI   923016
   LIACEH   830425
   NJLHCO   398547

8. ECILAJ   346809
    YNHOJC   136794
    OLYNCH   781340

9. LYNOEJ   813729
    IYACOL   610478
    CALNHE   408352

10. JONYAL   973108
    NELCIY   328461
    OLHAJE   785092

Test 5

Time: 12 minutes. 10 questions.

Code Table

Code letters:	T	E	L	U	S	Q	N	I	X	C
Corresponding numbers:	8	1	5	3	7	6	2	0	4	9

DIRECTIONS: *The Table above provides a corresponding number for each of the 10 letters used as codes in the questions. On the first line there are 10 selected letters. On the second line there are the 10 numerals, including zero. Directly under each letter on the first line there is a corresponding number on the second line. Every question consists of three pairs of letter and number codes. Each pair of codes is on a separate line. Referring to the Code Table above, determine whether each pair of letter and number codes is made up of corresponding letters and numbers. In answering each question, compare* all *three pairs of letter and number codes. Then mark your answers as follows:*

A. *if in* none *of the three pairs of codes do* all *letters and numbers correspond*
B. *if in only* one *pair of codes do* all *letters and numbers correspond*
C. *if in only* two *pairs of codes do* all *letters and numbers correspond*
D. *if in* all three *pairs of codes do* all *letters and numbers correspond*

1. LUXQIT   534608
   XUTLSN   468572
   EXUTIC   143809

2. ELTUNX   156324
   QUELTS   631587
   USISQT   370768

3. ITENXQ   081236
   TNXQIL   924601
   NUISET   230748

4. CUSTEL   937815
   ECQUIX   196304
   UQENTS   361287

5. LQITES   460817
   TIXLUC   804539
   STINEQ   780216

6. IQXTUL   064835
   CUTESI   938170
   LEXQIT   514608

7. UQESTX   361782
   TINCLS   802957
   NESTIL   217805

8. QINTEX   602814
   CEUSIT   923708
   SUNEQL   732165

9. XIEQTL   601685
   TSUNCE   873091
   EUNIXT   182048

10. LITENS   508127
   NLQXCU   256493
   IQENTC   061289

Test 6

Time: 12 minutes. 10 questions.

Code Table

Code letters:	N	E	Z	S	O	R	L	H	A	T
Corresponding numbers:	0	1	2	3	4	5	6	7	8	9

DIRECTIONS: The Table above provides a corresponding number for each of the 10 letters used as codes in the questions. On the first line there are 10 selected letters. On the second line there are the 10 numerals, including zero. Directly under each letter on the first line there is a corresponding number on the second line. Every question consists of three pairs of letter and number codes. Each pair of codes is on a separate line. Referring to the Code Table above, determine whether each pair of letter and number codes is made up of corresponding letters and numbers. In answering each question, compare all three *pairs of letter and number codes. Then mark your answers as follows:*

A. *if in* none *of the three pairs of codes do* all *letters and numbers correspond*
B. *if in only* one *pair of codes do* all *letters and numbers correspond*
C. *if in only* two *pairs of codes do* all *letters and numbers correspond*
D. *if in* all three *pairs of codes do* all *letters and numbers correspond*

1. TNZAHL   902856
   ROSELN   543160
   LANSZE   680321

2. SZENLA   321068
   ROTAHL   549876
   ZTOLRS   294653

3. HTORZS   894523
   ENLART   106857
   OSZTRA   432968

4. THESOR   971345
   OSAZRE   438251
   ALHOEZ   867412

5. TALHRO   986754
   ZSRNTH   235097
   NLAHSE   068731

6. ORTELZ   459163
   ELRSAH   165387
   SEZONT   312408

7. AHLTON   875940
   RENTSZ   510932
   SANTOZ   380942

8. SNATZE   308921
   THOLRA   974652
   ZONEAR   240185

9. SONATE   340891
   AERNLS   815063
   NEATRO   018954

10. HORTEA   745908
    OZSRTN   423591
    LOTHER   649815

Answer Key for Matching Letters And Numbers Practice Tests

Test 1

1. D	6. C	11. D	16. C
2. C	7. D	12. C	17. B
3. A	8. A	13. E	18. E
4. E	9. E	14. B	19. A
5. B	10. B	15. C	20. D

Test 2

1. B	6. D	11. C	16. A
2. D	7. B	12. E	17. D
3. E	8. C	13. A	18. D
4. A	9. E	14. D	19. C
5. A	10. E	15. C	20. E

Test 3

1. C	5. A	9. C	13. B
2. B	6. A	10. A	
3. A	7. D	11. C	
4. D	8. B	12. D	

Test 4

1. C	3. D	5. A	7. B	9. D
2. D	4. B	6. C	8. A	10. D

Test 5

1. C	3. A	5. C	7. C	9. A
2. C	4. D	6. D	8. C	10. D

Test 6

1. C	3. A	5. D	7. C	9. D
2. D	4. D	6. B	8. C	10. A